AF719245

OWNERSHIP AND DEVELOPMENT

# OWNERSHIP AND DEVELOPMENT:
# A COMPARISON OF DOMESTIC AND FOREIGN FIRMS
# IN COLOMBIAN MANUFACTURING

by

Brian F. Wallace

Ohio University Center for International Studies
Center for Latin American Studies

Monographs in International Studies
Latin America Series Number 12

Athens, Ohio 1987

**Library of Congress Cataloging-in-Publication Data**

Wallace, Brian F.
Ownership and development.

(Monographs in international studies. Latin America series; no. 12)
Bibliography: p.
1. Colombia—Manufactures. 2. Investments, Foreign—Government policy—Colombia. 3. International business enterprises—Government policy—Colombia.
I. Title. II. Series.
HD9734.C62W35 1987 332.6′7322861 86-33255
ISBN 0-89680-145-4



ISBN 0-89680-145-4

# PREFACE

This study is based on the premise that the proper role of government is to enhance the well-being of the governed. It is based on the additional premise that one of the most important goals of social science research is to evaluate government policies in terms of how well they meet the basic needs and add to the well-being of citizens. Although this study has gone through many changes, this normative orientation has remained the same. Using as its focus a policy of the Colombian government, this study has sought to evaluate government policies in terms of their potential effects on the population. The purpose is to determine, in effect, whether government policy is likely to benefit the governed.

Although I bear full responsibility for the content of this work, I must share credit for it. Over the past years this study has gone through many transformations. I owe thanks to several people and organizations for the financial, intellectual, and personal support which enabled me to complete my research and writing:

I would like to thank the University of South Carolina for providing me with a dissertation fellowship to begin my research. I would like to express my thanks to Richard Walker for nominating me and to the Scaife Foundation for awarding me an H. B. Earhart Fellowship, which allowed me to do field research in Colombia. I owe a debt of gratitude to Joseph Love and the National Endowment for the Humanities for providing me with a summer fellowship to revise this study.

I would like to thank Robert Rood and Larry Herman for their comments on the drafts of this research. For their friendship and personal support, I would like to thank Ellen Still, Amy Pitts, Joyce Leahy, Anne Bostwick, Diane Bennett, Starr Huffman, and Cheryl Enders. I want to give a special thanks to Katie Wallace, who has been a constant source of inspiration for my writing (especially last month when she asked me what I was going to be when I grew up). I would also like to thank my parents, whose unquestioning support made this work possible.

Finally I would like to thank Moss Blachman--mentor, fellow scholar, and friend--whose constant intellectual challenges and personal support enabled me to complete this research and to grow in the process.

## TABLE OF CONTENTS

PREFACE....................v

Chapter | Page

1. Introduction....................1
2. Policies Toward Direct Foreign Investment....................5
3. Direct Foreign Investment In the Colombian Economy....................19
4. Domestication and Well-Being: Background to the Study....................35
5. Domestication and Growth....................47
6. Domestication and Distribution....................61
7. Domestication and the Balance of Payments....................81
8. Nonmaterial Effects of Domestication....................101
9. Conclusion....................133

Appendix A: Direct Foreign Investment in Colombia....137

Appendix B: Foreign, Domestic and National Plants in Colombia....................145

List of Works Cited....................163

## LIST OF TABLES


Table Page

1. Estimated Total Direct Foreign Investment in Colombia, by Sector, 1914....20
2. U.S. Direct Foreign Investment in Colombia, 1929....21
3. Portfolio and Direct Foreign Investment in Colombia, 1945....25
4. U.S. Direct Foreign Investment in Colombia, 1943....26
5. Estimated Total Direct Foreign Investment in Colombia....27
6. Approved Nonpetroleum Direct Foreign Investment, 1967-77....28
7. Registered Nonpetroleum Direct Foreign Investment in Colombia, End of 1976, by Investing Countries....29
8. Estimated Sectoral Distribution of DFI in Colombia, 1976....31
9. Registered Direct Foreign Investment in the Colombian Manufacturing Sector, 1976....32
10. Method of Entry of U.S. Firms in Colombia....42
11. Plants with DFI as a Percentage of Total National Plants, 1974....45
12. Value Added/Assets, 1972....49
13. Production/Employee, 1974....51
14. Value Added/Employee, 1974....53
15. Value Added/Remuneration, 1972....54
16. Growth Rates of Production and Incidence of Foreign Plants, by Industry....57
17. Growth Rates of Value Added and Incidence of Foreign Plants, by Industry....58
18. Growth Rates of Employment and Incidence of Foreign Plants, by Industry....59
19. Estimates of Income Distribution in Colombia....62
20. Per Capita Remuneration to All Personnel, 1972....64
21. Per Capita Remuneration to Foreign Managerial Personnel, 1972....65
22. Per Capita Remuneration to National Managerial Personnel, 1972....66
23. Per Capita Remuneration to Office Workers, 1972....67
24. Per Capita Remuneration to Laborers, 1972....68
25. Distribution of Remuneration by Category of Employee, 1972....70
26. Remuneration as a Percentage of Value Added, 1972....72
27. Geographic Distribution of Production, 1973-1974....73
28. Geographic Distribution of Employment, 1973-1974....74
29. Assets/Employee for Foreign and National Plants, 1972....77

30. Negative Balance of Payments Effects as a Percentage of Sales....84
31. Foreign Debt as a Percentage of Total Debt....85
32. Technical Payments as a Percentage of Sales....86
33. Balance of Trade Effects of Large Importers, 1970....88
34. Distribution of Exports, Foreign and Domestic Plants, 1974....89
35. DFI Plants as a Percentage of Production and Exports, 1974....90
36. Manufactured Direct Exports as a Percentage of Production, 1974....92
37. Export Restrictions in Technology Transfer Contracts....94
38. Distribution of Raw Material Imports, 1970....96
39. Imported Raw Materials as a Percentage of Total Raw Materials, 1970....97
40. Favorable Attitude towards U.S. Investment....103
41. Overall Importance and Desirability of Foreign Investment....105
42. Preferred Government Policy toward Foreign Investment....106
43. Cultural Aggregates....110
44. Salary Increases Recommended by Nationality of Managers....111
45. Percentage of Managers Ranking the Life Goal of Service among Top Three in Importance....112
46. Satisfactions Sought by the Entrepreneur....113
47. Willingness to Spend Money for Five Needs....115
48. Opinions about Colombian Politics....121
49. Technological Dependence of Foreign and Domestic Plants in Colombia....123
50. Local Innovation by Domestic and Foreign Firms in Colombia....124
51. Use of Domestic and Foreign Administrators and Engineers....125
52. Interlocking Directorates of Thirteen Foreign Firms in Colombia....128
53. Interlocking Directorates....131
54. United States Direct Foreign Investment in Colombia, 1897-1977....139
55. Cumulative Nonpetroleum Registered Direct Foreign Investment in Colombia....140
56. Registered Nonpetroleum Foreign Investment in Colombia, by Country of Origin....142
57. Registered Nonpetroleum Direct Foreign Investment in Colombia, by Sector....143
58. International Uniform Industrial Classification System....146
59. National Manufacturing Industries....147
60. 421 Plants with Direct Foreign Investment....153
61. Domestic Plants, 1974....159
62. 421 Plants as a Percentage of Total Manufacturing...162

# CHAPTER 1

## INTRODUCTION

Latin American governments have long sought to control economic activities within their countries in order to secure desired governmental goals. During the colonial period, the crown attempted to monopolize trade with the Americas. In the early 1900s governments attempted to encourage raw material exports, only to find that they were increasing the vulnerability of their countries without any obvious increase in wealth. The post-war attempts to erect high tariff barriers through import substitution industrialization (ISI) had another unanticipated effect: the companies doing much of the new industrial production were subsidiaries of multinational corporations.

For nearly two decades debate has raged over the effects of these multinational corporations and their direct foreign investment (DFI) in developing countries. Raymond Vernon (1973-4) summed up the controversy when he wrote:

> According to its critics, the multinational enterprise is the cause of unemployment, maldistribution of income, and financial drain in the poor countries. According to the public relations departments, the multinational enterprise is the instrument of material progress and global harmony. Each protagonist draws upon its little collection of favorite studies, deaf to the evidence that does not seem to fit its simple case (p. 111).

The proponents of the multinational corporations claim that they bring technology, capital, managerial knowledge, and market access to developing nations. In the process they create jobs, provide needed revenues to governments, and train foreign nationals in managerial skills. In short, the multinational corporation "has proven to be the only really effective instrument of economic development" (Diebold, 1973: 84). This contribution to development is greatest when the host-country is poor. Jacoby writes:

> The economic, political, technological, and cultural effects of multinational corporate investment are most striking when the host country is less developed than when it is advanced, for it is in less developed lands that investment has made a strong impact on development. This conclusion emerges clearly from thirteen case studies.... In all cases the American

> corporation played an innovating and catalytic role, founding new industries, transmitting technological and managerial skills as well as infrastructures of schools, housing, health facilities, and transportation in order to conduct its business (p. 43).

Others see the multinational corporation and its associated direct foreign investment as a mixed bag of costs and benefits. Albert Hirschman (1971) writes that direct foreign investment

> shares to a very high degree the ambiguity of most human inventions and institutions: it has considerable potential for both good and evil. On the one hand, there are the celebrated and undoubted contributions of private international investment to development: the bringing of capital, entrepreneurship, technology, management and other skills, and of international market connections.... On the other hand, foreign investment brings not only the dangers of economic plunder and political domination which are the stock-in-trade of the various theories of imperialism, but a number of other, more subtle, yet serious effects and side effects which can handicap the development efforts of countries placing prolonged and substantial reliance on private investment from abroad (p.226).

Eric Kierans (1973) has pointed out one of the costly side-effects of the efficiency of MNCs. He states that MNCs sell mass production techniques and

> profitable mass production...requires mass consumption, i.e., the homogenization of tastes, needs, values and priorities of all nations within which the the firm and its subsidiaries operate. In the name of technical efficiency, we erase the differences among persons, the style and the art of their living (p.179).

Critics of the multinational corporations argue that they retard the development of poor countries. They argue that MNCs import little capital into developing countries, that they buy out existing local firms rather than starting new enterprises, that they reap excess profits, that they evade taxes, and that they import technology that is inappropriate for the needs of developing countries. Their cumulative effect is the further impoverishment of developing countries and a greater maldistribution of income. After reviewing his findings on MNCs in Latin America Ronald Muller (1973-4) says that "it is impossible to see how the MNC's financial impact on Third World countries could possibly assist in the alleviation of their underdevelopment" (p.89). Barnet (1973-4) says that studies of multinational corporations "suggest strongly that the overall impact of global companies throughout Latin America in the last twenty years has been adverse with respect to income concentration and unemployment" (p.120).

Just as Raul Prebisch's theories in the 1940s caused governments to reconsider previous policies and switch to import substitution industrialization, so the studies of the 1960s and 1970s made Latin American governments reevaluate the desireablity of direct foreign investment. This time government policy came in the form of attempts to limit the sectors in which foreign investment could be located, to alter the behavior of foreign firms, and to phase out foreign ownership entirely.

These economic policies are based on certain assumptions about the relationship between the nationality of ownership and the effects of firms. The ISI policy of encouraging any investment, provided it was located within the country, was based on the assumption that the behavior and effects of productive enterprises were related to the location of production, not the location of ownership, of a firm. More recent policies assume that behavior is strongly related to the location of ownership. The question begged by all of these policies is whether there are any differences in the effects of firms that are attributable to the foreignness of the firm or whether nationality of ownership is irrelevant to the effects of companies. That is the question that is studied in this work, which uses a case study of the industrial sector of Colombia to test whether nationality of ownership is related to the effects of a firm.

This research did not take place in a vacuum. It took place in Colombia, a real country. It deals with the lives of real people. Colombia is famous for its emeralds, its coffee, and its drugs. It was a country I grew to love and hate. A land of horror and beauty, of contradictions within contradictions. It was a country that has had a lasting impact on my life. It was my hope that this work would have some impact on the lives of people; now I am not so sure.

North American social scientists are often accused of approaching Latin American issues in such a way that our well-intentioned studies are irrelevant to the concerns of Latin America. A story is told of a Colombian balloonist whose craft was swept into a terrible storm. After days of being whirled about, the winds eased and he began to drift towards earth, uncertain of his location. As he neared the ground, he saw a rather pleasant fellow (a North American social scientist, it turns out) and shouted out to him: "Can you tell me where I am?" "Certainly," the voice answered him, "you're in a balloon."

So it goes. The topic of this research is one I believe to be important for the future of Colombia. It should be kept in mind, however, that for Colombia's un- and under-employed adults and malnourished children, a complex comparison of domestic and foreign industrial firms is about as useful as counting angels on the heads of pins. I hope this is not just an elaborate way of telling them they are in a balloon.

# CHAPTER 2

# POLICIES TOWARDS DIRECT FOREIGN INVESTMENT

The regulation of direct foreign investment (DFI) by individual countries is by now a generally accepted principle of international relations. On December 12, 1974, the United Nations General Assembly passed (by a vote of 120 to 6, with 10 abstentions) the Charter of Economic Rights and Duties of States. Article 2 of the Charter states that every state has the right:

> (a)to regulate and exercise authority over foreign investment within its national jurisdiction in accordance with its laws and regulations and in conformity with its national objectives and priorities...
> (c)To nationalize, expropriate or transfer ownership of foreign property (Erb & Kallab, 1975: 205-6).

Even the United States--the single largest source of the world's direct foreign investment--has accepted this right of countries to regulate direct foreign investment. This is epitomized by the statement of Under Secretary of State for Economic Affairs Richard N. Cooper in addressing the Council of the Americas:

> It is not our policy to insist that other countries let American investors in. Nor do we try to dictate the terms under which others should receive American companies. We respect the right of every sovereign government to establish conditions for foreign investment that will best meet its own development needs (Cooper, 1977: 2).

Developing countries are increasingly viewing direct foreign investment as a mixed blessing. For the most part, they now share J. J. Puthucheary's view (Freeman, 1968: 30) that to open their economies indiscriminately to foreign investment is like "holding open the door of a bird cage in the expectation that more birds will fly in than out" or Albert Hirschman's characterization that foreign investment "shares to a very high degree the ambiguity of most human inventions and institutions: it has considerable potential for both good and evil" (Hirschman, 1971: 226).

Indicative of this mixed view of foreign investment was the Declaration of Bogota of 1966, which established the basic principles of the Andean Subregional Pact. In the Declaration the Presidents and representatives of Colombia, Chile, Peru, Ecuador and Venezuela stated as follows:

> We consider that private external capital can play a considerable role in the economic development of Latin America provided that it stimulates the capitalization of the country where it locates, facilitates greater participation of national capital in this process and does not create obstacles to regional integration (Tironi, 1978: 966).

Because of their awareness of the limitations and benefits of direct foreign investment (DFI), the governments of developing countries have sought to gain greater control over the operations of foreign investors in their countries. This control progresses through three conceptually distinct stages:

(1) Acquiring more knowledge about the operations of direct foreign investment within the host country
(2) Requiring new DFI to be approved before it can enter the host-country
(3) Using a formal approval mechanism in order to evaluate and place restrictions upon the type of direct foreign investments that will be allowed to enter the host-country

A first step in the ability to control direct foreign investment is the acquisition of greater knowledge about DFI within the host-country. Writing on this in 1973, Constantine Vaitsos noted:

> Ten years ago the only place with reliable information on foreign investment in Peru was to be found in the United States embassy. Three years ago, in the drafting of the Decision 24, the major source of information was the data published by tha U.S. Department of Commerce.... Next year, the Andean Pact and Mexico will have their own systems of information and analysis on the flow and effects of foreign investment in their region (Vaitsos, 1973: 639-40).

In 1945 the Colombian government carried out its first census of foreign investment, but the results were questionable because, in the words of the government, it

> was not possible to check the validity and seriousness of the information given by the investors. In most cases the information came unilaterally from the companies themselves; therefore the evaluation was approximate (Boyce & Lombard, 1976: 8).

Some of the conclusions of the census were that the government needed to establish better control over foreign investment, that it needed to require foreign investors to sell their foreign exchange to the Central Bank (Banco de la Republica), and that foreign investors should register their capital with the Foreign Exchange Board (Boyce & Lombard, 1976: 9).

The government attempted to follow these suggestions in the next few years. Resolution 175 of 1947 required new foreign capital to be registered with the Office of Exchange Control if the investor wanted to retain the rights to repatriate the capital or export its profits. Decree 1949 of 1948 required foreign investors to sell their imported foreign exchange to the Central Bank (Lopez Arias, 1977: 132-5). Decree 545 of 1951 required the registration of all capital that was imported before 1951. Capital that did not comply was to be considered nonregistered and the Office of Exchange Control was not to allow it the right to export dividends. These laws provided an opportunity for the government to obtain accurate information on direct foreign investment by requiring foreign investors to register and by threatening those who did not do so by refusing to allow them to export profits. All of this effort came to naught when Law 1A of 1959 took the enforcement provisions out of the registration of DFI by allowing nonregistered direct foreign investment to export dividends (DANE, 1971: 60-1).

In spite of these earlier efforts to gain accurate knowledge of the operations of DFI in Colombia, it was not until Decree Law 444 of 1967 was promulgated that the government of Colombia had the ability to compel foreign investors to register and provide information on their operations. Decree Law 444 required foreign investments to be registered with the Exchange Office of the Central Bank. The Exchange Office was also to register the movement of investments, the reinvestment of remittable profits, and the repatriation of capital. Registration with the Exchange Office gave the foreign investor the right to remit profits and repatriate the original investment and any authorized reinvestment. In order to remit profits or repatriate capital, the investor was required to provide the Exchange Office with the following information: name of the investors, value of the initial investment, value of additional investments, value of reinstated profits, amount of profit remittances, amount of repatriated capital, and anything else required by the Exchange Office (Presidente, 1967: articulos 106-26). Decree Law 1900 of 1973, under which Colombia implemented the foreign investment code of the Andean Pact, restated this registration requirement. It required substantial additional information from the foreign investor, such as details of financial resources, technical knowledge to be supplied; justification of the project in terms of adding to domestic savings, foreign exchange, technical knowledge, or entrepreneurial spirit; balance of payments effects; effects on employment, and effects on pollution (Presidente, 1973: capitulo 1-5).

A second step in gaining control over direct foreign investment is the requirement that new DFI be approved by the host government before it could enter the country. Even in cases where this approval is simply pro forma, the procedure itself establishes at least the potential for the government to control DFI in the future.

In Colombia it was Decree 444 of 1967 that first established the requirement that new DFI be approved by the government. Under Article 107 of the law, the Administrative Planning Department (later called the National Planning Department, or DNP) was required to approve all new foreign investment as well as any increase in existing foreign investments. Under Resolution 17 of 1972 of the National Council of Economic and Social Policy, the National Planning Department was allowed 60 days to decide on each foreign investment application. In particularly complex cases, the DNP was allowed to extend this deadline to 120 days. However, if no decision were reached within 120 days, the proposed investment would be considered approved. Approved investments still had to be registered with the Exchange Office of the Central Bank (Consejo, 1972: articulo 5).

Taking into account the existance of greater knowledge about DFI activities in the host country and the host government's own formal control over the entry of direct foreign investment, many governments of developing nations proceed to the third stage in the control over DFI: trying to change the nature and operations of foreign investment within their borders. One tactic that host governments have used has been to negotiate an entry contract with prospective foreign investors. In the process, the government tries to exact as many concessions as possible in return for the approval of the foreign investment application. In the bargaining process, the major asset of the host government is its power to provide access to local productive resources and to the local (usually protected) market. Indonesia was the first country to have such a system of negotiating entry contracts (Lombard, 1978: 66).

In a similar procedure, called "screening," the government weighs the perceived costs and benefits of a foreign investment proposal and allows entry only to those investments that have the greatest net benefit or that meet certain pre-determined requirements. Walter Chudson has noted that, through the screening process,

> government authorities are increasingly turning to some form of systematic project appraisal as a means of combining in a single calculation various economic criteria that indicate those projects that can increase output as much as possible, using abundant resources (such as labor) intensively and economizing on scarce resources (such as financial and skilled human capital and foreign exchange) (Chudson, 1975: 134).

Under Decree Law 1900 of 1973 the Colombian government gave the National Planning Department the responsibility for screening foreign investment applications and approving them. However, in the process of screening these foreign investments, the DNP is pursuing two distinct goals. The first is an attempt to alter the behavior of foreign firms in such a way that their potential benefits are maximized and their potential costs are minimized. The second goal is an attempt to domesticate the economy by transforming foreign investments to majority-domestic investments.

## Behavior Alteration

In behavior alteration, the government offers a series of carrots and sticks to foreign investors. The incentives are offered to encourage specific behavior that is perceived as beneficial. The restrictions are offered to curb certain behavior of direct foreign investment that is viewed as harmful to national goals. Among the behavior alteration policies of the Colombian government are the following:

### A. Tax Discrimination

Colombia, like many other developing countries, taxes foreign firms at a higher rate than domestic ones. The country did this under Decree Law 3191 of 1963, which established a twelve percent tax on the payment of dividends abroad. This tax was in addition to the income tax on investments (Wurfel, 1965: 228-30). The rationale for such a policy can be varied. It may be an attempt to subsidize domestic businesses by taxing the foreign competition more heavily. It may be that foreign investments are more visable and are an easy source for increasing government revenues. It may be an attempt to reduce the outflow of capital and the drain on foreign exchange that comes from the remittance of profits from direct foreign investments. Whatever the justification, the result of this policy is likely to be all of the above: an increase in government revenues, a subsidization of domestic businesses, and a reduced demand for foreign exchange.

### B. Balance of Payments

The balance of payments has long been an area of concern for the Colombian government. The scarcity of foreign exchange, combined with the balance of payments problems of the 1960s and the government's belief that direct foreign investment was exacerbating the outflow of capital, caused the government of Carlos Lleras Restrepo to adopt the first effective restrictions on DFI in Colombia: Decree Law 444 of 1967 (see Maullin, 1972 and Hayter, 1971). Since that time, concern with the balance of payments impacts of direct foreign investment has continued, and so have attempts to alter the behavior of DFI so as to improve its balance of payments effects. In general, the government has tried to get DFI to increase its exports of goods (a balance of payments credit) and has discouraged imports of goods (a balance of payments debit). At the same time, the government has adopted policies to restrict capital exports (a balance of payments debit) and to increase imports of capital (a balance of payments credit). To increase its knowledge of the foreign exchange dealings of direct foreign investors, the Colombian government has funnelled all of its foreign exchange dealings through the Exchange Office of the Central Bank. One of the factors that the National Planning Department was to take into account in screening foreign investment applications was the "net effect on the balance of payments" (Presidente, 1967: articulos 106-26).

One of the factors listed in Decree Law 444 of 1967 was the "ratio between imported capital and the necessary investment required by the company" (Presidente, 1967: art. 110). It appears clear that one of the reasons for this was the desire to insure that direct foreign investments did indeed import most of the capital used for their investment, rather than obtaining most of the necessary capital through local borrowing.

The capital exports of direct foreign investment were also limited. Under Resolution 17 of 1972 of the National Council of Economic and Social Policy, direct foreign investments were allowed to remit abroad as profits only 14 percent of the registered value of their investment (Consejo, 1972: art. 8). Decree 170 of 1977 increased this limit to 20 percent (Presidente, 1977: art. 10). However, the purpose remained the same: to limit the export of capital by foreign investors. The country also has a restrictive policy for allowing royalty payments for technology (see below), part of the purpose of which is to reduce capital exports.

Another aspect of the Colombian government's policies of behavior alteration has to do with the balance of trade effects of prospective foreign investors. These effects are scrutinized thoroughly as part of the National Planning Department's screening process. As part of the Application Form for Direct Foreign Investment, prospective investors are required to state how much of their production will be exported, how much of their raw materials and intermediate goods will be imported, and whether the goods that they produce will be substituting for goods that are currently imported (DNP, 1973: 15-9). Those proposed investments that would have a direct negative effect on the balance of trade (i.e., imports exceeding new exports) were either rejected <u>or</u> required to increase the exports over the projected amounts until the direct balance of trade effect is at least neutral. These projects are then required to sign export contracts with the Institute of Foreign Trade (INCOMEX), which will then monitor their export performance (DNP, 1977).

C. Local Borrowing

Colombia has a government policy of limiting the degree to which direct foreign investors can use local credit. This policy was probably an attempt, in part, to insure that foreign investors did conduct their investment by bringing capital into the country (and thus aiding the balance of payments). Part of this policy was probably also caused by the desire of the government to prevent foreign investors from absorbing much of the investment capital available in the country and, in so doing, depriving the domestic investors of potential capital (Business International, 1970: 71). Decree 1031 of 1963 prevented foreign subsidiaries from obtaining loans for more than 100 percent of their assets (Wurfel, 1965: 228-30). Decree Law 1900 of 1973 allowed direct foreign investors access to short-term (one year or less) credit only. In Decree 170 of 1977 DFI was also allowed access to medium-term credit (3 years duration or less) (Presidente, 1977: art. 6).

D. Transfer of Technology

The government of Colombia requires the Committee on Royalties to approve all contracts for the transfer of technology and trademarks. This Committee screens technology contracts in a similar manner to that used by the DNP to screen DFI applications. The government also forbids firms with direct foreign investment from signing technology contracts with parent or affiliate firms (Moreno, 1976: 26-7).

In addition to the types of policies listed above, the Colombian government uses behavior alteration to bring about a series of other results: to increase the backward linkages (i.e., local supply of raw materials and intermediate products) of direct foreign investment, to reduce environmental pollution of DFI, to create employment within Colombia, to reduce the prices of products produced, to decentralize DFI outside of the three major industrial zones of the country--Bogota, Medellin, and Cali, and to keep foreign investors from buying out existing national enterprises except to prevent imminent bankruptcy (Presidente, 1973: art. 3; DNP, 1973: 13-20; DNP, 1977).

In all of these policies of behavior alteration, the perceived benefits and costs are explicit. These policies may have stated questionable or contradictory objectives, but in each case the perceived benefits are clear: increased employment of Colombians, decentralization of industry, increased government revenues, increases in the importation of capital and the export of goods, decreases in the export of capital and the import of goods, less foreign borrowing from domestic supplies of capital, lower prices of goods, and less pollution. It can still be argued that these goals do not correspond with national development, but the goals themselves are explicit and can be clearly analyzed. The other major goal of the DNP screening process--that of transferring control over DFI from foreign investors to domestic ones--is much more nebulous in its perceptions of cost and benefit to the nation . It is all the more intriguing for that reason.

## Domestication

Some countries have followed policies of limiting the participation of foreign investors to minority-ownership of companies in which majority ownership resides with private national investors. Leslie Rood (1976) refers to this policy as "indigenization," and he defines it as "the process by which a government limits participation in a particular industry to citizens of a country, thus forcing alien owners to sell" (p. 430). In the case of the countries of East Africa, "alien" owners may also include Asians who have long been residents of the area. Hence, indigenization may differ slightly from domestication. The transfer of ownership from Asian residents of Kenya or Uganda to African residents would be an example of indigenization, but it would not be considered domestication inasmuch as ownership was being transferred from one domestic group to another. In countries such as Indonesia and Malaysia, where government policy distinguishes between different groups of residents on the basis of ethnicity, there may also be differences between domestication and indigenization. In Colombia, however, these two approaches would be identical. Albert Hirschman (1971) has long been an advocate of this process of "phasing out" direct foreign investment. He refers to this policy as "divestment" (p. 225). In these pages I will use the term "domestication" to refer to these policies of (a) prohibiting new majority-owned direct foreign investment in the economy (or in certain sectors of it) and reserving these sectors to majority private-national investment or (b) requiring existing majority-owned direct foreign investments to phase out and transform into majority private-national investments.

Examples of such policies can be found throughout the developing world. Brazil (1975) restricts ownership of radio and television broadcasting to national citizens (p. 15). Indonesia restricts new foreign investments from several industries which it reserves for private national capital. Among these industries are paint, cigarettes, beverages, batteries, automobile assembly and distribution, and textile manufacturing. In addition, all new direct foreign investment in nonrestricted industries must begin as joint ventures in which local participation will be 51 percent within ten years (USDC, 1977a: 29).

In Malaysia the general policy norm is for direct foreign investment to be allowed, but in the form of joint ventures with majority participation going to local owners. In projects that cater mostly to the domestic market, majority equity must be nationally owned. In projects that sell mostly for export markets, majority equity may be held by the foreign investors.

In addition, the government has established a policy of transforming currently majority-owned foreign firms into majority-national firms. By 1990, 30 percent of the ownership of these companies must be held by ethnic Malays, 40 percent by nonethnic Malay citizens, and the remaining 30 percent by the foreign firms (USDC, 1977b: 17-8).

The Filipino government has selected a number of sectors of the economy to be reserved for majority-owned national firms. The government requires 60 percent Filipino ownership of companies involved in development of resources, public utilities, and finance. Commercial and private development banks must have 70 percent Filipino ownership. Investments in so-called "pioneer" areas may be 100 percent foreign-owned, but they must convert to joint venture status with Filipinos within thirty years (USDC, 1976: 22-4).

In Nigeria, twenty-two categories of enterprises (e.g., small retail operations, bakeries, newspapers, garment manufacturing) are reserved exclusively for Nigerians, as are small operations in some of the more complex industries. Larger companies in thirty-three other industries (including breweries and cement) must have a minimum of forty percent participation by Nigerians. In a similar policy, Ghana has reserved all small enterprises and companies in nineteen categories of simple industry to private Ghanian participation only. The government has also stated that large companies in forty-six categories of industry (including pharmaceuticals, automobile assembly, and plastics) must have Ghanian participation of forty percent to fifty percent (Rood, 1976: 432). Mexico has reserved certain sectors of the economy (e.g., radio, television, forestry) to private national investors only (USDC, 1977c: 19-20). In addition, foreign investment in the remainder of the economy is generally limited to 49 percent ownership (Poitras, 1974: 69).

One of the most famous examples of domestication policy has been the Andean Subregional Pact's Article 24, the "Common Regime for the Treatment of Foreign Capital and of Trademarks, Patents, Licenses, and Royalties." Article 27 of this regime prohibits majority-owned foreign firms from taking advantage of the Pact's trade liberalization program unless they are in the process of transforming to majority-local ownership. Article 30 requires new foreign investment to be minority-foreign-owned or in the process of transforming to majority-national ownership (Commission, 1973: 390-1).

The governmant of Colombia implemented the domestication policy of the Andean Pact under Decree Law 1900 of 1973. The law begins by distinguishing between "national," "mixed," and "foreign" companies. A "national" company is one in which more than 80 percent of the capital is owned by Colombian investors. A "mixed" enterprise is one in which national capital participation is between 51 percent and 80 percent. A "foreign" enterprise is defined as one in which national capital participation is less than 51 percent. In cases in which the state was one of the national investors and the state had a determining capacity in the company, an enterprise could be considered "mixed" even though national participation was less than 51 percent (Presidente, 1973: art. 1).

Articles 27 through 37 of Decree Law 1900 deal with the controversial issue of the fade-out (i.e., gradual domestication) of all new direct foreign investment and of existing foreign firms that wish to take advantage of the trade liberalization program of the Andean Pact. Under Article 27 of the law, only national and mixed companies, and those foreign enterprises which are in the process of transforming into national or mixed companies, may take advantage of the duty-free program of the Andean Subregional Pact. All existing foreign enterprises that wish to take advantage of the trade liberalization program were required to sign transformation agreements with the Colombian government within three years of the time when the statute entered into force (January 1, 1974). National participation of these companies must be at least 15 percent at the end of three years, 45 percent within ten years, and at least 51 percent within fifteen years (Presidente, 1973: art. 28-9).

More importantly, under Article 30 foreign enterprises which are established in Colombia after the agreement takes effect must sign agreements to transform into mixed companies within fifteen years. The taking effect of this requirement was delayed until January 1, 1974 (Presidente, 1977: art. 7). This transformation requirement for new DFI differed from that imposed on existing foreign companies, which had to transform only if they wanted to take advantage of the trade liberalization program of the Andean Pact. New foreign investors were required as part of the application procedure to sign an "Agreement of Transformation into a Mixed Enterprise for Foreign Corporations Existing After January 1, 1974," which stated:

(a) The period of time for compliance with the obligation to transform the foreign enterprise into a mixed one;
(b) The gradual scale for the transfer of shares, participation or rights to national investors, including in that scale at least the rules on minimum percentages referred to in Articles 28 and 30.
(c) Regulations that will ensure the progressive participation of national investors or their representatives in the technical, financial, commercial, and administrative management of the enterprise, at least as of the date the enterprise begins production;
(d) The method of determining the value of shares, participation of rights at the time of their sale; and
(e) The systems that will assure the transfer of shares, participation or rights to national investors

(Presidente, 1973: art. 31).

Under Decree Law 1900 of 1983, the government of Colombia began implementing a policy of domestication, of gradually transferring ownership and control over foreign investment to Colombian investors. A major implication of this policy is that ownership and control of the Colombian economy will ultimately be in the hands of Colombian citizens. This policy also raises two questions: (1) Why was it undertaken to begin with? (2) Will it improve the well-being of the population of Colombia?

Unlike the different policies of behavior alteration, in which the perceived costs and benefits to Colombia were explicit, domestication carries with it no prima facie justification. With policies of behavior alteration, there was a clear and logical connection between the means used (e.g., restrictions on the export of capital by direct foreign investors) and the goals to be achieved (e.g., the improvements of the country's balance of payments and freeing up of foreign exchange). With domestication the means are clear (i.e., transferring control over the economy to national citizens), but what remains unclear is the goal that is achieved by this policy. What difference would it make if control over the economy were to rest with national, rather that foreign, investors?

In studying the case of domestication policies in Mexico, Bennett and Sharpe (1976) posited three different justifications for transferring ownership and control over the economy from foreign to private national investors. The first justification, which they referred to as "parallelism," claimed that domestication is justified because the economic interests of national investors are more likely to run parallel to the national interest than are the interests of foreign investors. The second justification argued that national majority-owned firms are more easily controlled by the government than are foreign-owned firms. The final argument posited that in a predominantly private economy "the national interest is the interests of national capital" (p. 7).

The latter two justifications of domestication are truisms. They equate the national interest with greater state control or with the development of a national bourgeoisie. These justifications define "the national interest" in such a way that they have no direct connection to the well-being of the citizens of the nation. These justifications lead to the conclusion that the actions of national investors or those of the national government are, by definition, in the national interest. This leads to the _reductio ad absurdum_ that nationally owned companies could pollute the environment, charge extortionate prices for substandard products, pay subsistence wages for long hours of work in unhealthy conditions, and in doing all this still be operating in the national interest.

In the preface to this study it was asserted that the proper role of a government is to enhance the well-being of its citizens. It was further asserted that government policies can be judged according to this criterion. Given these premises, attempts to justify domestication in terms (such as state control or the development of the national bourgeoisie) that cannot be related to the well-being of the citizenry cannot be studied with this approach.

The parallelism justification is amenable to the approach stated in the preface. This argument asserts that the interests of national investors run parallel to the national interest more so than do the interests of foreign investors and, because of this difference, national firms are more likely to act in the national interest than are foreign firms. The parallelism justification is the only approach that allows one to evaluate the policy of domestication in terms of the well-being of the citizenry. This does not mean that the logic of parallelism is correct, but it does mean that it is amenable to empirical verification. In order to verify it, it is necessary to answer three questions:

(1) In what ways, related to the well-being of the citizens of a nation, could foreign and domestic firms act differently?

(2) Do they act differently?

(3) If there are differences, does the behavior of domestic firms enhance the well-being of the citizens more than the behavior of foreign firms?

Jack Behrman (1972) argues that such differences between foreign and domestic firms do not exist. He has asserted that, if domestication policies were implemented, "local owners would undoubtedly behave as similarly as possible to the (foreign) owners..." (p. 469). He goes on to argue:

> There is a major difficulty with 'solutions' that are concerned with the ownership of industry: they are not addressed to the real issues of economic growth and economic power....
> ...Mere change of ownership will not produce these results (economic growth and greater participation) automatically, and most of the desired benefits can be gained without the cost of changing ownership.
> ...If, however, nations insist that ownership is more important than behavior, and redistribution of ownership more important than expansion of investment, then they probably should be left to develop only at the rate which their own efforts can produce (p. 487).

What Behrman overlooks is the possibility that ownership and behavior are related, and that changes in ownership will bring changes in behavior.

In a similar vein, Little and Mirlees (1974) mention that

developing countries approach foreign private investment with a fear and resentment that is

> aroused and sustained by easily found examples of the behavior of foreign corporations which appear to have economic consequences at variance with the interests of the host country. It is seldom asked whether such behavior has anything to do with the foreignness of the corporation; whether the behavior is not caused by the host government's own policies; or whether the economic consequences were not inevitable (pp. 119-120, my emphasis).

The remainder of this study will focus on these issues. Specifically, it will study the case of the manufacturing sector in Colombia to try to determine whether the logic of parallelism is accurate. The study will assume the following counterfactual argument: that the government of Colombia has been successful in bringing about domestic ownership and control over the Colombian manufacturing sector. (For the purposes of this study, I will be assuming that the transfer of majority ownership to domestic citizens will also transfer effective control over the investment). Assuming that domestication of manufacturing has taken place, would this improve the well-being of the citizenry of the country? The primary hypothesis of this study is that of the parallelism argument itself:

> H1: Domestication will enhance the well-being of the Colombian citizenry because the behavior of domestic firms runs closer to the best interests of the citizenry than does the behavior of foreign firms.

This hypothesis assumes that there are differences between foreign and domestic investments, and that domestic investments have a more beneficial effect upon citizen well-being.

As another explanation I am positing Behrman's assumption of the null hypothesis:

> H0: Domestication will have no effect upon the well-being of the Colombian citizenry because foreign and domestic firms have no differences in behavior or effects.

The other possible explanation is that domestication is harmful:

> H2: Domestication will harm the well-being of the Colombian citizenry because the behavior of foreign firms enhances the welfare of citizens more than the behavior of domestic firms.

This hypothesis assumes that there are differences between domestic and foreign investment, and that foreign investments have a more beneficial effect upon citizen well-being. The remainder of this study will study these hypotheses as they relate to the case of the domestication of the Colombian manufacturing sector.

# CHAPTER 3

## DIRECT FOREIGN INVESTMENT IN THE COLOMBIAN ECONOMY

Foreign investment in Colombia is as old as the republic itself, and it has mirrored trends in the worldwide development of DFI. Throughout the nineteenth century direct foreign investment in Colombia was small-scale and directed primarily towards mineral extraction, agricultural production, and transportation. Mineral investments were directed towards exploiting emeralds, silver, and platinum. Most agricultural investments went into the growing of bananas, sugar, and coffee. The largest of these investments was United Fruit Company's 13,000-acre tract for banana production (Adams, 1914: 91). Transportation investments went towards the development of steamship lines, railroads, and the French effort to build a canal across Panama (then a province of Colombia) (Rippy, 1947: 13 & 61-71; United Nations, 1955: 5).

In the late nineteenth century the amount of direct foreign investment increased, and by 1914 it had reached an estimated $60 million (Table 1). Of this amount, an estimated $31 million was from Great Britain, (Lopez Arias, 1977: 43) with the United States accounting for about $24 million and the remainder coming from France and Germany (Matter, 1977: 119-20; Rippy, 1947: 13 & 53). Internationally, Britain was also the world's largest investor (Wilkins, 1970: 201).

As can be seen from Table 1, direct foreign investment in 1914 was still directed towards the sectors of transportation, mining, and agriculture. From the estimates in the table, no more that three percent of DFI could possibly have been in the manufacturing sector, indicating that foreign investment was not involved significantly in the industrialization that Colombia underwent between 1880 and World War I (Berry, nd a: 27a). McGreevey (1971) estimates that in 1914 about 15 percent of unemployment and 10 percent of GNP in Colombia came from manufacturing (p.299), and he concluded that foreign involvement played an insignificant role in Colombia's economy in 1914:

> There was virtually no foreign investment in manufacturing; thus the earliest phase of industrial development was achieved almost completely without the assistance of foreign capital.... Investments in agriculture (bananas) and mining (placers) were physically in Colombia but far from the population centers and generally unrelated to the domestic economy..., in any event those investments were not

decisive in the achievement of development (p.204).

The decade that followed the First World War was a period of tremendous economic growth in Colombia. This rapid growth was stimulated almost entirely by external factors: the rapid increase in exports of coffee and petroleum, a sharp increase in the country's foreign debt (Randall, 1977: 56), and an equally rapid increase in direct foreign investment. United States DFI in Colombia, for example, increased from $45 million in 1919 to $124 million in 1929 (see Table 54). Most of the U.S. investments went into the petroleum sector. Direct foreign investment in the petroleum sector accounted for 45.0 percent of U.S. DFI in Colombia by 1929 (see Table 2). Public utilities, agriculture, and mining also accounted for significant portions of U.S., and presumably total, DFI in Colombia. The only sectors with minimal involvement were manufacturing (2.9 percent of the total) and trade (3.0 percent of the total). This low participation by DFI in manufacturing led Konrad Matter to state that "the insipient industrialization that occurred in the years 1924-29 and 1929-32 was financed almost exclusively with Colombian capital" (Matter, 1977: 131).

TABLE 1
ESTIMATED TOTAL DIRECT FOREIGN INVESTMENT IN COLOMBIA, BY SECTOR, 1914

| Sector | Amount | Percent of Total |
|---|---|---|
| Transportation | $24 million | 40.0 |
| Mining | $18 million | 30.0 |
| Agriculture | $16 million | 26.7 |
| Miscellaneous | $ 2 million | 3.3 |
| Total | $60 million | 100.0 |

SOURCE: (McGreevey, 1971: 204 & 299).

However, this period was the time during which the first modern foreign manufacturing firms were established in Colombia. General Electric de Colombia was formed in 1927 as one of the first foreign manufacturing investments in the country. Coca Cola was established in Colombia in 1928, and Otis Elevator began in 1929 (Aldana, 1977: 150-8). This period also saw DFI enter the Colombian banking sector. The Banco de Londres y Montreal was established in Colombia in 1920; the Banco Frances-Italiano in 1924, and the Royal Bank of Canada in 1925 (Boyce & Lombard, 1976: 21-2).

One characteristic of the direct foreign investment in Colombia during the decade of the 1920s was that U.S. investments began to surpass those of Great Britain. British direct investment reached $33 million in 1918, and it increased in the years following due to expanding investments in petroleum (Winkler, 1928: 129). However, after the early 1920s British investment began to decline in both relative and absolute amounts. Randall estimates British portfolio and direct foreign investment in Colombia declined from $55 million in 1923 to $42 million in 1930, and it seems likely that DFI alone declined by a similar rate. By 1930 U.S. DFI in Colombia had increased to 130 million, more than three times the value of total British foreign investment in Colombia (Randall, 1977: 11).

In spite of the tremendous amount of foreign investment in Colombia during the 1920s, the U.N. Economic Commission for Latin America concluded that this investment did not play a vital role in supplying capital for Colombia's economic growth, stating:

> Notwithstanding the important role that it played during this period, for both its direct and indirect effects, foreign investment was equivalent to only 15% of the total quantity of capital on which the country depended (Montana Cuellar, nd: 112).

TABLE 2
U.S. DIRECT FOREIGN INVESTMENT IN COLOMBIA, 1929

| Sector | Amount | Percent of Total |
|---|---|---|
| Petroleum | $ 55.8 million | 45.0 |
| Public Utilities | $ 24.9 million | 20.1 |
| Agriculture | $ 15.8 million | 12.7 |
| Mining and Smelting | $ 10.6 million | 8.5 |
| Trade | $ 3.7 million | 3.0 |
| Manufacturing | $ 3.6 million | 2.9 |
| Miscellaneous | $ 9.6 milliom | 7.7 |
| Total | $124.0 million | 100.0 |

SOURCE: (Wilkins, 1974: 57).

The 1920s were also marked by a series of disputes between Colombian workers and foreign companies. The first major dispute centered on oil workers for Tropical Oil Company, a subsidiary of Standard Oil of New Jersey, who began complaining about poor health conditions in their work camps near Barrancabermeja. They were also upset that Colombian employees had a lower pay scale than foreign workers. The workers went on strike in 1924 and again in 1927. Both strikes were put down violently by troops sent in by the Conservative government (Urrutia, 1969: 93-99).

The most violent and notorious dispute took place in 1928 between the United Fruit Company and banana workers on the northern coast of Colombia. United's 30,000 workers went on strike for better working conditions and better pay. The government sent in the army to put down the strike. The strike was crushed at the cost of the lives of many striking workers and their families. Estimates of casualties vary from 1,500 dead and 3,000 wounded (by labor leader Alberto Castrillon) to about 40 killed and over 100 wounded (by General Cortes Vargas, the army commander who crushed the strike) (Kepner & Soothill, 1935: 329). Colombian novelist Gabriel Garcia Marquez (1971) immortalized the massacre in his novel _One Hundred Years of Solitude_ when he described an event during the strike when several hundred strikers and their families were gunned down by the army in a town plaza:

> After his (Arcadio Segundo's) shout something happened that did not bring on fright but a kind of of hallucination. The captain gave the order to fire and fourteen machine guns answered at once. But it all seemed like a farce. It was as if the machine guns were loaded with caps, because their panting rattle could be heard and their incandescent spitting could be seen, but not the slightest reaction was perceived, not a cry, not even a sight among the compact crowd that seemed petrified by an instantaneous invulnerability. Suddenly, on one side of the station, a cry of death tore open the enchantment (p.283).

The killing of the banana workers, and the role of United Fruit and the Conservative government in their deaths, became the topic of a heated session of the Colombian Congress in September of 1929. Liberal representative Jorge Eliecer Gaitan rose to fame with his verbal attacks on United Fruit and the Government (Sharpless, 1978: 56-60). In his September 6, 1929, address to the Colombian Congress, Gaitan summed up the episode as follows:

> Here is the tragedy, provoked by United with the complicity of unscrupulous military men and of a government incapable of understanding ideas of responsibility. Magdalena is a state in which everything is controlled by United. Not only the workers, but also the merchants and the banana producers are the economic slaves of that company.... That prostituted company has corrupted consciences and bought officials.... The national producers have turned to the government, but they have obtained no solution to their problem. This is so because the Colombian government machine-guns the country's children and kneels on the ground for the Yankee gold (Gaitan, 1972: 131-3, my translation).

The massacre of the banana workers, and the role of the Conservative Party government in the whole affair, was partly responsible for the fall of the Conservative government in the election of 1930 (Urrutia, 1969: 108-9). This episode created a bitter attitude towards foreign investment on the part of many Colombians, especially those on the political left (Rodriguez Acosta, 1973: 228). Among the governing elites, however, this bitterness soon dissipated. A bipartisan commission appointed as a result of the banana massacre reached this conclusion on foreign investment:

> Colombia requires for its development and progress the immigration of capital to develop its industries and of people who will establish in our midst the technology which made possible the development of higher civilizations. It would be contrary to rational, constructive policy of national regeneration to erect obstacles which might divert the flow of capital and energy to other areas.... We must provide foreign investment with full guarantees (Randall, 1977: 137-8).

Just as the Colombian economy had boomed due to external influences during the 1920s, so the 1930s saw the temporary collapse of the Colombian economy due to a foreign influence: the Depression. Export earnings declined from 133 million pesos in 1928 to 103 million in 1930, and to 42 million in 1935. In 1931 and again in 1932 the government had to go into default on its foreign debt (Randall, 1977: 24 & 68). Later the peso had to be devalued (Chu, 1977: 3). Writing on the role of foreign petroleum companies in Colombia's economic instability during the 1930s, Randall (1977) states:

> The Colombian experience underlines the difficulty experienced by capital- and technology-poor nations anxious to develop natural resources without sacrificing sovereignty. Certainly the Colombian government would have been equally affected by international price fluctuations of crude petroleum had it introduced more rigid controls over production, exportation, and marketing. But in the absence of such controls the government was virtually at the mercy of corporate and government decisions beyond its borders, and its balance of payments tended to be unpredictable (p. 116).

In spite of the sharp drop in export earnings and the reduction in capital inflows, the country's economy managed to pull out of the Depression. Real gross domestic product declined less than three percent between 1929 and 1931, and the economy then resumed its growth at about 3.3 percent annually between 1929 and 1945 (Chu, 1977: 4). The manufacturing sector was not apparently harmed by the general slowdown in the economy. Between 1930 and 1945 the manufacturing sector grew at a real rate of 6.5 percent annually, almost twice the level for the entire economy (Berry, nd a: 34a). This growth was aided by higher tariffs, exchange restrictions, and by currency depreciation (Whyte, 1949: 249).

This growth of the Colombian manufacturing sector occurred at a time when direct foreign investment in the country was declining and when DFI in manufacturing was small. United States DFI, which made up most of direct foreign investment in Colombia, decreased from $124 million in 1929 to $107 million in 1936. This investment increased from 1936 onward, but in 1943 it was still below the 1929 level. Direct foreign investment in the petroleum sector increased in both relative and absolute amounts during this period. United States DFI in petroleum increased from $56 million and 45 percent of the total in 1929 to $77 million and 66 percent of the total in 1943 (Matter, 1977: 119-20).

Direct foreign investment in the manufacturing sector remained at low levels during this period. Even as late as 1943 only 5 percent of U.S. DFI in Colombia was in the manufacturing sector (see Table 4). However, there were some important foreign manufacturing companies that entered Colombia during the 1930s. Two U.S. drug companies, the Sidney Ross Company and Miles Laboratories, established Colombian subsidiaries in 1932 and 1936, respectively. St. Regis Paper established its first Colombian subsidiary, Empaques Bates de Colombia, in 1934. The Fleischman Company was one of the first foreign firms to market food products in Colombia. It was established in 1938 (Armendariz, 1977: 86-95).

Direct foreign investment in the Colombian economy began an upward climb in the late 1930s. United States DFI, for example, climbed to $112 million in 1940, to $117 million in 1943, and to $189 million in 1946 (Matter, 1977: 119-20). The United States was far and away the largest foreign investor in Colombia during this period. A 1945 study of total foreign investment in the country (including portfolio and direct investments) showed a total of $339 million invested (see Table 3). The United States accounted for over two-thirds of the entire foreign investment in Colombia in that year. The country of origin of this investment can be taken as generally indicative of the origin of direct foreign investment. One of the most striking features of DFI in Colombia was the decline of British direct foreign investments since the 1920s. The Depression and the Second World War forced the liquidation of a large number of British firms in Colombia. British investments in railways, for example, were eventually sold to the Colombian government (United Nations, 1955: 69). By 1946, British direct foreign investment amounted to only $25 million, or 81 percent of what British DFI in Colombia had been in 1914 (Matter, 1977: 129). Britain was still the second largest foreign investor in Colombia at the end of the Second World War, but accounted for only 12 percent of Colombia's foreign investment.

TABLE 3
PORTFOLIO AND DIRECT FOREIGN INVESTMENT
IN COLOMBIA, 1945

| Country of Origin | Amount | Percent of Total |
|---|---|---|
| United States | $242 million | 71.4 |
| United Kingdom | $ 43 million | 12.7 |
| Germany | $ 12 million | 3.5 |
| Canada | $ 11 million | 3.2 |
| Belgium | $ 7 million | 2.1 |
| Italy | $ 5 million | 1.5 |
| France | $ 3 million | 0.9 |
| Spain | $ 2 million | 0.6 |
| Sweden | $ 2 million | 0.6 |
| Switzerland | $ 1 million | 0.3 |
| Miscellaneous | $ 11 million | 3.2 |
| Total | $339 million | 100.0 |

SOURCE: (Whyte, 1949: 270)

By the mid-1940s, direct foreign investment in Colombia was concentrated into two sectors of the economy: petroleum and transportation. Using U.S. DFI in Colombia as indicative of all DFI (see Table 4), one can see that in 1943 almost two-thirds of DFI was invested in petroleum and another 15 percent in transportation and public utilities. Manufacturing accounted for only 5 percent of the total, as did trade, and agriculture had declined to only 2 percent. This sectoral distribution was to change in the following decades.

The post-World War II period was characterized by the continued expansion of the Colombian economy, the rapid increase in direct foreign investment, the increased concentration of DFI into manufacturing pursuits, and the continued dominance of the United States as the source of DFI in Colombia. This period was also characterized by the relative decline of the agricultural sector in the Colombian economy and by a corresponding increase in the importance of the manufacturing sector.

The Colombian economy has expanded rapidly since the mid-1940s. The gross national product increased by 4.1 percent per annum between 1946 and 1950 (Arrubla, 1977: 171). Diaz-Alejandro (1976) states that the average annual growth rates of the Colombian real gross domestic product (GDP) were 5.2 percent from 1950-56; 4.6 percent between 1956-67; and 6.1 percent between 1967 and 1972 (p. 2). Throughout the post-war period, agriculture continued to decline in terms of relative employment and output in the Colombian economy. In 1947 agriculture accounted for 40.3 percent of gross domestic product and 60.9 percent of employment (Currie, 1950: 30-3). This share of GDP declined to 25.1 percent in 1975 (ANDI, 1977: 1), and in 1970 only 39 percent of the labor force was engaged in agriculture (Blutstein, 1977: 47).

TABLE 4
U.S. DIRECT FOREIGN INVESTMENT IN COLOMBIA, 1943

| Sector | Amount | Percent of Total |
|---|---|---|
| Petroleum | $ 75 million | 64.1 |
| Transportation, Communication & Public Utilities | $ 18 million | 15.4 |
| Manufacturing | $ 6 million | 5.1 |
| Trade | $ 6 million | 5.1 |
| Mining and Smelting | $ 5 million | 4.3 |
| Agriculture | $ 2 million | 1.7 |
| Finance and Insurance | $ 1 million | 0.9 |
| Miscellaneous | $ 4 million | 3.4 |
| Total | $117 million | 100.0 |

SOURCE: (United Nations, 1955: 69)

Manufacturing remained the second largest sector of the economy in terms of GDP, but it has been growing more rapidly than agriculture in the post-was period. The average real growth rate of manufacturing was 6.1 percent percent per annum between 1950 and 1972, compared to 3.4 pecent per annum for agriculture (Diaz-Alejandro, 1976: 2). Manufacturing accounted for 15.3 percent of gross domestic product and 5.1 percent of employment in 1947 (Currie, 1950: 30-3). In 1975 manufacturing produced 19.2 percent of the GDP (ANDI, 1977: 1). By 1969-70, manufacturing (of both the cottage shop and industrial variety) was employing about 14 percent of the labor force (Berry, nd a: 6a).

The period from the mid-1940s to the mid 1970s was a time of tremendous growth for direct foreign investment in Colombia. Registered nonpetroleum DFI increased from $75 million in 1943 to $686 million in 1976. Adding U.S. DFI in petroleum to this figure, one can develop an estimate of total DFI in Colombia, which rose from $152 million in 1943 to $742 million in 1976 (see Table 5). What makes this increase surprising is that much of it took place during la Violencia (1946-57), a period of exceptional political instability and violence in Colombia.

Following the promulgation and implementation of the foreign investment regulations in 1967 and 1973, a number of doubts were raised about the ability of Colombia and other Andean Pact members to attract more direct foreign investment (Inter-American

Economic Affairs, 1971: 58). Contrary to early expectations, Colombia has managed to attract a considerable amount of DFI in the years following 1967. As Table 6 demonstrates, from the beginning of the approval requirement for direct foreign investment in Colombia in 1967, the National Planning Department has approved $507.2 million in new investments. From the evidence available in the table, there is no indication that foreign investment applications have declined. In fact, the trend may be in the other direction, towards increasing amounts of DFI approvals.

TABLE 5
ESTIMATED TOTAL DIRECT FOREIGN INVESTMENT IN COLOMBIA
(in millions of U.S. dollars)

| Year | Total Estimated DFI(a) | Registered Direct in Manufacturing $ | % | Foreign Investment in Petroleum $ | % |
|---|---|---|---|---|---|
| 1943 | $152 million | 37 | 24.3 | 77 | 50.7 |
| 1946 | $253 million | 91 | 36.0 | 126 | 49.8 |
| 1950 | $315 million | 132 | 41.9 | 112 | 35.6 |
| 1955 | $415 million | 144 | 34.7 | 178 | 42.9 |
| 1960 | $547 million | 201 | 36.7 | 233 | 42.6 |
| 1965 | $659 million | 245 | 37.2 | 269 | 40.8 |
| 1970 | $785 million | 268 | 34.1 | 334 | 42.5 |
| 1976 | $742 million | 454 | 61.2 | 56 | 7.5 |

Source: Tables 54 and 55.

(a) Estimated value of total DFI was developed by taking the value of registered nonpetroleum DFI and adding the value of U.S. DFI in Colombian petroleum (reported by the U.S. Department of Commerce). Since the U.S. has been the source of almost all DFI in Colombian petroleum, this estimate should be accurate.

Throughout most of the post-war period, petroleum continued to be a major sector for DFI activity. Although it declined gradually as a percentage of estimated DFI in Colombia (from 51 percent in 1943 to 43 percent in 1970), it continued to increase in absolute value until the early 1970s (increasing from $77 million in 1943 to $334 million in 1970). After this time the petroleum direct foreign investments suffered a severe decline, falling to about 8 percent of estimated DFI and $56 million in 1976 (see Table 5). This decline in petroleum DFI was offset by a gradual increase in the amount of direct foreign investment in the manufacturing sector. DFI in manufacturing stood at $37 million and about 24 percent of estimated DFI in Colombia in 1943. This increased to $201 million and 37 percent of the total in 1965 and to $454 million and 61 percent of estimated DFI in

1976 (Table 5). The rapid increase in manufacturing DFI is shown by a Harvard University study of 187 U.S.-based multinational corporations. In 1939 these 187 corporations had 3 manufacturing subsidiaries in Colombia. This number increased to 30 in 1955 and to 90 by 1967 (Vaupel & Cuhran, 1969: 123-33). Similar results were found by a survey of 412 manufacturing plants in Colombia that had DFI in them. Of these plants, 11 were founded before 1930, 50 between 1931 and 1944, and 360 were founded between 1945 and 1970 (DANE, 1976b: 138).

TABLE 6
APPROVED NONPETROLEUM DIRECT FOREIGN INVESTMENT, 1967-1977

| Year | Amount (Millions of U.S. $) |
|---|---|
| 1967 | 18.4 |
| 1968 | 20.0 |
| 1969 | 27.4 |
| 1970 | 40.0 |
| 1971 | 31.0 |
| 1972 | 16.8 |
| 1973 | 61.7 |
| 1974 | 129.0 |
| 1975 | 60.4 |
| 1976 | 77.6 |
| 1977 (6 months) | 24.9 |
| Total | 507.2 |

SOURCES: (Boyce & Lombard, 1976: 16; Aldana, 1977: 161; Latin American Newsletters, 1977: 3).

The period between 1943 and 1976 saw rapid increases in DFI in almost all areas of the manufacturing sector. Registered DFI increased substantially in chemicals (from $9 million in 1943 to $59 million in 1970), pharmaceuticals (from $2 million in 1943 to $30 million in 1970), paper ($1 million in 1943 to $46 million in 1976), rubber (no DFI in 1943 to $31 million in 1970), food (from $5 million in 1943 to $44 million in 1976), metal products (from $1 million in 1943 to $19 million in 1976), machinery and electrical articles (from $18 million in 1943 to $32 million in 1970), and in textiles (from no investment in 1943 to $28 million in 1976) (DANE, 1976b: 70-1 & 79-81; Banco, 1977).

The increase in foreign manufacturing investments in Colombia was the result of two phenomena: (1) an overall trend in direct foreign investment to concentrate in the manufacturing sector in the post-war period, and (2) a conscious policy of import substitution industrialization adopted by the Colombian government in the early 1950s (Boyce & Lombard, 1976: 9). By increasing tariffs on industrial goods, the government made it more profitable for firms to establish manufacturing facilities in Colombia instead of importing goods into the country, as they had done previously.

By the mid 1970s, the United States remained the largest single foreign investor in Colombia. As Table 7 shows, U.S. registered DFI (excluding petroleum) accounted for 49 percent of all registered DFI in the country. Panama, the second largest source of DFI, accounted for only 8 percent. The European countries together accounted for only 21.7 percent of DFI in Colombia in 1976 (see Table 56). The United Kingdom, which had once been the largest source of direct foreign investment in Colombia, accounted for only 2 percent of total DFI. Even these figures underestimate the dominance of U.S. investments in Colombia, since much DFI from Panama is controlled by U.S. firms (Business International Corp., 1977: 3). It appears likely that most DFI attributed to the Bahamas, Curacao, and Canada is controlled by the U.S. and European firms. Direct foreign investment in Colombia, then, is dominated by investors from the United States.

TABLE 7
REGISTERED NONPETROLEUM DIRECT FOREIGN INVESTMENT IN COLOMBIA, END OF 1976, BY MAJOR INVESTING COUNTRIES (MILLIONS OF $ AND %)

| Country | Amount (millions $) | Percent of Total |
|---|---|---|
| United States | 338.7 | 49.4 |
| Panama | 55.7 | 8.1 |
| Canada | 49.6 | 7.2 |
| Switzerland | 33.2 | 4.8 |
| France | 26.7 | 3.9 |
| Netherlands | 24.3 | 3.5 |
| Venezuela | 21.4 | 3.1 |
| Dutch Antilles | 20.8 | 3.0 |
| West Germeny | 20.0 | 2.9 |
| United Kingdom | 14.1 | 2.1 |
| Ecuador | 11.5 | 1.7 |
| Bahamas | 10.8 | 1.6 |
| Sweden | 10.0 | 1.5 |

Source: Table 56.

However, the U.S. position of dominance has been declining in recent years. In 1966, for example, United States direct foreign investment accounted for 71 percent of registered, nonpetroleum DFI in Colombia. By 1976 this had declined to 49 percent. In the same period, European investors increased from 16 percent to 22 percent of registered DFI and Central and South America (most notably Panama) increased from 12 percent to 21 percent (Adapted from Table 56).

The sectoral distribution of DFI in Colombia is hard to determine exactly due to the difficulty in obtaining accurate information on the amount of direct foreign investment in the petroleum sector. This occurs because foreign petroleum investment has been registered on a voluntary basis only. For example, in 1970 the government-registered petroleum DFI was listed at $173.1 million (DANE, 1971: 90), while in the same year the U.S. Department of Commerce listed the book value of U.S. petroleum DFI in Colombia at $334 million (Table 54). In order to estimate the sectoral distribution of DFI, I have added registered nonpetroleum DFI in Colombia with the value of U.S. DFI in petroleum in Colombia for the same year. The same procedure was used in Table 5 to estimate the total value of DFI in Colombia for the years since 1943. This may underestimate somewhat the value of DFI in petroleum. However, since most petroleum DFI is from the U.S., the error is not likely to be large. The resulting sectoral distribution can be seen in Table 8, which presents these figures for 1976. As can be seen from this table, manufacturing is the dominant sector for DFI activity in Colombia, accounting for 61 percent of estimated DFI in the country in 1976. The second leading sector was finance and insurance, which accounted for 14.2 percent of estimated DFI in 1976. According to this estimate, petroleum accounted for about 8 percent of total DFI in the mid-1970s, and commerce for about 9 percent of total DFI in Colombia.

As the table also shows, the sectoral distribution of estimated direct foreign investment in Colombia is very different from the distribution of the Colombian gross domestic product in the mid-1970s. The manufacturing sector, which accounted for only 19 percent of the GDP, contained 61 percent of estimated DFI. Finance and insurance accounted for only 5 percent of GDP, but 14 percent of direct foreign investment. Petroleum and mining made up only 1 percent of GDP, but 11 percent of DFI. At the other extreme was agriculture, which accounted for 25 percent of the gross domestic product but only 1 percent of direct foreign investment in Colombia.

Between 1970 and 1976 the National Planning Department approved $416.5 million in new DFI and reinvestments. These new investments tended to reinforce the trend towards the concentration of DFI into a few sectors. Of the approved investments, manufacturing accounted for 52.4 percent; finance and insurance for 15.3 percent; mining for 18.2 percent; commerce for 5.4 percent; agriculture for 4.6 percent; and others for 4.6 percent. Less than 2 percent of this approved new investment was for the exploitation of petroleum and natural gas (Aldana, 1977: 162-4). It seems likely that the trend of DFI will continue towards a greater concentration in manufacturing.

Just as direct foreign investment is concentrated among a

few sectors of the economy, so is it concentrated within these sectors. In the manufacturing sector, for example, DFI is concentrated heavily in the chemical industry, and to a smaller extent in the metal products and machinery, paper, and food industries. As Table 9 shows, the chemicals industry accounted for 43 percent of all DFI in the manufacturing sector. Metal products and machinery accounted for 20 percent; paper for 10 percent; and food products for 10 percent of direct foreign investment in the manufacturing sector. Textiles, which is one of the largest industries in the Colombian economy, accounted for only 6 percent of DFI in manufacturing.

TABLE 8
ESTIMATED SECTORAL DISTRIBUTION OF
DFI IN COLOMBIA, 1976

| Sector | Investment (millions of $) | Percent of Total | Percent of GDP, 1975 |
|---|---|---|---|
| Manufacturing | 454 | 61.2 | 19.2 |
| Finance and Insurance | 105 | 14.2 | |
| Petroleum | 56 | 7.5 | |
| | | | 1.3 |
| Mining | 26 | 3.5 | |
| Commerce | 65 | 8.8 | 16.7 |
| Transportation and Communication | 22 | 3.0 | 7.4 |
| Agriculture | 7 | 0.9 | 25.1 |
| Construction | 2 | 0.3 | 4.5 |
| Utilities | 1 | 0.1 | 1.6 |
| Services | 1 | 0.1 | |
| | | | 19.6 |
| Miscellaneous | 3 | 0.4 | |
| Total | 742 | 100.0 | 100.0 |

SOURCES: (Tables 54 and 55; ANDI, 1977: 1).
NOTE: Figures for direct foreign investment are estimated by adding the registered nonpetroleum DFI to the value of United States DFI in petroleum.

It is impossible to determine the precise impact of direct foreign investment on the Colombian economy. However, some general estimations may shed some light on the subject. In 1975 the gross national product of Colombia was estimated at $12,740 million (USDS, 1977b: 24). In the same year, the sales of majority-owned U.S. firms operating in Colombia were $1,698 million (USDC,1977d: 36). Assuming that U.S. direct foreign investment in Colombia accounts for between 50 percent and 75 percent of all DFI in that country (and assuming that non-U.S. DFI in Colombia has investment/sales ratios similar to those of U.S. firms), one can estimate total sales of foreign firms in Colombia in 1975 at somewhere between $2,264 million and $3,396 million or between 17.8 percent and 26.7 percent of Colombia's GNP for that year. (Table 7 lists U.S. direct foreign investment as accounting for 49.4 percent of all nonpetroleum DFI in Colombia. It appears likely that many U.S. firms operate in Colombia through subsidiaries or affiliates in third countries, but are still listed as U.S. investments by the Department of Commerce. Thus, it is possible that the sales of U.S. foreign investors listed by the Dept. of Commerce may account for as much as 75 percent of the sales of all direct foreign investors in Colombia.)

TABLE 9
REGISTERED DIRECT FOREIGN INVESTMENT IN THE COLOMBIAN MANUFACTURING SECTOR, 1976
(MILLIONS OF U.S. $)

| Industrial Grouping | Investment | Percent of Total |
|---|---|---|
| 31. Food Products | 43.8 | 9.6 |
| 32. Textiles & Apparel | 27.6 | 6.1 |
| 33. Wood & Products | 5.9 | 1.3 |
| 34. Paper & Products | 45.8 | 10.1 |
| 35. Chemical Products | 195.6 | 43.1 |
| 36. Non-Metallic Minerals | 31.2 | 6.9 |
| 37. Basic Metals | 10.5 | 2.3 |
| 38. Metal Products & Machinery | 89.9 | 19.8 |
| 39. Other Manufacturing | 3.5 | 0.8 |
| Total | 453.9 | 100.0 |

SOURCE: (Banco, 1977: 1).

## Summary

This chapter has reviewed the historical development of direct foreign investment in Colombia. Direct foreign investment has existed in Colombia since the beginning of the republic in 1819. In the first century after independence, DFI was dominated by the British and was involved primarily in the extraction of precious metals and the building of transportation facilities. These investments were primarily of the enclave type, affecting only a small part of the country. In the late nineteenth and early twentieth centuries, U.S. investors became involved in extractive direct foreign investments in Colombia, particularly in bananas and petroleum. By the 1920s petroleum had become the major sector for DFI activity, and the United States had become the largest single source of DFI in Colombia. The total amount of DFI, which had increased throughout the late nineteenth and early twentieth centuries, suffered a decline in the Depression of the 1930s and did not recover until the Second World War. By the mid-1940s direct foreign investment in Colombia began increasing at a rapid rate. It was dominated by investors from the United States, and it began concentrating more strongly in the manufacturing sector. By the 1970s, when the domestication policy of the Colombian government was first implemented, direct foreign investment in the country was an estimated $742 million (almost five times what it had been in 1943). In addition, this DFI was dominated by the United States as the largest source of investments and by the manufacturing sector, which by 1976 accounted for over 60 percent of estimated DFI (Table 5). The question still remains whether a policy of domestication, if implemented in a country like Colombia, would improve the well-being of the citizenry of that country.

# CHAPTER 4

## DOMESTICATION AND WELL-BEING: BACKGROUND TO THE STUDY

> The effects of foreign private investment in host LDCs (less-developed countries) are a subject on which there is considerable controversey and confusion. Not only does endless debate take place about the existence and magnitude of the various costs and benefits, but there is also fundamental disagreement about what constitutes a 'cost' or a 'benefit.' It is not uncommon to find different writers accusing each other of 'bias,' 'prejudice,' 'subjectivity' or even 'extremism' when discussing ... welfare effects..., each implying that his own approach is in some way more neutral and objecctive. No normative analysis (dealing, in this case, with judgements about what is 'good' or 'bad' for society) can be value-free and objective, and certainly economics, despite the pretensions of several 'rigorous' practitioners, does not provide us with neutral, scientific tools for tackling welfare problems. One may be more consistent or inconsistent in welfare arguments or be more or less persuasive--but ultimately there is no scientific test of right or wrong. For this reason, there cannot be a final objective judgement on the welfare implications... (Lall & Streeten, 1977: 47).

Defining the economics of human well-being is a difficult problem. For the purposes of this study, human well-being will be understood to include three factors: (1) economic growth, the increased production and consumption of goods and services; (2) equitable distribution, the more equal sharing of those goods and services; and (3) nonmaterial benefits, increasing the beneficial externalities associated with the firm. Samuelson (1970) defines "external economies" as a "favorable effect on one or more persons that emanates from the action of a different person or firm" (p.453). I have chosen this definition of human well-being because economists and political economists have generally viewed human well-being in these terms (Clark, 1975; W. Weisskopf, 1977; Adelman & Morris, 1974; Myrdal, 1970; and Scitovsky, 1977), because the government of Colombia has accepted the first two of these factors as goals for its economic policies, and because it seems to be a reasonable way of comparing the costs and benefits of two different forms of ownership of firms.

Policy makers in Colombia, like those from almost every other country, have placed a great importance upon economic growth. The government development plan of 1975 took the position that lowered government involvement in the economy would achieve its goal of increasing economic growth (USDS, 1977A: 4). Finance Minister Rodrigo Botero Montoya stated in 1976 that the Colombian development policy was based on five points, the first of which was stable economic growth (US FBIS, 1976: F1).

Like most other developing countries, Colombia has accepted as a matter of government policy the general goal of the more equitable distribution of income. The title of the government's 1975 development plan was "Para cerrar la brecha" (To Close the Gap), a reference to reducing the disparities between rich and poor that exist in Colombia (USDS, 1977a: 4). In 1974, then-President Alfonso Lopez Michelson stated:

> The members of the government...have declared that...we assign a special priority to those investments and expenditures destined to improve the condition of the 50 percent of the population less favored by fortune (OAS, 1975: 34).

Zschock (1977) confirms this, noting that in its national strategies "Colombia has repeatedly committed herself to an equitable development process" (p.68). Added support for this view was given in 1976, when the Finance Minister listed the third priority of the country's development policy as income distribution (US FBIS, 1976: F1).

Direct foreign investment has been studied with a variety of methods to determine its effects upon growth and distribution. Among the predominant methodologies have been cross-national studies, single-country studies, pairing studies, and industry-aggregated studies. Each of these methods has advantages and limitations, and each has its own biases. The following pages will review each of these methods for studying direct foreign investment (and its alternetives).

## Cross-National Studies

Among the best-known studies of the effects of direct foreign investment in developing countries have been the cross-national studies. These studies try to gather a limited amount of information about a large number of separate countries using data at a high level of aggregation. The most prevalent methodology has been to measure direct foreign investment in terms of its stocks of and flows into developing countries, and then to correlate DFI with such variables as economic growth rates and levels of income distribution.

The advantage of these studies is that they provide a coverage of a large number of countries. For example, Bornschier, et. al. (1978) use a sample of 76 less-developed countries, Rubinson (1976) includes 39 countries, and Chase-Dunn (1975) and Gobalet & Diamond (1979) include all countries which in 1955 had a per capita GNP of less than $406. Additional studies including large samples are Alschuler (1976), Ray & Webster (1978), and McGowan & Smith (1978). The disadvantages of this methodology are numerous. The level of aggregation is such that no distinction is made as to whether the foreign investment is in the mining sector, in agriculture, or in manufacturing. Little attention is given to the nature of the economy in each developing country being studied, other than the rate of growth of GNP and the level of income distribution. Smith (1977) criticizes this reliance on results of studies using information aggregated from many countries and then "mixed without regard to the actual circumstances prevailing in any particular case" (p.116-8).

This approach also overlooks the problems of incomparability of data across nations. Especially where developing countries are concerned, reliability of data may be a problem; and when the comparison is made among a large group of such countries, the problem of lack of comparability may make any results meaningless. Partly as a result of these factors, the results of these cross-national studies are contradictory. One paper surveyed fourteen cross-national studies of the effects of foreign investment dependence upon economic growth in developing countries. Of the fourteen studies, six found that higher dependence on foreign investment had positive effects on economic growth, while eight studies found negative effects (Bornschier, et. al., 1978).

## Single-Country Studies

Another frequently used method of evaluating direct foreign investment is that which takes an in-depth look at DFI within a single developing country, without comparing it to domestic investment in the same country. In the case of Colombia, there are several studies of this type. They provide a detailed but descriptive account of the role of direct foreign investment in the Colombian economy. One study looks at the effects of direct foreign investment in the manufacturing sector with regard to four factors: income effect, public savings effect, private savings effect, and balance of payments effect (see Matter, 1977; Camacho Guizado, 1977).

Unlike the cross-national studies, these single-country studies provide substantial detail about direct foreign investment in the country. They give a great deal of information about its relative importance in the economy, which foreign firms are involved, whether foreign investment is primarily extractive or manufacturing (and about its distribution within extractive and manufacturing sectors), and about the exports and imports of firms with foreign investment (see Silva, 1976).

However, these studies share one thing in common with the

cross-national studies: they view alternatives to direct foreign investment in an empirical (although not necessarily a theoretical) vacuum. Empirically, there is no investigation of alternatives to DFI, particularly investment by domestic firms. Theoretically, many of these studies do take into account alternatives to DFI; they do consider the question of what would happen if the foreign investment were phased out or if it had never taken place.

First, it is sometimes assumed that the alternative to direct foreign investment is no investment. Iyanda (1975) refers to this as the "classical assumption," which views direct foreign investment as a supplement to domestic production and investment, as a generator of additional employment of domestic resources (p.32). This assumes that foreign investment does not displace production by domestic firms, and that the absence of DFI would require the host country to import all of the production stemming from the foreign investment (Lall & Streeten, 1977: 159). Herbert May (nd) generally accepts this approach to foreign investment. Edfelt (1975) epitomizes this approach in his statements about foreign firms:

> Because most of the products of these firms would not be manufactured by local firms, or on some cases not manufactured as efficiently or abundantly, there are direct benefits in terms of additional employment and the accompanying diffusion of knowledge, skills and attitudes that would not be generated in their absence... (p.132).

It is also sometimes assumed that the alternative to direct foreign investment would be for the production of the foreign firm to be replaced by an identical locally owned company (Lall & Streeten, 1977: 159). This approach, which Iyanda calls the "reverse classical assumption," views direct foreign investment as a substitute for domestic investment, not a supplement to it. Geraffi (1978) uses this argument with regard to the steroid hormone industry in Mexico, arguing that the industry was started by Mexican citizens and that foreign firms merely substituted for the production of national firms (pp. 254-5). Biersteker (1978), in his study of Nigeria, argues that local entrepreneurs and technicians did possess the knowledge, skill and resources to pose an alternative to investment by foreign corporations. He argues that, if foreign firms did not invest, some of this investment would be effected by Nigerians (pp. 96-101).

Third, it can be assumed that the alternative to direct foreign investment lies somewhere between the "classical" and "reverse classical" approaches. Lall and Streeten describe the assumption of "most likely" local replacement of DFI. This view of direct foreign investment takes into account the development of local economic forces in order to estimate how much of the production of foreign firms would be taken over by domestic industry, how much would be replaced by imports, and how much would not take place at all (Lall & Streeten, 1977: 159).

The cross-national and single-country studies of DFI seldom address the question of what is the "most likely" alternative to direct foreign investment. Silva, for example, has three separate estimates of how much of the value of DFI production would have to be imported in the absence of foreign investment (they range from 90 percent to 60 percent) (Silva, 1976: 119). Yet his model does not take into account that domestic firms (and not imports) may represent the alternative to direct foreign investment. Neither the cross-national nor the single-country studies have the ability to study domestication empirically, since they do not compare DFI to domestic investments. There are two methodologies that do consider domestic investment to be as alternative to DFI: pairing and industry-aggregated studies.

## Pairing Methodology

The pairing approach assumes that if foreign investment were replaced, it would be replaced by national firms of similar size, age, and technological level. (This assumption is not always acknowleged in the studies). This methodology attempts to compare pairs of firms that are similar in size, age, and products produced, but different in nationality of ownership (Ingles & Fairchild, 1977: 61) in order to determine how much of the behavior of foreign firms is attributable to the fact that they are foreign and how much can be explained by other characteristics.

The most noteworthy of these studies was that done under the auspices of Cornell University's Program on Policy for Science and Technology in Developing Nations, which includes studies of ninety-eight pairs of firms from Brazil, Central America, Colombia and Mexico (see DeCarvalho, 1977; Ingles & Fairchild, 1977; Fairchild, 1977). Edfelt (1975) uses a similar methodology, studying pairs of foreign and domestic firms that were matched according to product, number of employees, size of sales, and size of assets.

The advantage of the pairing methodology is that it provides detailed information about the operations of foreign and domestic firms at a low level of aggregation (i.e., the individual firm). This methodology also has disadvantages. Because of the detailed information required, the number of firms to be used in the study is limited by the resources of the study team. Even the Cornell study was limited to ninety-eight pairs, and the largest number of pairs from a single country (Mexico) was twenty-nine (DeCarvalho, 1977: 59). Because of the small size of these samples, it is difficult to obtain differences between foreign and national firms that are statistically significant.

Another disadvantage of the method is that, by pairing foreign firms and national firms according to product, size, and age, there are many firms for which there are no possible pairings. Ingles and Fairchild argue that this underestimates the contributions of foreign firms.

> The most critical shortcoming of the methodology is...that it tends to avoid precisely those cases where there is a clear foreign advantage. The point is simple: where the foreign advantage is great there will not exist a domestic counterpart. Thus there are no automobile manufacturers...in any of the country studies. In general...it is fair to object that the 'highest technology' sectors have been automatically ruled out of the analysis... (Ingles & Fairchild, 1977: 27).

This type of analysis obviously excludes many large foreign firms for which there is no equivalent domestic firm. It also excludes many small domestic firms for which there is no foreign equivalent. It is not obvious, as Ingles and Fairchild have asserted, that there is a "clear foreign advantage" in those cases where no pairs can be developed. They assume incorrectly that the likely alternative to a foreign firm with which no domestic firm of equivalent size, age, and industry can be paired, is no investment at all. One can assume with equal validity that the likely alternative to such foreign firms are domestic firms of much smaller size. Their approach also ignores any possible foreign alternative to domestic firms of fairly small size. In this case the likely alternative could be assumed to be foreign firms in the same industry, but with much larger size. The pairing methodology is thus limited to comparing a small range of foreign and domestic firms.

### Industry-Aggregated Studies

The second approach that looks empirically at alternatives to direct foreign investment is the industry-aggregated study. Instead of comparing individual foreign and domestic firms (as the pairing method does), the industry-aggregated approach lumps together all domestic firms operating in a certain industry and compares their characteristics with those of all foreign firms operating in that same industry. This approach views the likely alternative to foreign investment to be investment by domestic companies in the same industry, but not producing identical products.

This approach can look at very specific industries or more

general ones. Fajnzylber has compared foreign and domestic firms in Mexico in 230 very specific industries (Fajnzylber, 1975: 903-31). Iyanda (1975) uses samples of foreign and domestic firms in Nigeria, also at this very detailed level. Biersteker (1978) uses a similar approach for Nigeria, comparing all foreign and domestic companies in four industries. Tambunlertchai (1976) uses a similar approach in comparing foreign and domestic firms in Thailand.

It has been argued that this methodology aggregates data at too general a level, that it is comparing firms that are in the same industry but are not producing the same product. It has also been argued that this approach puts too much emphasis on the domesticness or foreignness of a firm and ignores such factors as size and age as important variables in explaining the behavior of firms (Ingles & Fairchild, 1977: 59-61). On the other hand, industry-aggregated studies have several advantages. They are able to have much larger sample sizes, and sometimes are able to include almost all of the foreign and domestic firms operating in the manufacturing sector. This approach lacks the depth of the pairing studies (since its level of analysis is the industry and not the individual firm), but its scope is much broader.

The industry-aggregated approach views a firm strictly in terms of whether it is foreign or domestic, which is why it is nearly perfect for studying domestication. The policy of domestication implies that there are differences in the behavior and effects of foreign and domestic companies, and the industry-aggregated approach provides a framework for determining whether these assumed differences do exist. This study is not trying to explain the behavior of firms (in which case size and age might have greater explanatory power than nationality). Rather, this study is concerned only with the existence and nature of any differences between foreign and domestic firms.

If direct foreign investment in Colombia were domesticated, it seems that the most likely alternative would be for the same type of production to be undertaken by domestic firms in the same general industry, using many of the same resources (e.g., local capital, labor and technology as well as some imports of those factors) that were used by foreign firms, but using them in ways that domestic firms currently use them (including their factor intensity). Many domestic firms entered Colombia by taking over production that was previously operated by Colombians, so it seems likely the reverse could also happen.

For example, a large portion of the manufacturing subsidiaries of U.S.-based multinational corporations in Colombia entered the country through the acquisition of already existing, domestically - owned manufacturing companies. Vaupel and Cuhran's (1969) study of the manufacturing subsidiaries of 187 U.S. based MNCs shows that 44 out of 116 manufacturing subsidiaries in Colombia were acquired from existing nationally owned companies (see Table 10). In their sample, 38 percent of the U.S. owned subsidiaries were acquired, while 47 percent were newly formed. Matter's (1977) study of 65 manufacturing subsidiaries with DFI established between 1950 and 1973 found that 31 percent were founded by foreign owners, 32 percent were founded as joint ventures, and 37 percent by buying out existing local firms (pp.241-3).

This suggests that domestic firms could indeed provide an alternative to investment by foreign firms, since a large number of these domestic firms were already operating in the same industry when they were acquired by foreign investors. Other studies suggest that a substantial amount of the operating capital of foreign firms is already being provided by domestic sources. In the absence of foreign firms, it would be equally available to domestic firms. A study by Banco de la Republica (1974a) of over 75 percent of the foreign manufacturing companies in Colombia between 1969 and 1971 found that these foreign companies relied on domestic borrowing for 25-27 percent of total financing; on external credit for 25 percent to 32 percent; and upon their own resources for 43 percent to 48 percent of total financing (pp.24-7). Silva's (1976) study of foreign firms in 1973 found that these firms relied on domestic credit for 27 percent of their total financial resources. These firms relied on external credit for 32 percent of their financing (pp.166-70). This suggests that a good part of the operating capital of foreign firms could be just as available for domestic firms' use.

TABLE 10

METHOD OF ENTRY OF U.S. FIRMS IN COLOMBIA

| Industry | Total | New Firms | Acquired Firms | Other |
|---|---|---|---|---|
| Food and Beverages | 20 | 8 | 12 | 0 |
| Textiles | 6 | 4 | 2 | 0 |
| Paper & Products | 6 | 3 | 2 | 1 |
| Chemicals & Related | 52 | 27 | 19 | 6 |
| Glass Products | 4 | 1 | 3 | 0 |
| Metal Products & Machinery | 12 | 7 | 1 | 4 |
| Other | 16 | 5 | 5 | 6 |
| Total | 116 | 55 | 44 | 17 |

SOURCE: Vaupel & Cuhran, 1969: 316-363, 502-509.

In order to determine the likely effects of domestication upon citizen well-being, one needs to compare the behavior and characteristics of foreign firms operating in Colombia with the behavior of domestic firms in the same general industry. The remainder of this study presents such a comparison.

## The Study

The primary methodology of this study consists of an industry-aggregated comparison of the behavior and effects of domestic and foreign firms in the Colombian manufacturing sector. The major comparison is between two groupings:

FOREIGN PLANTS (Set F): a sample of 421 plants with some degree of direct foreign investment. This sample accounted for 95 percent of the value added of all manufacturing plants with DFI in 1970, so the coverage is nearly complete (DANE, 1976b: 153).

DOMESTIC PLANTS (Set D): a population of manufacturing plants (5,645 plants in 1974) that have virtually no direct foreign investment. Because of the way in which the original data were made available, it was not always possible to develop a complete set of data on domestic plants. For variables where these data were lacking (e.g., most of 1972 data), I relied instead of the population of all manufacturing plants in Colombia which in 1972 or 1974 employed at least ten people.

These sets of plants were aggregated at the level of the three-digit industrial grouping according to the International Uniform Industrial Classification system (see Table 58). The plants were grouped into 28 separate industries, so that foreign and domestic plants in the same general industry were being compared. One industry (314, Tobacco Industries) was dropped from the study because it had no plants with DFI. However, this industry was an insignificant part of the entire study, accounting for only 2.0 percent of the production of all national manufacturing plants in 1974.

The data comes from the period 1970-1974. It was originally gathered by the Colombian government's National Department of Statistics (DANE), and the data were gathered at the level of the "establishment," or plant, and not at the level of the firm. It is possible for one firm to have several plants. The 421 foreign plants in the study were controlled by 363 different firms. The number of firms in the domestic population of plants is not known. The plants in this study include a very small number (398 out of 6,066 plants in 1974) that employed fewer that 10 people, so the study effectively excludes the small cottage shop type of production in Colombia (DANE, 1976a: 12). This is in keeping with the purpose of this study, which is to determine the effect of domestication. Since the larger more modern domestic plants in Colombia are the ones that are most likely to replace any foreign investment, it is with these larger plants (and not with populations that include smaller cottage industries) that foreign plants should be compared.

Two caveats need to be made about the data and the nature of the comparative study. First, the set of foreign plants includes 421 plants which have some amount of DFI, but it does not differentiate according to the degree of foreign participation. Of the 421 plants, 294 (or 69.8 percent) were majority-foreign. An additional 58 (13.8 percent) had foreign participation of more than 25 percent but less than 50 percent, while 66 (15.7 percent) had foreign participation of less than 25 percent. For three plants the degree of foreign participation was unknown (DANE, 1976b: 185-8). This tells very little, however, about the number of these plants that were actually controlled by foreign investors. The remainder of this study will assume that these 421 plants are, in effect, controlled by foreign investors. The danger is that some domestically controlled plants may be included in this sample. The effect of this would be to understate differences between foreign and domestic plants (inasmuch as some domestically controlled plants were included in the foreign set).

Second, because data on the set of domestic plants were not available for some variables, a comparison had to be made between foreign plants (Set F) and national plants (Set N). Because foreign plants were a part of the set of national plants (and it was impossible to determine precisely what part, for 1972), foreign plants (Set F) were being compared to domestic plants and foreign plants (Set N). It was impossible in this case to determine the degree of difference between foreign plants and domestic plants, but it was possible to determine the direction of difference (i.e., whether foreign plants in a certain industry had a value that was higher or lower that domestic plants).

Appendix B presents ths data for foreign plants (Set F), domestic plants (Set D), and for total manufacturing (Set N). Table 11 shows the percentage of total manufacturing (Set N) that was accounted for by plants with direct foreign investment (Set F). For all industries combined, the 421 plants with DFI accounted for 43.4 percent of manufacturing production, 44.7 percent of value added, 28.5 percent of employment, and only 6.9 percent of the number of plants (see Table 11).

The relative incidence of foreign plants (Set F) varied substantially by industry. Foreign plants accounted for only 3.2 percent of national production in beverage industries, and for only 6.0 percent of production in the industries of furniture and printing. On the other hand, foreign plants accounted for 84.0 percent of national production in the glass products industry, for 82.1 percent of production in rubber products, and for over 79 percent in transportation equipment, industrial chemicals and paper industries (see Table 11).

The relative importance of foreign plants (Set F) is greater in the more advanced industries such as chemicals, nonmetallic minerals, basic metals, and metal products and machinery. Foreign plants' participation is lower in those industries that are less advanced in terms of technology and skill, such as food products, textiles, and wood products. Table 11 also reveals that in almost every industry, foreign plants make up a much smaller share of the number of plants than of production, employment or value added. For all industries combined, foreign plants (Set F) accounted for 6.9 percent of the number of plants in national manufacturing (Set N), but for 43.4 percent of production and 44.7 percent of value added. This indicates a larger scale of production for foreign plants relative to domestic ones.

TABLE 11
PLANTS WITH DFI AS A PERCENTAGE OF TOTAL NATIONAL PLANTS, 1974
(BY INDUSTRY)

| Industrial Grouping | Production | Value Added | Employment | Number of Plants |
|---|---|---|---|---|
| Total | 43.4% | 44.7% | 28.5% | 6.9% |
| Food Products | 22.1 | 29.7 | 17.8 | 4.6 |
| Beverages | 3.2 | 2.4 | 6.6 | 1.6 |
| Textiles | 62.0 | 61.4 | 46.1 | 8.0 |
| Apparel | 9.4 | 10.2 | 8.3 | 1.5 |
| Leather & Products | 18.5 | 18.8 | 9.8 | 1.2 |
| Footwear | 22.7 | 24.1 | 11.3 | 1.1 |
| Wood & Products | 33.6 | 38.6 | 21.8 | 2.0 |
| Furniture | 6.0 | 4.0 | 3.2 | 0.9 |
| Paper & Products | 79.3 | 81.7 | 53.4 | 13.7 |
| Printing/Publishing | 6.0 | 8.7 | 6.1 | 2.0 |
| Industrial Chemicals | 79.5 | 77.8 | 51.3 | 47.9 |
| Other Chemicals | 60.3 | 68.1 | 51.8 | 23.1 |
| Petroleum Refineries | 22.0 | 18.9 | 10.1 | 53.8 |
| Petroleum Derivatives | 10.0 | 16.0 | 2.3 | 22.2 |
| Rubber Products | 82.1 | 83.7 | 70.2 | 8.3 |
| Plastic Products | 47.3 | 54.8 | 27.8 | 4.9 |
| Clay & Porcelain | 16.6 | 18.9 | 15.5 | 5.6 |
| Glass & Products | 84.0 | 85.8 | 57.7 | 14.6 |
| Other Nonmetallic | 56.7 | 58.8 | 28.3 | 5.7 |
| Basic Iron & Steel | 49.9 | 42.2 | 29.8 | 15.7 |
| Basic Nonferrous | 73.6 | 82.2 | 63.3 | 19.2 |
| Metal Products | 42.8 | 44.4 | 23.7 | 6.8 |
| Nonelect. Machinery | 29.6 | 31.2 | 17.6 | 8.4 |
| Electric Machinery | 67.3 | 68.8 | 47.6 | 15.2 |
| Transport Equipment | 79.8 | 78.3 | 39,5 | 5.7 |
| Gauges/Optical Equip | 38.4 | 35.5 | 20.2 | 13.2 |
| Other Manufacturing | 23.4 | 27.1 | 14.9 | 5.4 |

SOURCE: Adapted from Tables 59 and 60.

## Summary

This chapter began by introducing a three-part definition of human well-being. It was argued that there are three areas in which possible effects of domestication could be compared: economic growth, equitable distribution, and nonmaterial factors. The chapter then reviewed four different methodologies for studying the effects of direct foreign investment (DFI). It was argued that the first two approaches, the cross-national and single-country studies, failed to study empirically the alternatives to direct foreign investment. It was also argued that the pairing methodology, although it studied an actual alternative to DFI, was inaccurate in its view that the most likely alternative to direct foreign investment consisted of domestic firms of smaller size, age, and industry. It was then argued that the industry-aggregated study (which compares foreign and domestic forms in the same general industry and in the same country) provides a more realistic view of the most likely alternative to direct foreign investment once domestication has been implemented.

The remainder of this chapter introduced the industry-aggregated method that will be used in the following three chapters. Using a single country (Colombia) for a short period of time (1970-1974), this study will compare two sets of plants. The first is a set of 421 plants with direct foreign investment in them (Set F). These foreign plants will be compared to a set of domestic plants (Set D) that have virtually no DFI. In those cases where data for Set D (domestic plants) could not be developed, foreign plants will be compared to all national manufacturing plants (Set N).

# CHAPTER 5

# DOMESTICATION AND GROWTH

This chapter will examine two ways in which domestication could conceivably increase economic growth. First, if domestic plants have a greater total factor productivity than foreign plants, then the transfer of control over the economy to these plants with a greater factor productivity (i.e., domestic ones) would, other things being equal, increase overall growth within the economy. Second, if some intangible aspect of the nature of domestic plants contributes more to increased growth (e.g., by stimulating competition) than do foreign plants, then domestication could be said to increase economic growth. This chapter will begin by investigating the factor productivity of foreign and domestic plants in Colombia. It will then see if the intensity of foreign or domestic plants in specific industries is related to the levels of growth in those industries.

## Factor Productivity

In looking at factor productivity, I will be using an economic model which assumes that domestic and foreign plants are producing a given output (Q) by using two factors of production: capital (K) and labor (L). I will also be assuming that the factors used by these plants are identical, so that one unit of labor used by domestic plants is qualitatively the same as a unit of labor used by foreign plants. The costs of these factors will be assumed to be the same for the two types of plants, so that one unit of K will cost the domestic plant precisely what it costs for a foreign plant. I will also be assuming that there are constant returns to scale, so that the increased or decreased size of a plant will not affect the productivity of a given factor. These foreign and domestic plants will also be assumed to be producing similar products that allow for the same substitutability of capital for labor in their production. Finally, in the comparisons of domestic and foreign plants, I will be looking at their average factor productivity in a given industry (i.e., total output/total input of the factor being studied). Average factor productivity will be assumed to be equal to marginal factor productivity (i.e., the amount of additional input of the specific factor which is required to produce each additional unit of output).

These assumptions do not all mesh with the reality of the manufacturing sector in Colombia. Thoumi (nd), for example, mentions that capital is cheaper for the larger plants in Colombia. Foreign plants tend to be larger than domestic ones (p.5). However, these assumptions are necessary in order to begin this comparison of foreign and domestic manufacturing plants in Colombia. As the analysis proceeds, some of these assumptions will be relaxed.

## A. Output/Capital

The output/capital (Q/K) ratio is one way of comparing the relative factor productivity of foreign and domestic plants in Colombia. The hypothesis suggested by the domestication policy (i.e., the logic of parallelism), would read as follows:

H1: Domestic plants will have a greater output to capital (Q/K) ratio than will foreign plants in the same industry.

HO: The null hypothesis suggests that there are no systematic differences in the Q/K ratios of domestic and foreign plants in the same industry.

H2: The alternative hypothesis holds that foreign plants will have greater Q/K ratios than domestic plants in the same industry.

As suggested by Lall and Streeten and Tambunlertchai, I will be using the ratio of value added/fixed assets as a measure of output/capital (Lall & Streeten, 1977: 110-1; Tambunlertchai, 1976: 214). Table 12 presents a comparison of these ratios for foreign plants and national plants for 1972. National plants (Set N) is being used as a substitute for domestic plants (Set D). As a result, the degree of the difference between the foreign plants and the national plants is meaningless (since foreign plants constitute an unknown part of national plants in each industry for 1972). However, the direction of the difference is indicative of the differences between foreign plants and domestic plants.

Of the twenty-seven industries for which foreign plants were compared to national plants, foreign plants had a higher output/capital ratio in sixteen industries, national plants had a higher Q/K ratio in five, and there was no difference in six industries. The evidence obviously disconfirms the primary hypothesis, that domestic plants have a greater Q/K ratio than foreign plants. The only remaining question is whether the null hypothesis or the alternative hypothesis best explains the relationship shown in the table. In order to determine this, a signs test was run to determine whether the observed relationship could be explained under the null hypothesis. The signs test is a two-sample test. It looks at the direction of score differences between two samples under different conditions in order to determine whether the samples are different from one another. It assumes that the samples are related. In this case

TABLE 12
VALUE ADDED/ASSETS, 1972

| Industry | (Set F) Foreign Plants | (Set N) National Plants | Difference |
|---|---|---|---|
| Food Products | 2.5 | 1.2 | + |
| Beverages | 3.3 | 2.4 | + |
| Textiles | 1.7 | 1.6 | + |
| Apparel | 3.6 | 2.3 | + |
| Leather & Products | 3.1 | 2.4 | + |
| Footwear | 3.2 | 2.3 | + |
| Wood & Products | 1.1 | 1.1 | 0 |
| Furniture | 0.6 | 1.9 | − |
| Paper & Products | 0.8 | 0.9 | − |
| Printing/Publishing | 1.5 | 1.5 | 0 |
| Industrial Chemicals | 1.4 | 0.5 | + |
| Other Chemicals | 4.9 | 3.1 | + |
| Petroleum Refineries | 2.2 | 0.9 | + |
| Petroleum Derivatives | 1.3 | 1.3 | 0 |
| Rubber Products | 2.3 | 2.2 | + |
| Plastic Products | 1.0 | 1.2 | − |
| Clay & Porcelain | 0.7 | 1.1 | − |
| Glass & Products | 1.4 | 2.2 | − |
| Other Nonmetallic | 0.9 | 0.9 | 0 |
| Basic Iron & Steel | 1.2 | 0.7 | + |
| Basic Nonferrous | 1.2 | 1.2 | 0 |
| Metal Products | 1.6 | 1.5 | + |
| Nonelectric Machinery | 2.0 | 1.7 | + |
| Electric Machinery | 1.7 | 1.7 | 0 |
| Transport Equipment | 2.9 | 2.2 | + |
| Gauges/Optical Equip | 2.7 | 1.9 | + |
| Other Manufacturing | 2.0 | 1.6 | + |
| Mean | 1.96 | 1.61 | |

SOURCE: Tables 59 and 60.
NOTE: Signs test was significant at .008 for a one-tailed test.

the samples are related by industry (Champion, 1970: 161-5). If there were at least a 5 percent chance that these observed relationships could be explained by the null hypothesis, then this null hypothesis would be accepted. The signs test showed that the relationship was significant at the .008 level, so the null hypothesis was rejected and the alternative hypothesis accepted.

The primary and null hypotheses were both rejected. Foreign plants have a significantly greater output/capital ratio than do domestic plants. Other studies of the output/capital ratios of domestic and foreign firms have also found higher ratios for the foreign firms. A study using twenty-six pairs of firms in Colombia found foreign firms to have greater output/capital than domestic firms. Using Q/K such as profits/total assets, 1970-74 and 1974; profits/net worth, 1974; cash flow/total assets, 1970-74 and 1974; and cash flow/net worth 1970-74 and 1974, they found foreign firms to be significantly higher at the .01 level (and at the .05 level for profits/net worth 1970-74). DeCarvalho found somewhat less significant foreign advantages for the sample that included Colombia with Brazil and Mexico (DeCarvalho, 1977: 96 & 226).

While these data tend to disconfirm the domestication hypothesis, it is still possible that foreign plants in Colombia have a greater Q/K because they are more labor intensive. The smaller the amount of capital used, the more productive each unit of capital is (in terms of Q/K). If this were true, then domestic plants could be expected to have a much higher output/labor (Q/L) ratio than foreign plants.

## B. Output/Labor

The domestication hypothesis posits that total factor productivity of domestic plants is greater than that for foreign plants. The comparison of output/capital ratios of foreign and domestic plants shows, on the contrary, that foreign plants have a significantly higher Q/K ratio than domestic plants. In order for the domestication hypothesis to be correct, domestic plants would have to have a substantially higher output/labor (Q/L) ratio in order to compensate for the higher Q/K ratio for foreign plants. In keeping with the recommendations of Fajnzylber (1975: 912), Tambunlertchai (1976: 214), and Lall and Streeten (1977: 110-1), I will be using as measures of output/labor the following: production/employee, value added/employee, and value added/personnel payments. As Tables 13 through 15 demonstrate, domestic plants had a lower output/labor using all three measures. Table 13 compares the production/employee of foreign and domestic plants for 1974. Of the twenty-seven industries for which a comparison was made, only two (beverages and printing and publishing) showed an advantage for domestic plants. The other twenty-five industries had a higher production/employee for foreign plants. From these results, the domestication hypothesis

TABLE 13
PRODUCTION/EMPLOYEE, 1974
(THOUSANDS OF PESOS)

| Industry | Foreign Plants | Domestic Plants | Difference | Rank of Difference |
|---|---|---|---|---|
| Food Products | 766 | 584 | 182 | 10 |
| Beverages | 294 | 638 | -344 | -21 |
| Textiles | 422 | 222 | 200 | 12 |
| Apparel | 139 | 119 | 20 | 3 |
| Leather & Products | 516 | 249 | 277 | 17.5 |
| Footwear | 229 | 99 | 130 | 7 |
| Wood & Products | 245 | 135 | 110 | 6 |
| Furniture | 202 | 104 | 98 | 4 |
| Paper & Products | 1026 | 306 | 720 | 24 |
| Printing/Publishing | 205 | 208 | -3 | -1 |
| Industrial Chemicals | 1575 | 427 | 1148 | 26 |
| Other Chemicals | 525 | 371 | 154 | 8 |
| Petroleum Refineries | 2423 | 960 | 1463 | 27 |
| Petroleum Derivatives | 750 | 157 | 593 | 23 |
| Rubber Products | 457 | 236 | 221 | 13.5 |
| Plastic Products | 562 | 241 | 321 | 19 |
| Clay & Porcelain | 128 | 118 | 10 | 2 |
| Glass & Products | 299 | 78 | 221 | 13.5 |
| Other Nonmetallic | 499 | 150 | 349 | 22 |
| Basic Iron & Steel | 589 | 251 | 338 | 20 |
| Basic Nonferrous | 605 | 374 | 231 | 15 |
| Metal Products | 413 | 171 | 242 | 16 |
| Nonelect Machinery | 380 | 193 | 187 | 11 |
| Electric Machinery | 497 | 220 | 277 | 17.5 |
| Transport Equipment | 924 | 153 | 771 | 25 |
| Gauges/Optical Equip | 294 | 120 | 174 | 9 |
| Other Manufacturing | 252 | 145 | 107 | 5 |
| Mean | 563.5 | 260.3 | 303.2 | |

SOURCE: Tables 60 and 61.

NOTE: Wilcoxon Test was significant at .001 level for one-tailed test.

can immediately be rejected. The only question is whether these results are consistent with the null hypothesis or with the alternative hypothesis (that foreign plants have a greater output/labor). In order to determine the significance of these differences, I used the Wilcoxon Matched-pairs Signed-ranks Test. This test is designed to look at the magnitude of difference between matched pairs. In this case the industry in which the plants are located serves as a basis for matching groups of plants. This test assumes interval-level data, which are available for comparing sets F (foreign plants) and D (domestic plants) (Champion, 1970: 165-9). This test is more precise than the signs test, and it can be used in this case because in comparing Sets D and F, the differences in the values of the two sets can be measured for each industry, and these differences can then be ranked. The results of the test allow one to reject the null hypothesis at the .001 level of significance.

Table 14 uses value added/employee in 1974 as a measure to compare the Q/L ratios of foreign and domestic plants in the same industry. In this comparison only one of the twenty-seven industries shows a higher Q/L ratio for domestic plants, so we can immediately rule out the domestication hypothesis. The other twenty-six industries showed advantages for foreign plants. The Wilcoxon Matched-pairs Signed-ranks test also allows one to reject the null hypothesis (at the .001 level of significance) and to support the alternate hypothesis.

Table 15 presents a different measure of output/labor, comparing the value added/remuneration of foreign and national plants for 1972. Of the twenty-seven industries for which comparisons were made, seventeen showed foreign plants with a higher ratio of value added/remuneration, seven showed a higher ratio for national plants (and, by deduction, domestic plants), and three industries had no difference. Again the data do not support the domestication hypothesis. A signs test was then run, proposing the alternate hypothesis, and it allowed the rejection of the null hypothesis (at the .01 level of significance) and the acceptance of the alternate hypothesis.

From the results of this analysis, it appears clear that foreign plants have a higher output/capital and output/labor ratio. The higher output/capital ratios of foreign plants can be explained if foreign plants were more labor intensive, and the higher output/labor ratios of foreign plants could be explained if they were more capital intensive. However, these two arguments cannot be made at the same time. Obviously, the greater output of both labor and capital cannot be explained solely in terms of factor intensities.

It could be that foreign plants are managed more efficiently than domestic plants, and both labor and capital can be more productive. Another possible explanation is that there are increasing returns to scale and that, since foreign plants tend to produce at a larger scale, they are more likely to benefit from this. In order to see if these explanations could account

TABLE 14
VALUE ADDED/EMPLOYEE, 1974
(THOUSANDS OF PESOS)

| Industry | Foreign Plants | Domestic Plants | Difference | Rank of Difference |
|---|---|---|---|---|
| Food Products | 250 | 128 | 122 | 15 |
| Beverages | 146 | 416 | -270 | -23.5 |
| Textiles | 172 | 93 | 79 | 9 |
| Apparel | 57 | 45 | 12 | 1 |
| Leather & Products | 151 | 71 | 80 | 10 |
| Footwear | 98 | 39 | 59 | 5 |
| Wood & Products | 135 | 60 | 75 | 8 |
| Furniture | 62 | 49 | 13 | 2 |
| Paper & Products | 360 | 93 | 267 | 22 |
| Printing/Publishing | 132 | 89 | 43 | 4 |
| Industrial Chemicals | 669 | 201 | 468 | 27 |
| Other Chemicals | 272 | 137 | 135 | 18 |
| Petroleum Refineries | 857 | 411 | 446 | 26 |
| Petroleum Derivatives | 500 | 61 | 439 | 25 |
| Rubber Products | 195 | 89 | 106 | 13 |
| Plastic Products | 267 | 85 | 182 | 20 |
| Clay & Porcelain | 77 | 60 | 17 | 3 |
| Glass & Products | 172 | 39 | 133 | 17 |
| Other Nonmetallic | 284 | 78 | 206 | 21 |
| Basic Iron & Steel | 233 | 136 | 97 | 12 |
| Basic Nonferrous | 222 | 83 | 139 | 19 |
| Metal Products | 175 | 68 | 107 | 14 |
| Nonelect Machinery | 175 | 83 | 92 | 11 |
| Electric Machinery | 210 | 87 | 123 | 16 |
| Transport Equipment | 330 | 60 | 270 | 23.5 |
| Gauges/Optical Equip | 114 | 53 | 61 | 6 |
| Other Manufacturing | 137 | 64 | 73 | 7 |
| Mean | 239.0 | 64 | 73 | 7 |

SOURCE: Tables 60 and 61.

Note: Wilcoxon Test was significant at .001 level for a one-tailed test.

TABLE 15
VALUE ADDED/REMUNERATION, 1972

| Industry | Foreign Plants | Domestic Plants | Sign of Difference |
|---|---|---|---|
| Food Products | 3.85 | 3.45 | + |
| Beverages | 8.33 | 5.88 | + |
| Textiles | 2.94 | 2.56 | + |
| Apparel | 2.17 | 2.17 | 0 |
| Leather & Products | 1.96 | 2.27 | − |
| Footwear | 1.85 | 1.72 | + |
| Wood & Products | 2.27 | 2.17 | + |
| Furniture | 1.32 | 1.64 | − |
| Paper & Products | 2.78 | 2.86 | − |
| Printing & Publishing | 2.08 | 2.04 | + |
| Industrial Chemicals | 4.17 | 3.13 | + |
| Other Chemicals | 3.33 | 3.33 | 0 |
| Petroleum Refineries | 12.50 | 5.88 | + |
| Petroleum Derivatives | 5.56 | 4.00 | + |
| Rubber Products | 2.56 | 2.63 | − |
| Plastic Products | 3.13 | 2.86 | + |
| Clay & Porcelain | 2.38 | 1.59 | + |
| Glass & Products | 2.50 | 2.63 | − |
| Other Nonmetallic | 2.86 | 2.56 | + |
| Basic Iron & Steel | 2.44 | 1.85 | + |
| Basic Nonferrous | 2.13 | 2.22 | − |
| Metal Products | 2.22 | 2.22 | 0 |
| Nonelect Machinery | 2.27 | 2.17 | + |
| Electric Machinery | 2.17 | 2.27 | − |
| Transport Equipment | 4.35 | 3.03 | + |
| Gauges/Optical Equip | 2.94 | 2.56 | + |
| Other Manufacturing | 3.57 | 2.33 | + |
| Mean | 2.69 | 2.48 | |

SOURCE: Tables 59 and 60.

NOTE: Signs test was significant at .03 level for one-tailed test.

for the greater value added/employee in 1974 (Q/L) of foreign plants, a partial correlation was run of sets D (domestic) and F (foreign) for the twenty-seven industries involved. The foreign plants in each industry were given a dummy variable of 1 for foreignness, the domestic plants a value of 0 for the same variable. A regression was then run correlating this dummy variable for foreignness with the value added/employee (Q/L) in 1974: r = .4217, r2 = .1778; significant at .001. A partial correlation was then run to determine whether other intervening variables could account for the correlation between foreignness and VA/employee. This was looking for a variable that would reduce to insignificance the differences between foreign and domestic plants. One indicator of scale of operations (value added/plant, 1974) was able to reduce the difference between foreign and domestic: the r = .2743; r2 = .0752; and significant at .023. Another measure, remuneration/employee 1974, was also able to reduce the differences explained by foreignness: r = .2654; r2 = .0704; significant at .027. These partial correlations suggest that it may be the larger scale of operations of foreign plants that accounts for the greater factor productivity of labor and capital, and that the labor used by foreign plants may be qualitatively different than that used by domestic plants (since remuneration/employee seemed to explain many of the differences between the Q/L ratios of foreign and domestic plants). However, the differences between foreign and domestic plants remained significant at the .03 level. Controlling for these two variables simultaneously did not reduce the significance of the differences between foreign and domestic plants.

Other studies have shown similar results with regard to output per unit of labor. DeCarvalho's study of Colombia shows significant differences (at the .01 level) between foreign and domestic firms with regard to value added/employee for 1970-74 and 1970. The aggregated data from paired firms in Mexico, Brazil, Central America and Colombia also found differences in the value added/employee of foreign and domestic firms, with foreign firms having a greater value added/employment ratio, significant at the .01 level (DeCarvalho, 1977: 96 & 226). Tambunlertchai (1976) found that foreign firms in Thailand had higher sales/employee ratios than did domestic firms, but that domestic firms had higher value added/employee ratios than foreign firms. In both cases, there were substantial variations by industry (p.215). Fajnzylber's (1975) study of Mexico found that foreign firms had production/employee ratios that were two times greater than those of domestic firms in the same industries (p.912). Mason's (1973) study of paired firms in the Philippines and Mexico found foreign firms to have greater value added/employee ratios than domestic firms. These differences were significant at the .006 level (p.351).

The results found in this study of Colombia seem to be consistent with those reported by Fajnzylber, DeCarvalho, and Mason. In the case of both output/capital and output/labor, this study must reject the domestication hypothesis (that there is an advantage for domestic plants) and the null hypothesis (that there were no significant differences between foreign plants and domestic ones), and accept the alternate hypothesis (that foreign plants have greater ratios of output/capital and output/labor).

## Growth Rates and Industrial Groupings

The only other way in which the domestication hypothesis could have any accuracy is if domestic plants aid in some intangible way the growth of the economy (e.g., by increasing competition within the economy). In order to test this, correlations were run using as an independent variable the relative incidence of foreign plants (i.e., foreign plants as a percentage of total national production, employment, and value added). The dependent variable in these correlations was the growth of production, value added, or employment in that industry between 1970 an 1975.

H1 (the domestication hypothesis): Rates of growth will be greatest in those industries where the incidence of foreign plants is lowest (and of domestic plants is highest).

HO (the null hypothesis): There will be no significant differences in the rates of growth of industries based on the incidence of foreign plants.

H2 (the alternative hypothesis): There will be greater rates of growth in those industries where the incidence of foreign plants is greatest.

The results of the correlations are shown in Tables 16-18. Table 16 correlated the incidence of foreign plants in total national production in each industry with the rate of growth of production in that industry. The resulting correlation (r = -.1327; r2 = .0176) indicates a negative correlation between incidence of foreign plants and rates of growth. This allows us to rile out the alternative hypothesis. However, the significance level of the correlation (.255) will not allow us to accept the domestication hypothesis. The null hypothesis is accepted. Table 17 shows a similar correlation for growth of value added, and Table 18 for growth of employment. In both cases, the relationship between incidence of foreign plants and growth was negative (r = -.0868 for value added; r = -.0746 for employment). In both cases the differences were not significant at the .05 level, so the null hypothesis is accepted.

The available evidence indicates that there is no significant relationship between the incidence of foreign or domestic plants and the rates of growth of a specific industry. It cannot even be argued that foreign or domestic plants gravitate towards industries with rapid rates of growth.

TABLE 16
GROWTH RATES OF PRODUCTION AND INCIDENCE OF FOREIGN PLANTS, BY INDUSTRY

| Industry | Growth of Production 1970-1975 | Foreign Plants as a Percent of National Production, 1974 |
|---|---|---|
| Food Products | 267.9 | 22.08 |
| Beverages | 228.7 | 3.15 |
| Textiles | 181.1 | 61.95 |
| Apparel | 192.1 | 9.37 |
| Leather & Products | 197.7 | 18.45 |
| Footwear | 278.5 | 22.66 |
| Wood & Products | 122.1 | 33.55 |
| Furniture | 122.5 | 5.95 |
| Paper & Products | 294.6 | 79.34 |
| Printing/Publishing | 224.2 | 5.99 |
| Industrial Chemicals | 425.3 | 79.52 |
| Other Chemicals | 214.7 | 60.29 |
| Petroleum Refineries | 307.4 | 22.00 |
| Petroleum Derivatives | 1900.0 | 10.00 |
| Rubber Products | 209.3 | 82.05 |
| Plastic Products | 415.6 | 47.25 |
| Clay & Porcelain | 212.8 | 16.61 |
| Glass & Products | 352.6 | 84.04 |
| Other Nonmetallic | 173.8 | 56.66 |
| Basic Iron & Steel | 238.1 | 49.89 |
| Basic Nonferrous | 170.3 | 73.62 |
| Metal Products | 211.6 | 42.79 |
| Nonelect Machinery | 169.9 | 29.64 |
| Electric Machinery | 227.6 | 67.28 |
| Transport Equipment | 366.1 | 79.76 |
| Gauges/Optical Equip | 484.3 | 38.41 |
| Other Industries | 159.7 | 23.41 |
| Mean | 309.2 | 41.69 |

SOURCES: Table 62; ANDI, 1976: 1-2.
NOTE: The results of the regression were r = -.1327; r2 = .0176; significant at .255 for a one-tailed test.

TABLE 17
GROWTH RATES OF VALUE ADDED AND THE INCIDENCE OF FOREIGN PLANTS, BY INDUSTRY

| Industry | Growth of Value Added, 1970–1975 | Foreign Plants as a Percentage of National Value Added, 1974 |
|---|---|---|
| Food Products | 233.0 | 29.67 |
| Beverages | 209.6 | 2.41 |
| Textiles | 164.2 | 61.35 |
| Apparel | 185.1 | 10.17 |
| Leather & Products | 180.9 | 18.80 |
| Footwear | 268.0 | 24.11 |
| Wood & Products | 137.5 | 38.60 |
| Furniture | 106.5 | 3.98 |
| Paper & Products | 248.6 | 81.70 |
| Printing/Publishing | 198.8 | 8.71 |
| Industrial Chemicals | 410.9 | 77.76 |
| Other Chemicals | 200.1 | 88.08 |
| Petroleum Refineries | 483.8 | 18.90 |
| Petroleum Derivatives | 1642.9 | 16.00 |
| Rubber Products | 180.1 | 83.73 |
| Plastic Products | 373.6 | 54.79 |
| Clay & Porcelain | 185.9 | 18.95 |
| Glass & Products | 306.9 | 85.79 |
| Other Nonmetallic | 191.4 | 58.77 |
| Basic Iron & Steel | 208.7 | 42.20 |
| Basic Nonferrous | 161.7 | 82.15 |
| Metal Products | 223.9 | 44.38 |
| Nonelect Machinery | 149.4 | 31.23 |
| Electric Machinery | 251.8 | 68.83 |
| Transport Equipment | 547.4 | 78.26 |
| Gauges/Optical Equip | 506.3 | 35.51 |
| Other Industries | 147.8 | 27.10 |
| Mean | 300.2 | 43.40 |

SOURCES: See Table 16.
NOTE: The results of the regression were r = –.0868; r2 = .0075; significant at .333 for a one-tailed test.

CHAPTER 18
GROWTH RATES OF EMPLOYMENT AND INCIDENCE OF FOREIGN PLANTS, BY INDUSTRY

| Industry | Growth of Employment 1970-1975 | Foreign Plants as a Percent of National Employment, 1974 |
|---|---|---|
| Food Products | 23.1 | 17.77 |
| Beverages | 34.7 | 6.58 |
| Textiles | 27.4 | 46.13 |
| Apparel | 43.3 | 8.27 |
| Leather & Products | 64.3 | 9.84 |
| Footwear | 40.5 | 11.29 |
| Wood & Products | 1.2 | 21.78 |
| Furniture | 7.1 | 3.15 |
| Paper & Products | 37.8 | 53.38 |
| Printing/Publishing | 35.3 | 6.08 |
| Industrial Chemicals | 66.6 | 51.29 |
| Other Chemicals | 27.9 | 51.75 |
| Petroleum Refineries | 83.9 | 10.05 |
| Petroleum Derivatives | 181.1 | 2.27 |
| Rubber Products | 18.9 | 70.21 |
| Plastic Products | 79.6 | 27.80 |
| Clay & Porcelain | 28.7 | 15.46 |
| Glass & Products | 90.1 | 57.70 |
| Other Nonmetallic | 8.0 | 28.25 |
| Basic Iron & Steel | 20.2 | 29.81 |
| Basic Nonferrous | 46.5 | 63.29 |
| Metal Products | 20.2 | 23.67 |
| Nonelect Machinery | 23.8 | 17.64 |
| Electric Machinery | 53.3 | 47.63 |
| Transport Equipment | 85.8 | 39.48 |
| Gauges/Optical Equip | 89.1 | 20.22 |
| Other Industries | 12.2 | 14.90 |
| | Mean | 46.3 20.29 |

SOURCES: See Table 16.
NOTE: The results of the regression were r = -.0746; r2 = .0056; significant at .356 for a one-tailed test.

A rank-order correlation was computed of the growth of industries in the Colombian manufacturing sector in 1945-57 and 1957-68 (adapted from Berry, nd a: 34a) with the incidence of foreign plants in each industry's production, 1974. The correlation for 1945-57 was rs = .4228 (significant at the .05 level for a one-tailed test); and growth during the 1957-68 period correlated even higher with the incidence of foreign plants in each industry (rs = .5212; significant at the .02 level for a one-tailed test). Because of the lack of usable data on the incidence of foreign plants in these earlier periods, it is not possible to argue a causal relationship for foreign plants upon growth in manufacturing.

## Conclusion

The question addressed in this chapter is whether domestication would lead to more growth in the Colombian economy. The domestication hypothesis argued that domestication would benefit economic growth because domestic plants have a higher factor productivity for both capital (Q/K) and labor (Q/L) and that domestic plants cause the industries in which they concentrate to be more dynamic. The alternate hypothesis argued that the reverse was true, that foreign plants had the advantages of greater factor productivity and more dynamism. The null hypothesis stated that there were no significant differences between domestic and foreign plants in the same industries.

With regard to both output/capital (Q/K) and output/labor (Q/L), the alternative hypothesis was accepted. The greater factor productivity for foreign plants can be attributed to their greater size and the resulting economies of scale and to the fact that foreign plants were employing qualitatively different (i.e., more highly skilled) labor. Yet, even when controlling for these variables, the higher output/labor ratio of foreign plants remained significant. With regard to domestication causing greater dynamism in the manufacturing sector, the evidence in this chapter has tended to confirm the null hypothesis. The incidence of foreign plants (or of domestic plants) in a specific industry is not related in a significant manner to the levels of growth of production, employment, or value added in that industry. It seems likely that domestication will retard economic growth of the Colombian manufacturing sector. It will not add a dynamic element to the growth of industries where it locates, and it will result in lower factor productivity of labor and capital.

# CHAPTER 6

# DOMESTICATION AND DISTRIBUTION

Colombia has a highly regressive distribution of income. That statement can sound inane and trivial (particularly when summarized in the figures below) unless one realizes what this inequality means. It means that a large share of the population have only limited access to adequate health care, good housing, proper nutrition, and honorable employment. Please keep this in mind when looking over the figures on the following pages to remember the human faces behind them.

As one can see from Table 19. In 1964 the poorest 9 percent of the economically active population earned less that 1 percent of all income, the poorest 25 percent earned less than 5 percent of all income, and the poorest 60 percent earned less than 20 percent of all income. On the other hand, the richest 3 percent earned almost 30 percent of all income, the richest 10 percent received about 45 percent of all income, and the richest 20 percent received over 63 percent of all income.

The Gini ratio is a numerical index of income inequality. It compares the cumulated shares of income from poor to richer and compares those shares with what would occur in conditions of perfect equality. It ranges from 1.0 (complete inequality) to 0 (complete equality) (R. Weisskopf, 1976: 30). Using this measure we can see that Colombia's income distribution in the early 1960s among active workers (Gini = .586) was less equal than those of many other Latin American countries (e.g., Argentina, Chile, Mexico, and Venezuela) and more equal than only Brazil (Cline, 1972: 111). Lin's study of the Gini ratios of thirty-five developing countries in the late 1960s found that Colombia had a less equal distribution of income than twenty-seven of those countries (Lin, 1978: 119-22). Berry and Urrutia (1976) argue that Colombia's distribution of income worsened between the mid-1930s and the early 1950s (Gini of .553 in 1934-6 and of .602-.633 in 1951) and then improved by the mid-1960s (Gini of .57 in 1964) (p.114).

Domestication could have a number of possible effects on income distribution in Colombia. To the extent that foreign plants' operations involve capital inflows, they can be expected to lower the incomes of local capitalists and raise the real incomes of labor (Reuber, 1974: 140). If foreign and domestic plants differ with regard to their wage levels, the distribution of remuneration between labor and management, the labor share of value added, the creation of employment, of their geographic distribution within Colombia, then domestication will have some effects upon distribution. The domestication hypothesis argues the following:

H1: Domestic plants pay higher wage levels, they pay a greater part of remuneration to workers, a higher share of value added to labor, they create more employment through the production of a given unit of value added, and they are distributed more equally than foreign plants in a geographic sense.

The null hypothesis argues the following:

H0: There are no significant differences between domestic and foreign plants with regard to any of these factors.

The alternate hypothesis argues:

H2: Foreign plants pay higher wage levels, pay a greater part of remuneration to labor (vs. management), pay a higher share of value added to labor (vs. capital), create more employment through the production of a given unit of value added, and are distributed geographically more equally than are domestic plants.

TABLE 19
ESTIMATES OF INCOME DISTRIBUTION IN COLOMBIA

| Berry-Urrutia: Active Population, 1964 w | z | McClure-Musgrave: Active Workers, 1964 w | z |
|---|---|---|---|
| 8.75 | 0.54 | 37.2 | 10.3 |
| 25.06 | 4.01 | 54.2 | 17.4 |
| 42.21 | 9.61 | 64.6 | 22.9 |
| 52.55 | 14.49 | 86.8 | 39.5 |
| 60.87 | 19.63 | 92.3 | 48.7 |
| 66.86 | 24.13 | 96.0 | 57.7 |
| 76.71 | 33.16 | 99.0 | 74.2 |
| 86.06 | 45.27 | 99.9 | 88.4 |
| 91.70 | 55.59 | 100.0 | 100.0 |
| 95.61 | 66.29 | | |
| 97.28 | 72.94 | | |
| 99.41 | 87.41 | | |
| 100.00 | 100.00 | | |

SOURCE: (Cline, 1972: 204).
NOTE: w = cumulative percentage of recipient units.
z = cumulative percentage of income.

## Wage Levels

Tables 20 through 24 provide a comparison of the remuneration per employee of foreign and national plants for different categories of employees in 1972. Foreign plants in each category of employee paid an average remuneration by industry that was greater than that paid by national plants. Because foreign plants (Set F) were being compared to national plants (Set N), it was impossible to determine the degree of difference between the levels of remuneration in the two sets, but a signs test was used to determine the direction of any differences.

For per capita remuneration to all personnel (Table 20), foreign plants paid higher remuneration in twenty-three out of the twenty-seven industries for which a comparison was made. In only four industries (beverages, petroleum refining, clay and porcelain objects, and iron and steel) did national plants pay higher levels of remuneration to all personnel. These data obviously disconfirm the domestication hypothesis. The results of the signs test show that this difference is significant at the .001 level for a one-tailed test, giving substantial support for the alternative hypothesis.

A comparison of the per capita remuneration to foreign managers (Table 21) shows that foreign plants have higher remuneration in twenty-one of the twenty-six industries for which a comparison was made; national plants had a higher remuneration in four industries (footwear, industrial chemicals, clay and porcelain objects, and glass products); and there was no difference in petroleum refining. One industry, manufacture of petroleum and carbon derivatives, was omitted because there were no foreign managerial personnel in the industry. The signs test shows this relationship to be significant at the .001 level for a one-tailed test, giving support to the alternative hypothesis.

Per capita remuneration to national managers showed a similar relationship between foreign plants and national plants, with foreign plants paying higher remuneration in twenty-five out of twenty-seven industries, a relationship that was also significant at the .001 level for a one-tailed test (Table 22). Remuneration to office workers (Table 23) showed a similar relationship, with foreign plants paying higher remuneration in twenty-three of the twenty-seven industries for which a comparison was made, again significant at the .001 level. For per capita remuneration to laborers, foreign plants paid more than national plants in twenty-one of twenty-seven industries, national plants paid more in five industries, and there was no difference in one. This relationship was significant at the .001 level, again giving support to the alternative hypothesis (Table 24).

In each of these five cases of remuneration, the domestication hypothesis and the null hypothesis had to be rejected in favor of the alternative hypothesis. Foreign plants

TABLE 20
PER CAPITA REMUNERATION TO ALL PERSONNEL, 1972
(THOUSANDS OF PESOS)

| Industry | Foreign Plants | National Plants | Sign of Difference |
|---|---|---|---|
| Food Products | 46 | 27 | + |
| Beverages | 35 | 50 | – |
| Textiles | 45 | 37 | + |
| Apparel | 32 | 17 | + |
| Leather & Products | 42 | 27 | + |
| Footwear | 37 | 21 | + |
| Wood & Products | 37 | 20 | + |
| Furniture | 25 | 19 | + |
| Paper & Products | 64 | 45 | + |
| Printing/Publishing | 42 | 35 | + |
| Industrial Chemicals | 59 | 52 | + |
| Other Chemicals | 59 | 43 | + |
| Petroleum Refineries | 123 | 129 | – |
| Petroleum Derivatives | 42 | 22 | + |
| Rubber Products | 54 | 44 | + |
| Plastic Products | 35 | 25 | + |
| Clay & Porcelain | 20 | 26 | – |
| Glass & Products | 47 | 35 | + |
| Other Nonmetallic | 53 | 32 | + |
| Basic Iron & Steel | 45 | 47 | – |
| Basic Nonferrous | 45 | 35 | + |
| Metal Products | 43 | 26 | + |
| Nonelectrical Machinery | 51 | 34 | + |
| Electric Machinery | 52 | 36 | + |
| Transport Equipment | 45 | 30 | + |
| Gauges/Optical Equip | 33 | 23 | + |
| Other Manufacturing | 29 | 22 | + |
| Mean | 45.9 | 35.5 | |

SOURCES: Tables 59 and 60.
NOTE: The Signs Test was significant at the .001 level for a one-tailed test.

TABLE 21
PER CAPITA REMUNERATION TO FOREIGN MANAGERIAL PERSONNEL, 1972
(THOUSANDS OF PESOS)

| Industry | Foreign Plants | National Plants | Sign of Difference |
|---|---|---|---|
| Food Products | 215 | 164 | + |
| Beverages | 194 | 186 | + |
| Textiles | 218 | 165 | + |
| Apparel | 165 | 70 | + |
| Leather & Products | 193 | 184 | + |
| Footwear | 162 | 178 | − |
| Wood & Products | 243 | 107 | + |
| Furniture | 381 | 130 | + |
| Paper & Products | 271 | 232 | + |
| Printing/Publishing | 200 | 181 | + |
| Industrial Chemicals | 183 | 185 | − |
| Other Chemicals | 244 | 220 | + |
| Petroleum Refineries | 621 | 621 | 0 |
| Petroleum Derivatives | -- | -- | |
| Rubber Products | 414 | 313 | + |
| Plastic Products | 150 | 119 | + |
| Clay & Porcelain | 57 | 67 | − |
| Glass & Products | 112 | 119 | − |
| Other Nonmetallic | 384 | 249 | + |
| Basic Iron & Steel | 202 | 86 | + |
| Basic Nonferrous | 272 | 221 | + |
| Metal Products | 218 | 163 | + |
| Nonelect Machinery | 449 | 260 | + |
| Electric Machinery | 211 | 193 | + |
| Transport Equipment | 159 | 145 | + |
| Gauges/Optical Equip | 173 | 118 | + |
| Other Manufacturing | 234 | 154 | + |
| Mean | 243.3 | 185.8 | |

SOURCES: Tables 59 and 60.
NOTE: The Signs Test was significant at the .001 level for a one-tailed test.

TABLE 22
PER CAPITA REMUNERATION TO NATIONAL
MANAGERIAL PERSONNEL, 1972
(THOUSANDS OF PESOS)

| Industry | Foreign Plants | National Plants | Sign of Difference |
|---|---|---|---|
| Food Products | 186 | 112 | + |
| Beverages | 161 | 191 | – |
| Textiles | 160 | 137 | + |
| Apparel | 149 | 62 | + |
| Leather & Products | 260 | 134 | + |
| Footwear | 206 | 55 | + |
| Wood & Products | 231 | 76 | + |
| Furniture | 201 | 79 | + |
| Paper & Products | 197 | 151 | + |
| Printing & Publishing | 197 | 122 | + |
| Industrial Chemicals | 164 | 142 | + |
| Other Chemical Products | 161 | 132 | + |
| Petroleum Refineries | 203 | 178 | + |
| Petroleum Derivatives | 123 | 106 | + |
| Rubber Products | 183 | 148 | + |
| Plastic Products | 157 | 108 | + |
| Glass & Porcelain Objects | 56 | 66 | – |
| Glass & Products | 177 | 130 | + |
| Other Nonmetallic Minerals | 163 | 113 | + |
| Basic Iron & Steel | 232 | 87 | + |
| Basic Nonferrous Metals | 188 | 142 | + |
| Metal Products | 152 | 98 | + |
| Nonelectrical Machinery | 128 | 107 | + |
| Electric Machinery | 150 | 109 | + |
| Transportation Equipment | 150 | 103 | + |
| Gauges & Optical Equipment | 138 | 89 | + |
| Other Manufacturing | 144 | 87 | + |
| Mean | 171.0 | 113.5 | |

SOURCES: Tables 59 and 60.
NOTE: The Signs Test was significant at the >001 level for a one-tailed test.

TABLE 23
PER CAPITA REMUNERATION TO OFFICE WORKERS, 1972
(THOUSANDS OF PESOS)

| Industry | Foreign Plants | National Plants | Sign of Difference |
|---|---|---|---|
| Food Products | 53 | 41 | + |
| Beverages | 50 | 65 | - |
| Textiles | 64 | 53 | + |
| Apparel | 50 | 33 | + |
| Leather & Products | 69 | 41 | + |
| Footwear | 58 | 40 | + |
| Wood & Products | 48 | 34 | + |
| Furniture | 42 | 26 | + |
| Paper & Products | 84 | 68 | + |
| Printing & Publishing | 41 | 47 | - |
| Industrial Chemicals | 68 | 71 | - |
| Other Chemical Products | 68 | 54 | + |
| Petroleum Refineries | 92 | 89 | + |
| Petroleum Derivatives | 59 | 43 | + |
| Rubber Products | 92 | 73 | + |
| Plastic Products | 47 | 39 | + |
| Glass & Porcelain Objects | 33 | 48 | - |
| Glass & Products | 67 | 60 | + |
| Other Nonmetallic Minerals | 65 | 46 | + |
| Basic Iron & Steel | 57 | 51 | + |
| Basic Nonferrous Metals | 61 | 53 | + |
| Metal Products | 49 | 38 | + |
| Nonelectrical Machinery | 52 | 42 | + |
| Electric Machinery | 68 | 53 | + |
| Transportation Equipment | 63 | 47 | + |
| Gauges & Optical Equipment | 41 | 34 | + |
| Other Manufacturing | 52 | 40 | + |
| Mean | 59.0 | 49.2 | |

SOURCES: Tables 59 and 60.
NOTE: The signs Test was significant at the .001 level for a one-tailed test.

TABLE 24
PER CAPITA REMUNERATION TO LABORERS, 1972
(THOUSANDS OF PESOS)

| Industry | Foreign Plants | National Plants | Sign of Difference |
|---|---|---|---|
| Food Products | 31 | 20 | + |
| Beverages | 14 | 33 | – |
| Textiles | 37 | 31 | + |
| Apparel | 23 | 14 | + |
| Leather & Products | 32 | 22 | + |
| Footwear | 29 | 19 | + |
| Wood & Products | 29 | 18 | + |
| Furniture | 12 | 17 | – |
| Paper & Products | 45 | 33 | + |
| Printing & Publishing | 35 | 27 | + |
| Industrial Chemicals | 40 | 38 | + |
| Other Chemical Products | 31 | 24 | + |
| Petroleum Refineries | 53 | 132 | – |
| Petroleum Derivatives | 23 | 15 | + |
| Rubber Products | 41 | 34 | + |
| Plastic Products | 24 | 19 | + |
| Glass & Porcelain Objects | 16 | 22 | – |
| Glass & Products | 39 | 29 | + |
| Other Nonmetallic Minerals | 44 | 28 | + |
| Basic Iron & Steel | 36 | 42 | – |
| Basic Nonferrous Metals | 34 | 27 | + |
| Metal Products | 31 | 21 | + |
| Nonelectrical Machinery | 29 | 27 | + |
| Electric Machinery | 34 | 24 | + |
| Transportation Equipment | 31 | 24 | + |
| Gauges & Optical Equipment | 20 | 16 | + |
| Other Manufacturing | 17 | 17 | 0 |
| Mean | 30.7 | 28.6 | |

SOURCES: Tables 59 and 60.
NOTE: The Signs Test was significant at the .001 level for a one-tailed test.

paid significantly higher levels of remuneration in all five categories than did national plants. This corresponds with data from other sources which compared the wages paid by foreign and domestic firms. The International Labor Office cites studies from Mexico, Argentina, Brazil, Chile, Peru, Colombia, India, Pakistan, Korea, and the Philippines which found that foreign firms paid higher wages than domestic ones (International Labor Office, 1976: 22-3).

Biersteker's (1978) study of Nigeria found that foreign firms paid higher wages than domestic companies in all of the four different categories of workers that were studied (p.142). Tambunlertchai's (1976) study of foreign and domestic firms in Thailand found that foreign firms paid higher average salaries overall, but domestic firms paid higher salaries to Thai workers (pp.232-3). Fajnzylber's (1975) study of Mexico found that foreign firms paid levels of remuneration that were 1.7 times higher than domestic firms in the same sector (pp.912-3). Wells' (1973) study of Indonesia showed that foreign plants in his sample paid higher wages to skilled and unskilled workers than did domestic plants (p.323). Mason's (1973) study of paired foreign and domestic firms in the Philippines and Mexico found that foreign subsidiaries paid significantly higher wages (at the .02 level) to five out of six categories of personnel (p.352).

There are several possible explanations for the significantly greater remuneration paid by foreign plants in Colombia and other developing countries. It is possible that foreign plants pay higher wages as a political decision to reduce criticism of their operations. They may pay higher wages in order to attract a loyal and stable work force. It is also possible that foreign plants may be employing qualitatively different workers, as was suggested in the last chapter, and that greater levels of remuneration are due to differences in skill levels among employees in the same general category. The nature of the data in this study make it impossible to determine whether foreign plants do, in fact, employ workers of greater skill levels than those employed by domestic plants.

## Distribution Between Labor and Management

Another way of comparing the distributional effects of domestication is to compare the distribution of remuneration among the different categories of employees. As can be seen from Table 25, foreign plants pay a greater share of their total remuneration to foreign managers, to national managers, and to clerical workers than do domestic plants. Domestic plants pay a greater share of their total remuneration to laborers than do foreign plants. As Table 25 shows, foreign plants paid 3.4 percent of their total remuneration to foreign managers, compared to only 1.1 percent for domestic plants. Foreign plants paid 15.0 percent of total remuneration, compared with only 11.3 percent for domestic plants, to national managers. Foreign

TABLE 25
DISTRIBUTION OF REMUNERATION BY CATEGORY
OF EMPLOYEE, 1972

| Category of Employee | Foreign Plants (Amount) | (Percentage) | Domestic Plants (Amount) | (Percentage) |
|---|---|---|---|---|
| Foreign Managers: | | | | |
| # of Employees | 707 | (0.7) | 737 | (0.3) |
| Remuneration | 171 | (3.4) | 83 | (1.1) |
| National Managers: | | | | |
| # of Employees | 4,568 | (4.5) | 8,864 | (3.3) |
| Remuneration | 749 | (15.0) | 878 | (11.3) |
| Subtotal: Managers | | | | |
| # of Employees | 5,275 | (5.1) | 9,601 | (3.6) |
| Remuneration | 920 | (18.4) | 961 | (12.4) |
| Office Workers: | | | | |
| # of Employees | 24,056 | (23.5) | 46,080 | (17.0) |
| Remuneration | 1,535 | (30.7) | 1,927 | (24.9) |
| Laborers | | | | |
| # of Employees | 73,252 | (71.4) | 214,694 | (79.4) |
| Remuneration | 2,550 | (50.9) | 4,851 | (62.7) |
| Total: | | | | |
| # of Employees | 102,583 | (100.0)a | 270,375 | (100.0)a |
| Remuneration | 5,005 | (100.0)a | 7,739 | (100.0)a |

SOURCES: (Tables 21-24; DANE, 1976b: 217-8).
NOTE: Figures are in millions of current pesos and percentage.
(a) May not equal 100 due to rounding.

plants paid 30.7 percent of total remuneration, compared with 24.9 percent for domestic plant, to clerical workers. Finally, foreign plants paid only 50.9 percent of total remuneration to laborers, while domestic plants paid 62.7 percent of total remuneration to laborers.

To the extent that a greater share of foreign plants' remuneration goes to foreign managers, to national managers, and to clerical workers, and to the extent that these categories of workers are paid more than laborers, then foreign plants are contributing to the unequal distribution of income. Managers, the highest paid of the categories of personnel, receive 18.4 percent of the foreign plants' remuneration and only 12.4 percent of domestic plants' total remuneration. Laborers, the lowest paid of the four categories, account for 50.9 percent of foreign plants' total remuneration and 62.7 percent of domestic plants' total remuneration. Domestic plants have a more equal effect on income distribution in terms of the distribution of remuneration to their employees. This evidence tends to support the domestication hypothesis.

## Labor Share of Value Added

Domestication could also affect distribution if foreign and domestic plants have differences in the share of value added that goes to labor. The greater the share of value added that accrues to labor, the stronger the effects towards a more equal distribution of income. Table 26 presents an industry-aggregated comparison of the remuneration/value added ratios of foreign and national plants in Colombia for 1972. Of the twenty-seven industries being compared, domestic plants had a higher labor share of value added in seventeen, foreign plants had a higher ratio in seven, and there was no difference in three. This evidence tends to support the domestication hypothesis, which argues that domestic plants will have a more equitable effect on the distribution of income than will foreign plants. A signs test was run for this relationship, and it was found to be significant at the .02 level for a one-tailed test. This allows us to reject the alternative hypothesis and the null hypothesis and to accept the domestication hypothesis.

Similar results were found in other studies. Fajnzylber (1975) has noted in his study of Mexico that domestic firms in Mexican manufacturing had ratios of remuneration/value added that were 1.2 times higher than those of foreign firms in the same sector (p. 913). DeCarvalho's (1977) study of paired domestic and foreign firms in Colombia found that domestic firms had a much higher wage share of value added (45.5 percent for 1974 and 45.3 percent for 1970-74) than did foreign firms (27.7 percent for 1974 and 32.2 percent for 1970-74). These differences were significant at the .01 level (p. 230).

TABLE 26

REMUNERATION AS A PERCENTAGE OF VALUE ADDED, 1972

| Industry | Foreign Plants | National Plants | Sign of Difference |
|---|---|---|---|
| Food Products | 26 | 29 | – |
| Beverages | 12 | 17 | – |
| Textiles | 34 | 39 | – |
| Apparel | 46 | 46 | 0 |
| Leather & Products | 51 | 44 | + |
| Footwear | 54 | 58 | – |
| Wood & Products | 44 | 46 | – |
| Furniture | 76 | 61 | + |
| Paper & Products | 36 | 35 | + |
| Printing & Publishing | 48 | 49 | – |
| Industrial Chemicals | 24 | 32 | – |
| Other Chemical Products | 30 | 30 | 0 |
| Petroleum Refineries | 8 | 17 | – |
| Petroleum Derivatives | 18 | 25 | – |
| Rubber Products | 39 | 38 | + |
| Plastic Products | 32 | 35 | – |
| Clay & Porcelain Objects | 42 | 63 | – |
| Glass & Products | 40 | 38 | + |
| Other Nonmetallic Minerals | 35 | 39 | – |
| Basic Iron & Steel | 41 | 54 | – |
| Basic Nonferrous Metals | 47 | 45 | + |
| Metal Products | 45 | 45 | 0 |
| Nonelectrical Machinery | 44 | 46 | – |
| Electric Machinery | 46 | 44 | + |
| Transportation Equipment | 23 | 33 | – |
| Gauges & Optical Equipment | 34 | 39 | – |
| Other Manufacturing | 28 | 43 | – |
| Mean | 37.1 | 40.4 | |

SOURCES: Tables 59 and 60.

NOTE: Signs Test was significant at the .02 level for a one-tailed test.

## Geographic Distribution

Domestication could also have a large effect on distribution in Colombia if foreign and domestic plants had substantial differences in their geographic concentration. To the extent that domestic plants are distributed geographically similar to the distribution of population, and to the extent that foreign plants are not distributed this way, domestication would improve distribution. A brief look at Tables 27 and 28 shows that foreign plants are indeed concentrated geographically within Colombia. The four largest metropolitan areas (Bogota, Medellin, Cali, and Barranquilla), accounted for 27.9 percent of the Colombian population in 1974. They accounted for 76 percent of the gross production and 78 percent of the employment of foreign manufacturing plants in Colombia (DANE, 1976a: 9). National plants exhibit almost the same level of concentration in the four major cities, accounting for 70 percent of production and 72 percent of the employment of all national manufacturing plants.

TABLE 27
GEOGRAPHIC DISTRIBUTION OF PRODUCTION, 1973-74

| Mertopolitan Area | Foreign Plant Production | National Plant Production |
|---|---|---|
| Bogota | 23.5% | 26.2% |
| Medellin | 24.1 | 21.4 |
| Cali | 19.8 | 14.2 |
| Barranquilla | 8.1 | .8.5 |
| Subtotal | 75.5% | 70.2% |
| Cartagena | 6.2 | 3.8 |
| Manizales | 0.8 | 1.7 |
| Pereira | 1.7 | 2.0 |
| Bucaramanga | 0.2 | 1.8 |
| Subtotal | 8.9% | 9.3% |
| All Other Areas | 15.6% | 20.5% |

Sources: Adapted from (DANE, 1976b: 223; DANE, 1976a: 108)
NOTE: Figures for foreign plants are from 1973, those for national plants are from 1974.

Of the eight largest cities in the country, foreign plants'production (Set F) was more concentrated than that of national plants (Set N) in the cities of Medellin, Cali, and Cartagena. Foreign plants' production was less concentrated than that of national plants in the cities of Bogota, Barranquilla,

Manizales, Pereira, and Bucaramanga. What is striking about the figures in Tables 27 and 28 is not that there are slight differences between the distribution of foreign and national plants, but that there is a general similarity in that both sets of plants are extremely concentrated into a few metropolitan areas. The rest of Colombia (excluding the largest eight cities) accounts for 67 percent of Colombia's population, but it makes up only 21 percent of the production and 19 percent of the employment of national manufacturing plants and even less (16 percent of production and employment) of foreign plants.

TABLE 28
GEOGRAPHIC DISTRIBUTION OF EMPLOYMENT, 1973-1974

| Metropolitan Area | Foreign Plant Employment | National Plant Employment |
|---|---|---|
| Bogota | 23.9% | 28.9% |
| Medellin | 29.5 | 23.2 |
| Cali | 17.3 | 12.3 |
| Barranquilla | 7.7 | 7.8 |
| Subtotal | 78.4% | 72.2% |
| Cartagena | 1.2 | 1.9 |
| Manizales | 1.3 | 1.9 |
| Pereira | 2.5 | 2.9 |
| Bucaramanga | 0.4 | 2.5 |
| Subtotal | 5.4 | 9.2 |
| All Other Areas | 16.2% | 18.6% |

SOURCES: See Table 27.
NOTE: Figures for foreign plants are from 1973, those for national plants are for 1974.

In the past several years, the government of Colombia has followed a policy of requiring many new foreign plants to locate outside of the Bogota, Medellin, and Cali metropolitan areas. No such similar policy has been directed towards domestic firms. This policy is one of behavior modification rather than of domestication. In practice the two policies are used hand-in-hand in Colombian government policy. In addition to being required to sign transformation agreements with the government, foreign investors are usually not allowed in the areas of Bogota, Medellin, or Cali unless there is substantial justification. This policy may be caused by the government's recognition that geographic decentralization of industry is desirable. It may also stem from the government's desire to keep the population from migrating to a few large cities and overburdening municipal services there. In any case, the location of foreign plants may stem as much from government policy as it does from characteristics of foreign firms. Figure 2 presents a graphic comparison of the geographic distribution of foreign and national plants. As the chart indicates, national plants were distributed somewhat more equally than were foreign plants.

## Creation of Employment

> Without rapid growth in the industrial sector, the Colombian economy will not be able to solve the employment problem....It is manufacturing that will have to provide the increasing exports needed for a sustained growth of employment and it is only in this sector that the battle to free the Colombian economy from excessive dependemce on imports of capital and intermediate goods can in the end be won. More specifically, the manufacturing sector will have to absorb a bigger proportion of the labour force, and this means that its rate of expansion must be much faster than during recent years, and that the number of jobs it creates per unit of investment must be higher (International Labor Office, 1971: 107).

This statement by the International Labor Office's inter-agency team on Colombia points out another possible effect of domestication upon distribution: the degree to which domestication would effect the creation of employment in the factory manufacturing sector. The share of factory manufacturing in the total labor force has grown from a little over 3 percent in the mid-1920s to about 6 percent by 1970 (Berry & Thoumi, 1977: 90). It is uncertain whether the factory manufacturing sector can, as hoped by the International Labor Office, create more jobs and absorb some of the massive unemployment and underemployment in Colombia. In Colombia's four major cities in 1969, the rate of open unemployment was 10-12 percent (Berry, 1975: 278). There was also a substantial amount of underemployment in these urban areas, and it usually ran slightly higher than levels of unemployment (Fedessarrollo, 1976: 40).

The concern of this section is whether domestication will lead to the creation of more employment and, hence, a wider distribution of income (inasmuch as remuneration of factories would be spread among more workers). Vaitsos (1974a) has argued that "compared with the rest of the manufacturing sector foreign direct investments in developing countries provide less direct labor utilization per unit of capital committed" (pp. 336-7). Matter (1977) has argued with regard to Colombia that industries dominated by foreign firms are unable to generate employment because they are capital-intensive and rely too much on assembly (pp.318-9). Foreign investment has been accused of being more capital-intensive (higher K/L ratios) than local investment and thus creating fewer jobs (Lall & Streeten, 1977: 84). Jolly (1974) has noted that using capital-intensive techniques of production in capital-scarce countries will increase the share of capital in value added and concentrate the labor share into the hands of a small number of skilled workers (p. 171). This would explain why, in a relatively capital-scarce country like Colombia, foreign plants pay higher wages and have a lower labor share of value added. Foreign plants' production may also be more likely to mirror the factor endowments of the investing country (where labor is relatively more scarce and capital more abundant than in the recipient country) and this may result in production techniques that emphasize high capital intensity and create relatively fewer jobs.

What will be compared here is the ability of foreign and domestic plants to generate employment per unit of capital (L/K) and per unit of value added (L/Q). If domestic plants can generate more employment per unit of capital or per unit of value added, then the domestication hypothesis would be supported. Comparing the employment generated per unit of output (L/Q), one reaches conclusions that are the inverse of the output/labor ratios listed in Tables 13 and 14. Domestic plants create significantly more employment pet unit of output than do foreign plants.

Part of this labor/output of domestic plants may be due to their lower capital intensity (K/L). Capital intensity can be measured by fixed assets/employee or energy consumption/employee (Edfelt, 1975: 58; Vaitsos, 1974a: 337). Table 29 presents an industry-aggregated comparison of foreign and national plants in terms of their assets/employee. As the table shows, foreign plants had a higher capital intensity (K/L) in twenty-one of the twenty-seven industries for which a comparison was made. This difference was significant at the .002 level for a one-tailed test. This supports ths domestication hypothesis that foreign plants gemerate less employment per unit of capital than do domestic plants in the same industry.

In addition to this comparison of foreign and domestic plants in the same industry, a regression was run to determine whether foreign plants concentrate in those industries which were more capital intensive. There was a moderate and significant correlation between the incidence of foreign plants (i.e., foreign plants production/total plants production, 1974) in each industry and the industry's capital intensity (measured as electric consumption/employee): = .337, significant at .043. This evidence suggests that foreign plants do concentrate in industries that are more capital intensive and that, even within these industries, foreign firms were more capital intensive. It also corresponds with Vaitsos' findings that energy consumption/employee rose more rapidly between 1960 and 1967 for those industries where foreign firms concentrated (Vaitsos,

TABLE 29
ASSETS/EMPLOYEE FOR FOREIGN AND
NATIONAL PLANTS, 1972
(THOUSANDS OF PESOS)

| Industry | Foreign Plants | National Plants | Sign of Difference |
|---|---|---|---|
| Food Products | 69 | 79 | - |
| Beverages | 92 | 121 | - |
| Textiles | 78 | 59 | + |
| Apparel | 20 | 16 | + |
| Leather & Products | 27 | 25 | + |
| Footwear | 22 | 15 | + |
| Wood & Products | 75 | 40 | + |
| Furniture | 50 | 17 | + |
| Paper & Products | 209 | 135 | + |
| Printing & Publishing | 58 | 47 | + |
| Industrial Chemicals | 175 | 312 | - |
| Other Chemical Products | 40 | 45 | - |
| Petroleum Refineries | 712 | 768 | - |
| Petroleum Derivatives | 173 | 64 | + |
| Rubber Products | 59 | 51 | + |
| Plastic Products | 101 | 61 | + |
| Clay & Porcelain Objects | 63 | 37 | + |
| Glass & Products | 81 | 41 | + |
| Other Nonmetallic Minerals | 173 | 88 | + |
| Basic Iron & Steel | 90 | 129 | - |
| Basic Nonferrous Metals | 77 | 66 | + |
| Metal Products | 59 | 37 | + |
| Nonelectrical Machinery | 58 | 42 | + |
| Electric Machinery | 66 | 47 | + |
| Transportation Equipment | 67 | 40 | + |
| Gauges & Optical Equipment | 37 | 30 | + |
| Other Manufacturing | 50 | 32 | + |
| Mean | 103.0 | 90.5 | |

SOURCE:Tables 59 and 60.
NOTE: The Signs Test was significant at the .002 level for a one-tailed test.

1974a: 337).

Other studies of Colombia have shown mixed results. A Central Bank study found that foreign investment in Colombia was substantially more capital intensive than domestic investment (Silva, 1976: 234). DeCarvalho's (1977) study of paired firms Colombia found no significant differences in the capital intensity of foreign and domestic firms. Berry (nd b) has argued that a good deal of the technology used in the entire factory manufacturing sector of Colombia is borrowed from countries like the United States which have high capital/labor ratios. He has also argued that larger firms create relatively little employment (pp. 25 & 28). To the extent that foreign firms are somewhat larger than domestic ones, they might be expected to create less employment. To the extent that both foreign and domestic firms in the factory manufacturing sector are much larger than those in the handicrafts industries, neither foreign nor domestic firms in the factory sector can be expected to create much employment relative to the needs of the country.

Studies of other countries have generally found similar results to those found in Colombia. Iyanda's (1975) study of Nigeria found that foreign firms used more capital per employee than indigenous firms (p. 187). Biersteker's (1978) study of Nigeria found foreign firms to be slightly more capital intensive in the textile industry, but it found no significant differences in two other industries (pp. 123-4). Tambunlertchai (1976) found that foreign firms in Thailand were more capital intensive than domestic firms (p. 238). The ILO's study of Kenya found that, when industry was taken into account, domestic firms were slightly more capital intensive than foreign firms (Leys, 1977: 138-9). Forsyth and Solomon's (1977) study of Ghana found that foreign firms do not always tend to be more capital intensive than domestic firms (pp.265-78). Mason's (1973) paired sample of foreign and domestic firms in Mexico and the Philippines found that the foreign firms were significantly more capital intensive than domestic firms in terms of three out of five measures of capital intensity with no significant differences in the other two (p.351). Wells' (1973) study of Indonesia also found foreign firms to be more capital intensive than domestic firms (p. 323).

## Conclusion

The results of the comparison of the distributional effects of foreign and domestic plants in Colombia are generally in keeping with the domestication hypothesis, which argued that domestic plants would have more equitable effects on distribution than would foreign plants. In looking at wage rates, it was found that foreign plants paid significantly higher wages to all five categories of employees than did domestic plants. This supported the alternative hypothesis. In terms of the distribution of remuneration between labor and management, domestic plants were found to have a more equal distribution, and the domestication hypothesis was supported. Domestic plants also paid a higher share of value added as remuneration, and the domestication hypothesis was again supported. In terms of geographic distribution, foreign plants were distributed less equally than were national plants, so the domestication hypothesis was accepted. These results may have been the result of government policy. Domestic plants were found to create significantly mire employment per unit of capital used and per unit of output, and the domestication hypothesis was again accepted.

Given these characteristics of foreign and domestic plants in Colombia, the effective implementation of a policy of domestication would have the following likely results on distribution: the wages of all categories of employees in factory manufacturing would fall, and the share going to laborers would increase. The labor share of value added would increase, so income would be distributed from capital to labor. The geographic distribution of plants would not change substantially. Employment in the factory manufacturing sector would increase.

# CHAPTER 7

# DOMESTICATION AND THE BALANCE OF PAYMENTS

Differences between foreign and domestic plants in Colombia with regard to the balance of payments could have substantial effects on both economic growth and distribution. Exports of manufactured products have increased the growth of the Colombian industrial sector by providing markets for domestic industrial production. Balance of payments surpluses make available foreign exchange which can be used to import capital goods that can lead to increased growth of manufacturing. Conversely, the shortage of foreign exchange can act as a constraint on economic growth (Joshi, 1976: 336). Diaz-Alejandro (1976) demonstrates these points in the case of Colombia, noting that in the period 1950-1954 imports accounted for 94 percent of Colombian gross investment in machinery and equipment. Even though domestic output of machinery and equipment has increased rapidly, imports accounted for 68 percent of gross investment in machinery and equipment in the 1971-1972 period. He argues that a "substantial import capacity" is a necessary but not sufficient condition for investment in manufacturing (p.94). Sheahan (1968) also makes the point that investment in Colombia has been limited by a lack of foreign exchange and not by a lack of savings (p.98).

The balance of payments effects of foreign and domestic plants can also have an impact on distribution in Colombia. Constantine Vaitsos (1974b) concluded from his study of foreign pharmaceutical companies in Colombia that these foreign firms had income accruing to foreign sources (i.e., profits + royalties + import overpricing) that was 158.2 percent of the income accruing to domestic factors (p.65). If this were true of foreign firms in other industries of the Colombian manufacturing sector (and given the existing differences between foreign and domestic firms in their balances of trade), then foreign firms would have a more detrimental effect on the distribution of income between Colombia and the rest of the world.

Foreign and domestic plants in Colombia have four types of direct effects upon the balance of payments. The first consists of imports of capital. This includes the inflow of investment capital (for foreign plants only) and loans from abroad as well as payments from abroad on investments, loans, and technology contracts controlled by plants resident in Colombia. The second direct effect consists of exports of capital in the form of remission of profits and repatriation of investment (for foreign firms only) as well as payments for foreign loans, technology, trademarks, and managerial assiatance. Together these constitute the capital accounts effects on the balance of payments, with the inflows of capital being credits and the outflows debits.

The third direct effect on the balance of payments consists of exports of goods and services. The fourth is made up of imports of goods and services. Together these two constitute the balance of trade, with the exports comprising a credit on the balance of payments and imports a debit.

In addition to these direct effects, there are a number of indirect effects of foreign and domestic plants on the balance of payments. Koopman (1975) notes that the balance of payments effects of direct foreign investments could be determined exactly only if one could know (a) the extent to which foreign investment substituted local production for goods previously imported, (b) the degree to which domestic firms could have carried out the same investment, and (c) the relative export performances of domestic and foreign firms (p.351).

In Chapter 4 it was assumed that domestic firms would replace those investments currently conducted by foreign firms, but would do so by producing in a manner similar to that employed by domestic firms in the same industry. In order to find the likely effects of domestication, this chapter will compare foreign and domestic firms in terms of their capital accounts (i.e., imports and exports of capital) and their balance of trade (i.e., the imports and exports of goods). I am using the term "balance of trade" to refer to trade in goods only. The term "capital accounts" is used here to include investment and repatriation of capital, payments for services (e.g., royalties), and payments for capital (i.e., profit remittances and interest payments).

The domestication hypothesis argues the following relationship between foreign and domestic firms:

H1: The total balance of payments effects of domestic firms are more positive than those of foreign firms. Domestic firms will import more capital, export less capital, import fewer goods, and export more goods than foreign firms.

The null hypothesis argues the following:

H0: There are no significant differences in the balance of payments effects of foreign and domestic firms.

The alternative hypothesis argues:

H2: Foreign firms have a more positive balance of payments effect than do domestic firms.

Capital Accounts Effects

With regard only to the import and export of capital, foreign firms are likely to have far greater negative effects than domestic companies. Foreign firms invest in the expectation of recouping their original investment as well as gaining an acceptable return on their investment. While this may mean a net capital inflow into the host country in the early years of the investment, the long-term effect is bound to be a net debit on the capital accounts. It is not surprising, therefore, when it is found that the long-run effect of foreign investment in developing countries is (at least with regard to the capital account) a capital flow from developing host-countries to investing countries. Evans, for example, notes that:

> Recent examinations of financial relations between the United States and Latin America also suggest that less developed countries end up exporting more funds than they receive. From 1950 to 1956 remittances of income to United States parent companies exceeded net new private investment by $7.5 billion (Evans, 1971: 328).

There are only a few cases in which foreign firms could have a more positive effect on the capital accounts than domestic firms. If a foreign firm invested in a host country and never remitted capital equal to its original investment, it would have a more positive effect. Or if domestic firms borrowed or bought technology heavily from abroad and paid interest and royalty payments higher than the external payments of foreign firms, then foreign firms would have a more positive capital accounts effect. However, both of these situations are rare. Noting tha negative capital accounts effects of foreign investment, Falero has noted that:

> ...unless the foreign investment creates direct increases in exports and/or decreases in imports...the repatriation of profits and capital will overtake the inflow of dollars and cause a chronic balance of payments deficit.... (Falero, 1974: 84).

Lall and Streeten (1977) compared the direct balance of payments effects (exports + capital inflow - royalty payments - profit remittance - interest payments) for 159 firms in six different countries (Kenya, Jamaica, India, Iran, Colombia, and Malaysia) and found that foreign-controlled firms had greater negative balance of payments effects than locally controlled firms (see Table 30). A greater percentage of foreign-controlled firms had negative balance of payments effects than did locally controlled firms. In addition, the negative effects of foreign-controlled firms tended to be of greater magnitude. Only 26 percent of foreign-controlled firms (as opposed to 54 percent of locally-controlled ones) had negative effects equivalent to of 20 percent of sales or less. However, 43 percent of foreign firms and only 19 percent of local ones had negative effects between 20 percent and 50 percent of sales, and 23 percent of foreign controlled firms had negative effects of greater than 50 percent (compared with only 15 percent for locally controlled firms).

As noted earlier, unless foreign firms are unprofitable, their repatriation of capital and remission of profit will eventually exceed capital inflow. Domestic firms, with no profit to remit or capital to repatriate, have an advantage with regard to this part of the capital account. However, there are other ways in which the behavior of foreign and domestic firms may affect the capital account. These firms may use external credit at varying degrees, and payments for this credit will eventually have a negative effect on the balance of payments.

TABLE 30
NEGATIVE BALANCE OF PAYMENTS EFFECTS AS A PERCENTAGE OF SALES

| | # of Firms | % with Negative Effects | (Extent of Negative Effects) 0% to -20% | -20% to -50% | Greater than -50% |
|---|---|---|---|---|---|
| Foreign-controlled | 133 | 91 | 26 | 43 | 23 |
| Locally controlled | 26 | 88 | 54 | 19 | 15 |

SOURCE: (Lall & Streeten, 1977: 133).

Information on the external credit of the two sets of plants was not available. A Banco de la Republica (1974a) study of foreign firms in the Colombian manufacturing sector found that these firms obtained 31.6 percent of their financing from foreign loans in 1971 (p.20). Silva's (1976) figure for 1973 was 32.0 percent for foreign firms in manufacturing. However, these studies provided no comparison with domestic firms. DeCarvalho (1977) did compare pairs of foreign and domestic firms in the Colombian manufacturing sector in 1974. He found that foreign firms relied more on foreign sources for short-term debt than did domestic firms (24.1 percent to 17.2 percent), but that domestic firms relied on foreign sources for long-term debt (16.6 percent for domestic firms and 13.6 percent for foreign firms). However, neither of these differences was statistically significant due to the small size of the Colombian sample. For the sample of all countries in the study (Mexico, Brazil, and Central America as well as Colombia), there were significant differences, with foreign firms relying more on external credit for both long-term and short-term debt (see Table 31). The results from the total sample were significant at the 5 percent level. From these results, one would expect foreign firms to have a more negative effect on the capital account, since they will be exporting more capital to pay for foreign loans. From the Colombian sample, however, there is no evidence to suggest significant differences in the use of foreign capital between foreign and domestic firms.

In addition to remission of profit for foreign credit, domestic and foreign firms can affect the capital account by differential payments for imported technology. Fajnzylber's (1975) study of Mexico found that foreign firms accounted for 80 percent of all technology payments in the industrial sector. He also found that foreign firms had a ratio of technology payments/production that was approximately seven times higher than that of national companies (p.919). Lall and Streeten compared technical payments for their sample of foreign-controlled and locally controlled firms (see Table 32). Foreign firms (those with majority foreign ownership) generally paid higher levels of technical payments/sales than did locally controlled firms: 64 percent of locally controlled firms, as opposed to 54 percent of foreign-controlled firms, paid technical payments of 1 percent or less of sales. Only 8 percent of locally controlled firms, as opposed to 19 percent of foreign firms, had technical payments in excess of 3 percent of sales.

TABLE 31
FOREIGN DEBT AS A PERCENTAGE OF TOTAL DEBT

| | Domestic Firms | Foreign Firms | Significance Level |
|---|---|---|---|
| Short-term debt: | | | |
| Total Sample | 13.9 | 25.0 | .05 |
| Colombian Sample | 17.2 | 24.1 | -- |
| Long-term debt: | | | |
| Total Sample | 18.8 | 38.0 | .05 |
| Colombian Sample | 16.6 | 13.6 | -- |

SOURCE: (DeCarvalho, 1977: 86).

Vaitsos' (1974b) study of Colombia brought up further evidence that foreign firms pay greater royalties than domestic firms. He found that foreign firms in Colombia generally paid higher absolute levels of royalties than did national firms and that foreign firms had royalty payments in 1968 that were 3.2 times greater per company than payments of national firms. In the rubber and chemical industries, foreign firms paid a higher rate of royalties/reported profits than did national firms (pp.

86-7). DeCarvalho (1977) found that there were significant differences in the royalty payments of foreign and domestic firms. For all the countries in the study, the ratio of royalty payments to sales 1974 and 1970-74 was three times higher for foreign firms than domestic ones. These differences were significant at the 5 percent level (p.107).

From the evidence reviewed so far, it appears likely that foreign firms in Colombia will have effects on the capital account of the balance of payments that are substantially more negative than the effects of domestic firms. First, foreign firms must (if they wish to be profitable) remit profits and repatriate the invested capital to the investing country. It is likely that the initial period of the investment will bring a net inflow of capital to the host country, but this initial benefit to the recipient country will eventually be offset by an even greater outflow of capital. Since wholly domestic firms have no foreign owners, there is no capability to remit profits or repatriate capital abroad.

TABLE 32
TECHNICAL PAYMENTS AS A PERCENTAGE OF SALES

| | Total # | 0% | 0-1% | 1-3% | 3-5% | 5-7% | 7-10% | Over 10% |
|---|---|---|---|---|---|---|---|---|
| Foreign-controlled | 133 | 27 | 27 | 26 | 10 | 5 | 2 | 2 |
| Locally controlled | 25 | 24 | 40 | 28 | 8 | 0 | 0 | 0 |

SOURCE: (Lall & Streeten, 1977: 148).

This net-debit effect of foreign firms relative to domestic ones could be reduced if foreign firms exported less capital than domestic firms to service external debt, if foreign firms exported less capital to pay for external technology, of if foreign firms had a more beneficial balance of trade than domestic firms. The evidence from Colombia suggests thst there are no significant differences between foreign and domestic firms with regard to their use of external debt. DeCarvalho's (1977) study indicates that in Latin America, domestic firms use significantly less external credit. Evidence from Colombia, as well as several other developing countries, suggests that foreign firms also make greater payments for licensed technology (most of which is owned outside the host country). From this evidence it is likely that foreign firms have a substantially more negative effect on the capital account than domestic firms.

## Balance of Trade Effects

In addition to their effects on the capital account of the balance of payments, foreign and domestic firms can be compared according to their direct balance of trade effects. Because of certain limitations in the data for this study, no comprehensive camparison of the balance of trade effects can be made for the two sets of plants. This study will, however, compare the two sets of plants with regard to their import and export performance. It will also see if there is any relationship between industries dominated by foreign plants and export and import intensity. A few earlier studies have attempted to study the balance of trade effects of foreign and domestic firms in Colombia. Silva (1976) looked at the direct balance of trade effects of foreign firms only between 1967 and 1973. He found that in each of those years foreign firms had a pronounced negative direct balance of trade effect ranging from $59 million in 1967 to $227 million in 1973. In 1973 these foreign firms were importing over five times what they exported. Unfortunately, Silva made no comparison with domestic firms (p.175).

Diaz-Alejandro (1976) found that most of Colombia's exports and imports were made by a limited number of foreign and domestic firms. Studying the 320 largest importers in Colombia in 1970, he found that the 80 largest importing firms accounted for 30 percent of Colombia's registered imports and 50 percent of manufactured exports (excluding sugar). The largest 314 importers accounted for 77 percent of all manufactured exports and about 40 percent of all registered imports in 1970. The 320 largest importers included 134 majority-foreign companies and 186 majority-local firms. Diaz-Alejandro found that all these firms had a pronounced negative direct balance of trade effect. These 320 firms had combined imports of $361.5 million in 1970 and exports of $98.9 million (pp.155-8).

However, when broken down according to nationality of ownership, it was found that majority-local firms had smaller negative balance of trade effects than majority-foreign firms (See Table 33). Foreign firms had negative effects of $1.3 million per firm and $3,478 per employee, while majority-local firms had much smaller negative effects of $0.5 million per firm and $795 per employee. Even though these firms were selected because they were the largest industrial importers and their negative balance of trade effects may thus be overstated (for both majority-foreign and majority-local firms), it should be remembered that these firms also accounted for over three-fourths of all manufactured exports in 1970 and that any overstating of negative effects may be slight.

TABLE 33
BALANCE OF TRADE EFFECTS OF LARGE IMPORTERS, 1970: COLOMBIA

| | Majority-Foreign Firms | Majority-Local Firms |
|---|---|---|
| # of Firms | 134 | 186 |
| Manufactured Imports | $202.4 million | $159.1 million |
| Manufactured Exports | $26.8 million | $72.1 million |
| Balance of Trade Effect: | | |
| Aggregate Effect | -$175.6 million | -$87.0 million |
| Per Firm | -$1.3 million | -$0.5 million |
| Per Employee | -$3,478 | -$795 |

SOURCE: (Diaz-Alejandro, 1976: 155).

A. Exports

The following pages compare the export characteristics of foreign plants (Set F) and domestic plants (Set D) in 1974. Table 34 presents the distribution of exports for the two sets of plants. As the table shows, foreign plants and domestic plants exported about the same amount of goods in 1974: 4,722 million pesos for foreign plants and 4,788 million for domestic ones. The leading industries accounting for the exports of foreign plants were textiles (32.5 percent), industrial chemicals (11.9 percent), food products (10.0 percent), nonmetallic minerals (7.6 percent), metal products (7.5 percent), and paper and products (6.1 percent).

Whereas exports from foreign plants were distributed among several industries, the exports of domestic plants were concentrated into food products. This industry accounted for 43.9 percent of the exports of all domestic plants, and sugar exports undoubtedly accounted for most of the exports in this industry. Other industries that accounted for sizable shares of domestic plants' exports were textiles (16.2 percent) and apparel (8.0 percent). There was a limited tendency for DFI plants' exports to be high or low in the same industries where domestic plants' exports were high or low (rs = .4934; significant at .006 level for one-tailed test). This indicates that some industries tend to be export oriented (e.g., food products, textiles) while others (e.g., petroleum refining and petroleum and carbon derivatives) do not.

As Table 35 indicates, foreign plants in 1974 accounted for a greater portion of industrial exports (49.7 percent) than of

TABLE 34
DISTRIBUTION OF EXPORTS, FOREIGN AND DOMESTIC PLANTS, 1974
(in millions of pesos and percentages)

| Industry | Foreign Plants Exports | Foreign Plants Percent | Domestic Plants Exports | Domestic Plants Percent |
|---|---|---|---|---|
| Food Products | 473 | 10.0 | 2,101 | 43.9 |
| Beverages | 0 | 0 | 57 | 1.2 |
| Textiles | 1,535 | 32.5 | 775 | 16.2 |
| Apparel | 97 | 2.1 | 381 | 8.0 |
| Leather & Products | 48 | 1.0 | 213 | 4.4 |
| Footwear | 2 | 0 | 25 | 0.5 |
| Wood & Products | 40 | 0.8 | 54 | 1.5 |
| Furniture | 4 | 0.1 | 40 | 0.8 |
| Paper & Products | 287 | 6.1 | 183 | 3.8 |
| Printing/Publishing | 4 | 0.1 | 33 | 0.7 |
| Industrial Chemicals | 562 | 11.9 | 91 | 1.9 |
| Other Chemicals | 211 | 4.5 | 31 | 0.6 |
| Petroleum Refineries | 0 | 0 | 0 | 0 |
| Petroleum Derivatives | 0 | 0 | 0 | 0 |
| Rubber Products | 85 | 1.8 | 4 | 0.1 |
| Plastic Products | 142 | 3.0 | 50 | 1.0 |
| Clay & Porcelain | 25 | 0.5 | 46 | 1.0 |
| Glass & Products | 43 | 0.9 | 17 | 0.4 |
| Other Nonmetallic | 357 | 7.6 | 13 | 0.3 |
| Basic Iron & Steel | 72 | 1.5 | 64 | 1.3 |
| Basic Nonferrous | 10 | 0.2 | 4 | 0.1 |
| Metal Products | 354 | 7.5 | 76 | 1.6 |
| Nonelectric Machinery | 97 | 2.1 | 231 | 4.8 |
| Electric Machinery | 121 | 2.6 | 17 | 0.4 |
| Transport Equipment | 54 | 1.1 | 55 | 1.1 |
| Gauges/Optical Equip | 19 | 0.4 | 22 | 0.5 |
| Other Manufacturing | 18 | 0.4 | 99 | 2.1 |
| Total | 4,722 | 100.0 | 4,788 | 100.0 |

SOURCE: Tables 60 and 61.

TABLE 35
DFI PLANTS AS A PERCENTAGE OF PRODUCTION AND EXPORTS, 1974

| Industrial Grouping | Percentage of Exports | Percentage of Production | Difference |
|---|---|---|---|
| Food Products | 18.38 | 22.08 | -3.70 |
| Beverages | 0 | 3.15 | -3.15 |
| Textiles | 66.45 | 61.95 | 4.50 |
| Apparel | 20.29 | 9.37 | 10.92 |
| Leather & Products | 18.39 | 18.45 | -0.06 |
| Footwear | 7.41 | 22.66 | -15.25 |
| Wood & Products | 42.55 | 33.55 | 9.00 |
| Furniture | 9.09 | 5.95 | 3.14 |
| Paper & Products | 61.06 | 79.34 | -18.28 |
| Printing & Publishing | 10.81 | 5.99 | 4.82 |
| Industrial Chemicals | 86.06 | 79.52 | 6.54 |
| Other Chemical Products | 87.19 | 60.29 | 26.90 |
| Petroleum Refineries | no exports | 22.00 | --- |
| Petroleum Derivatives | no exports | 10.00 | --- |
| Rubber Products | 95.51 | 82.05 | 17.95 |
| Plastic Products | 73.96 | 47.25 | 26.21 |
| Clay & Porcelain | 35.21 | 16.61 | 18.60 |
| Glass & Products | 71.67 | 84.04 | -12.37 |
| Other Nonmetallic | 96.49 | 56.66 | 39.83 |
| Basic Iron & Steel | 52.94 | 49.89 | 3.05 |
| Basic Nonferrous | 71.43 | 73.62 | -2.19 |
| Metal Products | 82.33 | 42.79 | 39.54 |
| Nonelect Machinery | 29.57 | 29.64 | -0.07 |
| Electric Machinery | 87.68 | 67.28 | 20.40 |
| Transport Equipment | 49.54 | 79.76 | -30.22 |
| Gauges/Optical Equip | 46.34 | 38.41 | 7.93 |
| Other Manufacturing | 15.38 | 23.41 | -8.03 |
| Total | 49.69 | 43.37 | 6.32 |

SOURCE: Tables 59 and 60.

total industrial production (43.4 percent). This indicates that either foreign plants export a greater part of their production than domestic plants or that foreign plants concentrate in the more export-intensive industries, or both. Table 36 compares the manufactured direct exports/production ratios of domestic and foreign plants in 1974. As was suggested by the last table, foreign plants showed a relative advantage in the percentage of total production exported. Even when industry was taken into account, foreign plants were more export intensive. Of the twenty-five industries for which a comparison was made, foreign plants exported a greater percentage of production in fifteen, and domestic plants exported a greater portion in ten. Two industries were omitted because they had no exports at all. These results disconfirmed the domestication hypothesis, which argued an export advantage for domestic plants. A Wilcoxon matched-pairs signed-ranks test was run to determine whether the null hypothesis could be accepted or rejected. The results showed the relationship to be significant at the .05 level (see Table 36). The null hypothesis was rejected in favor of the alternative hypothesis. Foreign plants export significantly more of their total production than do domestic plants in the same industry.

While this comparison of foreign and domestic plants in Colombia found that foreign plants export a greater part of production than do domestic plants, other studies have come up with contradictory results. DeCarvalho's (1977) study of paired foreign and domestic firms in Colombia found that foreign firms exported more on the average than domestic firms, but the difference was not statistically significant. His sample of firms in Brazil found very small and statistically insignificant differences in the exports/sales of foreign and domestic firms. He also found small and statistically insignificant differences in the exports/sales of foreign and domestic firms in Mexico. However, for his Central American sample he found large and statistically significant (at the .01 level) differences between foreign and domestic firms, with foreign firms' exports/sales almost twice as high as those of domestic firms (pp.228-31).

Cohen (1973), in his study of foreign and local firms in Korea, found that foreign firms' exports grew at a faster rate than the exports of domestic firms (p. 196). Morgenstern and Muller (1976) compared the export performance of foreign and local firms in Latin America in the late 1960s, and found that foreign firms exported more than local firms. But when their data were disaggregated by industry, there were no significant differences in exports. They concluded that foreign firms tended to concentrate in industries that were export oriented (pp.405-6). In another article they found that 72 percent of foreign firms (as opposed to 40 percent of joint ventures and 14 percent of local firms) sold their exports to related companies. They also found that firms which exported to related firms had exports of $427.5 million less than firms which exported to

TABLE 36
MANUFACTURED DIRECT EXPORTS AS A PERCENTAGE
OF PRODUCTION, 1974

| Industry | Foreign Plants | Domestic Plants | Differ- ence | Rank of Differences |
|---|---|---|---|---|
| Food Products | 5.73 | 7.21 | -1.48 | -7 |
| Beverages | 0.00 | 0.49 | -0.49 | -5 |
| Textiles | 10.75 | 8.69 | 1.88 | 8 |
| Apparel | 21.45 | 8.71 | 12.75 | 24 |
| Leather & Products | 14.95 | 15.01 | -0.06 | -2 |
| Footwear | 1.05 | 3.88 | -2.83 | -15 |
| Wood & Products | 8.70 | 5.98 | 2.72 | 13 |
| Furniture | 8.16 | 5.16 | 3.00 | 16 |
| Paper & Products | 4.83 | 11.83 | -6.99 | -21 |
| Printing/Publishing | 1.89 | 0.99 | 0.90 | 6 |
| Industrial Chemicals | 6.40 | 4.02 | 2.38 | 10 |
| Other Chemicals | 3.27 | 0.73 | 2.54 | 11 |
| Petroleum Refineries | 0 | 0 | 0 | 0 |
| Petroleum Derivatives | 0 | 0 | 0 | 0 |
| Rubber Products | 2.88 | 0.62 | 2.26 | 9 |
| Plastic Products | 8.61 | 2.72 | 5.89 | 20 |
| Clay & Porcelain | 25.25 | 9.26 | 15.99 | 25 |
| Glass & Products | 3.93 | 8.17 | -4.24 | -19 |
| Other Nonmetallic | 13.15 | 0.63 | 12.52 | 23 |
| Basic Iron & Steel | 3.15 | 2.79 | 0.36 | 4 |
| Basic Nonferrous | 1.18 | 1.31 | -0.13 | -3 |
| Metal Products | 12.24 | 1.97 | 10.27 | 22 |
| Nonelec Machinery | 9.51 | 9.54 | -0.03 | -1 |
| Electric Machinery | 3.91 | 1.13 | 2.78 | 14 |
| Transport Equipment | 0.89 | 3.49 | -2.62 | -12 |
| Gauges/Optical Equip | 15.08 | 10.89 | 4.19 | 18 |
| Other Manufacturing | 5.81 | 9.76 | -3.95 | -17 |
| Mean | 7.13 | 5.00 | 2.13 | |

SOURCE: Tables 60 and 16.
NOTE: The Wilcoxon Matched-Pairs Signed Ranke Test showed this relationship to be significant at the .05 level for a one-tailed test.

unrelated buyers, and they argued that this difference constituted the amount of underpricing of exports. Given the heavy reliance of foreign firms on exports to related firms, they concluded that foreign firms are much more likely than joint ventures or local companies to engage in export underpricing (Morgenstern & Muller, 1974: 317). If these results were true for my sample of Colombia, then the export potential of foreign plants would be understated (although the balance of payments effects would remain the same, since export underpricing is merely another way of remitting profits).

Lall and Streeten (1977) compared the export performance of their sample of foreign-controlled and locally-controlled firms in six developing countries. They concluded that "foreign control does not generally seem to promote exports and may even inhibit it" (p. 135). Their subsample from India found that locally-controlled firms in that country exported significantly more (at the 5 percent level) than did foreign firms. Iyanda's (1975) study of Nigeria reached similar results. He found that indigenous firms in that country exported a higher percentage of sales than did foreign firms (p. 184). On the other hand, Fajnzylber's (1975) study of Mexico found that foreign firms had an exports/production ratio slightly higher than that of domestic firms: 2.8 percent compared to 2.6 percent (p. 918). Tambunlertchai (1976) also found that foreign firms in Thailand exported much more than did domestic firms (p. 170).

The studies just reviewed present different conclusions about the relative export performance of foreign and domestic firms, and many of them seem to contradict the results of this study (as shown in Table 36). On closer examination, many of these differences can be accounted for by the different methods used. Iyanda (1975), who found that local firms exported more, concluded that this export advantage resulted not from the foreignness of firms but rather from the fact that foreign firms concentrated less heavily in export-oriented industries. He stated that "export performance therefore is not much associated with foreign ownership but rather with the nature of industry" (p.185). Nor did Lall and Streeten's Indian subsample, which also showed a significant export advantage for locally controlled firms, take industry into account. So the differences between these studies and my study of Colombia may be due to the fact that many of these did not take industry into account.

Another factor which could explain the greater export propensity of foreign plants is the existence of export restrictive clauses in technology contracts which affect foreign and domestic firms differentially. Two studies which have been made of technology contracts and export restrictions in Colombia both suggest that domestic firms are affected more strongly than foreign firms by these contracts. Constantine Vaitsos studied restrictive clauses in 451 technology transfer contracts in Colombia, Bolivia, Peru, and Ecuador (see Table 37). The study included the industries of foods and beverages, textiles, chemicals, and pharmaceuticals.

TABLE 37
EXPORT RESTRICTIONS IN TECHNOLOGY
TRANSFER CONTRACTS

| Type of Company | # Firms | Prohibit Exports | Partial Permission | No Export Restrictions |
|---|---|---|---|---|
| Wholly Foreign: | | | | |
| Total Sample | 99 | 72% | 8% | 20% |
| Colombia | 34 | 67% | 4 | 29 |
| Joint Venture: | | | | |
| Total | 8 | 75% | 0% | 25% |
| Colombia | 7 | 71% | 0 | 29 |
| National Firms: | | | | |
| Total | 114 | 88% | 3% | 9% |
| Colombia | 51 | 86% | 0 | 14 |

SOURCE: (Vaitsos, 1974b: 55)

The table shows that national firms are more frequently the victims of clauses that totally prohibit export using the new technology. For Colombia, 86 percent of national firms (compared with 67 percent of wholly foreign firms and 71 percent of joint ventures) have clauses which prohibit exports. Only 14 percent of national firms in Colombia (compared with 29 percent of wholly foreign firms and joint ventures) had no export restrictions. The National Planning Department of Colombia conducted a study of export-restrictive clauses in three industries. For mixed and foreign firms (20 percent to 100 percent foreign ownership), 59 percent of the contracts explicitly prohibited imports. For national firms (less than 20 percent foreign ownership), 72 percent of the contracts prohibited exports explicitly (Matter, 1977: 288).

It is possible, therefore, that some of the export advantage of foriegn plants may stem from the fact that domestic plants are more hindered in their exporting due to technology contracts that restrict exports. However, one must consider that foreigners already exert effective managerial control over the export decisions of foreign plants, and can limit the exports of these plants without having explicit restrictions. It may be that apparent differences between foreign and domestic firms in terms of export restrictions may be more superficial than actual. Vaitsos states as much himself (1974b: 58). Regardless of the causality, the fact remains that foreign plants export a significantly greater percentage of their production than do domestic plants in the same industry, so the alternate hypothesis is confirmed.

## B. Imports

The second aspect of the balance of trade is imports. Table 38 shows the distribution of imported raw materials between foreign and domestic manufacturing plants in 1970. As the table indicates, foreign plants imported substantilly more raw materials than did domestic plants in that year. Plants in the industries of transport equipment, other chemicals, textiles, and industrial chemicals were responsible for most of the imports of foreign firms. Domestic plants in the industries of food products, beverages, transport equipment, industrial chemicals, and printing accounted for most of their imports of raw materials (Table 38).

Table 39 presents a comparison of the imported raw materials/total raw materials ratios of foreign and domestic plants. Of the twenty-five industries for which a comparison was made, domestic plants had lower levels of raw material imports in nineteen industries, foreign plants had lower levels in five, and there was no difference in one. This evidence disconfirms the alternative hypothesis, which argued that foreign plants would have lower levels of imports than domestic plants in the same industry. A Wilcoxon matched-pairs signed-ranks test was run to determine whether this relationship could be explained by the null hypothesis or whether it corresponded with the domestication hypothesis. The results showed the relationship to be consistent with the domestication hypothesis at the .001 level of significance. The null hypothesis was rejected, and the domestication hypothesis accepted.

Other studies have reached contrasting conclusions about the effects of foreign and domestic firms on imports. DeCarvalho (1977) found no significant differences in the imports of raw materials or of machinery between domestic and foreign firms in Colombia, Mexico or Central America. He did find that in Brazil foreign firms imported significantly more ( at the .05 level) machinery than domestic firms (pp. 228-30). Vaitsos (1974b) compared foreign and domestic firms in Colombia in terms of their import intensity for raw materials and intermediate goods for the pharmaceuticals and chemical industries. He found that foreign firms used more imports in the pharmaceuticals industry, but that domestic firms imported more in the chemical industry (p. 90).

Some research has found a greater import-intensity for foreign firms. Biersteker (1978) found that foreign firms imported a greater percentage of their inputs than did domestic Nigerian firms (p. 90). Iyanda (1975) also found that domestic firms in Nigeria obtained a higher percentage of their inputs locally (p. 186). Cohen's (1973) study of Korea found that foreign firms imported more and bought less from Korean firms than did Korean firms (p. 145). On the other hand, Lall and Streeten's (1977) six-country sample found no significant differences in the import intensities of foreign-controlled and

TABLE 38
DISTRIBUTION OF RAW MATERIAL IMPORTS, 1970
(MILLIONS OF PESOS)

| Industry | Foreign Plants (Amount) | Foreign Plants (Percent) | Domestic Plants (Amount) | Domestic Plants (Percent) |
|---|---|---|---|---|
| Food Products | 226 | 5.0 | 852 | 27.3 |
| Beverages | 1 | 0.0 | 347 | 11.1 |
| Textiles | 552 | 12.1 | 136 | 4.4 |
| Apparel | 0 | 0.0 | 8 | 0.3 |
| Leather & Products | 5 | 0.1 | 26 | 0.8 |
| Footwear | 0 | 0.0 | 2 | 0.0 |
| Wood & Products | 17 | 0.4 | 2 | 0.0 |
| Furniture | 0 | 0.0 | 0 | 0.0 |
| Paper & Products | 273 | 6.0 | 18 | 0.6 |
| Printing/Publishing | 10 | 0.2 | 250 | 8.0 |
| Industrial Chemicals | 509 | 11.2 | 21 | 0.7 |
| Other Chemicals | 601 | 13.2 | 306 | 9.8 |
| Petroleum Refineries | 14 | 0.3 | 8 | 0.3 |
| Petroleum Derivatives | 16 | 0.4 | 0 | 0.0 |
| Rubber Products | 259 | 5.7 | 46 | 1.5 |
| Plastic Products | 53 | 1.2 | 69 | 2.2 |
| Clay & Porcelain | 1 | 0.0 | 12 | 0.4 |
| Glass & Products | 5 | 0.1 | 11 | 0.4 |
| Other Nonmetallic | 58 | 1.3 | 73 | 2.3 |
| Basic Iron & Steel | 273 | 6.0 | 83 | 2.7 |
| Basic Nonferrous | 105 | 2.3 | 38 | 1.2 |
| Metal Products | 241 | 5.3 | 173 | 5.5 |
| Nonelec Machinery | 158 | 3.5 | 153 | 4.9 |
| Electric Machinery | 287 | 6.3 | 73 | 2.3 |
| Transport Equipment | 829 | 18.2 | 341 | 10.9 |
| Gauges/Optical Equip | 21 | 0.5 | 1 | 0.0 |
| Other Manufacturing | 33 | 0.7 | 54 | 1.7 |
| Total | 4,548 | 100.0 | 3,124 | 100.0 |

SOURCE: Tables 60 and 61.

TABLE 39
IMPORTED RAW MATERIALS AS A PERCENTAGE
OF TOTAL RAW MATERIALS, 1970

| Industry | Foreign Plants | Domestic Plants | Difference | Rank of Differences |
|---|---|---|---|---|
| Food Products | 12.8 | 11.0 | 1.8 | 5 |
| Beverages | 17.6 | 25.4 | -7.8 | -10 |
| Textiles | 21.6 | 8.5 | 13.1 | 13 |
| Apparel | 0.1 | 0.8 | -0.7 | -2 |
| Leather & Products | 7.0 | 7.8 | -0.8 | -3 |
| Footwear | 1.7 | 1.4 | 0.3 | 1 |
| Wood & Products | 19.1 | 1.0 | 18.1 | 14 |
| Furniture | 0.0 | 0.1 | 0.0 | |
| Paper & Products | 27.0 | 7.4 | 19.6 | 16 |
| Printing/Publishing | 55.1 | 46.5 | 8.6 | 12 |
| Industrial Chemicals | 58.2 | 21.6 | 36.6 | 22 |
| Other Chemicals | 61.2 | 41.1 | 20.1 | 17 |
| Petroleum Refineries | 2.7 | 1.5 | 1.2 | 4 |
| Petroleum Derivatives | 26.2 | --- | --- | |
| Rubber Products | 49.5 | 43.0 | 6.5 | 8 |
| Plastic Products | 35.0 | 29.7 | 5.3 | 7 |
| Clay & Porcelain | 15.1 | 21.8 | -6.7 | -9 |
| Glass & Products | 6.6 | --- | --- | |
| Other Nonmetallic | 18.7 | 21.7 | -3.0 | -6 |
| Basic Iron & Steel | 57.8 | 35.5 | 22.3 | 18 |
| Basic Nonferrous | 70.6 | 62.3 | 8.3 | 11 |
| Metal Products | 53.7 | 21.9 | 31.8 | 21 |
| Nonelec Machinery | 64.4 | 33.6 | 30.8 | 20 |
| Electric Machinery | 53.7 | 25.7 | 28.0 | 19 |
| Transport Equipment | 78.7 | 59.6 | 19.1 | 15 |
| Gauges/Optical Equip | 54.3 | 8.3 | 46.0 | 24 |
| Other Manufacturing | 70.8 | 25.7 | 45.1 | 23 |
| Mean | 36.3 | 22.5 | 13.8 | |

SOURCE: Tables 60 and 61.
NOTE: The Wilcoxon Matched-Pairs Signed-Ranks test showed this relationship to be significant at the .001 level for a one-tailed test.

domestically- controlled firms (p. 145). Those studies which found no significant differences in the import-intensity of foreign and domestic firms (i.e., DeCarvalho and Lall and Streeten) used samples that included primarily large firms. In the case of DeCarvahlo, the pairing methodology used required that foreign firms be paired with domestic firms of the same size. The Lall and Streeten study also seems to have chosen firms that were large, especially in its sample from Colombia (pp. 93-4). It could be that some of the differences between those studies and the present one could be accounted for by differences in the size of the plants studied. However, the central point remains that foreign plants are substantially and significantly more import-intensive than domestic ones in the same industry. It can be argued that the official figures overstate the reliance of foreign plants on imports. Foreign firms in Colombia have been known to use import overpricing to remit profits secretly. It has been shown that foreign firms in the Colombian pharmaceutical, rubber, chemical and electronics industries overpiced imports considerably more than domestic firms (Vaitsos, 1974b: 47).

## Conclusion

This chapter has studied the balance of payments effects of domestic and foreign firms in Colombia. In the beginning of the chapter it was suggested that, in terms of the flow of investment capital and profit remittances, foreign firms are more likely than domestic ones to have negative effects on the balance of payments. Evidence available on the foreign debt and on technology payments by foreign and domestic firms indicates that there are no major differences and that these factors will not be likely to reduce the capital accounts advantage of domestic firms.

A look at the balance of trade effects of foreign and domestic plants in Colombia showed mixed results. Foreign plants had a small but statistically significant advantage in exports. With regard to raw material imports, domestic plants had a moderate and statistically significant advantage (i.e., they imported less). It can be argued that the direct balance of trade effects do not show the substantial contribution that foreign firms make through import substitution (i.e., by producing domestically goods that would otherwise have to be imported). Silva (1976) estimates that between 60 percent and 90 percent of foreign manufacturing firms' production in Colombia was substitution for imports (p.119). It seems doubtful that the greater export intensity of foreign firms would compensate for the foreign firms' greater import intensity and for their tendency to have negative capital accounts effects.

The likely effects of the effective implementation of a policy of domestication would be a reduced inflow of investment capital, and a reduced outflow of capital repatriation, profit remittance, and royalty payments. There would be no likely changes in foreign debt. There would also be a slight decrease in exports in the manufacturing sector, and a somewhat larger decrease in raw material imports in that sector. The overall balance of payments would (given the assumptions of this study) likely be slightly positive.

# CHAPTER 8

## NONMATERIAL EFFECTS OF DOMESTICATION

> Even if it could be demonstrated that foreign investment is economically preferable to other alternatives, it would still be rational to opt for a secondbest economic alternative if the noneconomic gains attained thereby outweighed the economic losses entailed. In other words, assuming a negative trade-off, how much 'nationalism' might host countries be able to justify purchasing by foregoing economic benefits (Reuber, 1974: 144).

This question raises a key issue. Even if domestication were found to have no significant effects upon such material factors as economic growth and distribution, what effects would this policy have upon nonmaterial factors in Colombia? This chapter will investigate three possible areas in which domestication policies might have nonmaterial effects: attitudes, national autonomy, and the domestic socio-economic power structure.

In looking at the likely effects of domestication upon attitudes, this chapter will focus on the attitudes of the general public and upon those of the managers of firms in the Colombian economy. If domestication would lead to favorable changes in the attitudes of the general public or of managers of firms, then it could be said to benefit the country. In looking at effects of domestication upon national autonomy, this chapter will compare domestic and foreign firms in terms of their use of national administrative personnel, their responsiveness to national circumstances, and their dependence upon foreign sources of technology. This section will also study the possible effects of domestication upon the cultural domination of Colombia. This section will argue that, to the degree that domestication increases national autonomy and decreases cultural domination, it can be said to benefit the country.

The final factor to be studied in this chapter is the degree to which domestication is likely to effect the socioeconomic power structure in Colombia. Even if domestication were to bring about more autonomy and self-control for the domestic society, to whom in the domestic society would this control gravitate? Would domestication help to disperse power within Colombia, or would it concentrate power even more? Effects upon the concentration of power will be studied by comparing the interlocking directorates of foreign and domestic firms in colombia to see the degree to which these firms are tied into the economic power structure of the country. To the extent that domestication helps to diffuse the concentration of economic power, it can be said to benefit the country.

## Effects of Domestication on Attitudes in Colombia

This section of the chapter will look at the likely effects of domestication upon the attitudes of the general public, of elite groups, and of managers of firms in Colombia. It will begin by looking at general public and elite public attitudes. The remainder of this section will be devoted to comparing the attitudes of Colombian managers with those of managers from the major investing countries in Colombia (e.g., the U.S., Canada, etc.) to determine whether changing the nationality of managers in Colombia is likely to alter managerial attitudes.

### A. Public Opinion Towards Foreign Investment in Colombia

Opinion studies on foreign investment in Colombia are rather rare. Lombard (1979) conducted two studies of elite attitudes toward foreign investment. The first was a series of interviews with students and army officers (total n = 80). Only 15 percent of the students and none of the officers felt that foreign investment had a neutral or negative effect on the development of Colombia. Fifteen percent of the students and 13 percent of the officers felt that foreign investment had a "positive contribution with some reserve," and 70 percent of the students and 87 percent of the officers felt that the investment had "quite a positive contribution." His second study of elite attitudes consisted of a content analysis of the three leading daily newspapers in Colombia-- _El Tiempo_, _El Espectador_, and _El Siglo_--from Januatry 1971 through September 1973. The two papers associated with the Liberal party were more critical of foreign investment: in _El Espectador_ 100 percent of the articles on foreign investment were listed as "restrictive"; 26 percent of the articles in _El Tiempo_ were listed as "critical" and 84 percent "favorable." In the Conservetive paper _El Siglo_, 100 percent of the articles were listed as "favorable" (pp. 69-73). These papers probably are more indicative of splits within elite opinion than anything else, but they do represent possible avenues towards altering public opinion (or at least the opinions of the literate public).

The most extensive sampling of Colombian opinion on foreign investment consists of two polls jointly sponsored by the United States Information Agency and the Interamerican Action Committee of Bogota. One poll was conducted in 1971, the second in the fall of 1975. The first poll was a sample of general public and elite opinion, the latter of elite groups only. Because of sampling differences the two surveys are not comparable. The 1971 sample did not disaggregate most of the responses to differentiate between general public opinion and the opinions of specific elite groups, so I will discuss it only briefly. For the entire sample in 1971 (n = 990) there was a favorable predisposition towards foreign investment: 76 percent of the respondents felt that foreign investment was "very important" for the country; 60 percent felt that the country needed more foreign firms, as opposed to only 17 percent who said that there were already too many; 76 percent felt that the government should stimulate future foreign investment; 59 percent felt that foreign companies had either a "very good" or "good" effect on Colombia, while 39 percent ranked it as "not so good" or "bad" (USIA, 1971: 1-5).

TABLE 40
FAVORABLE ATTITUDE TOWARDS U.S. INVESTMENT

| Group | Number of Respondent | Percentage with Favorable Response |
|---|---|---|
| Military, Police | 61 | 62 |
| Business Executives | 202 | 56 |
| General Public | 210 | 53 |
| Intellectuals | 24 | 44 |
| Communications Leaders | 53 | 41 |
| Religious Leaders and Parish Priests | 46 | 41 |
| Labor Leaders | 18 | 37 |
| University Community (Professors and Students) | 123 | 36 |
| Government Officials and Legislators | 141 | 35 |

SOURCE: (USIA, 1971: b).
NOTE: Composite of each group's answers to two questions: role of DFI and whether U.S. DFI is desirable. Responses that the current effect of foreign investment was "good" or "very good" and that named the U.S. as a good source of future foreign investment were given the highest ranking. One hundred percent would be the maximum possible favorable score.

The only disaggregation of response groups was a response to U.S. foreign investment on particular. As Table 40 shows, the general public had one of the higher favorable responses to U.S. foreign investment. Its favorable attitude towards U.S. DFI ranked ahead of six of the eight elite groups and substantially ahead of that of government officials and legislators. (The general public was a sample from Bogota, Medellin, and Cali excluding the lowest economic-level districts and of the small city of Sogamoso) (p. v). Although the 1975 data do not include any samples of the public, this 1971 ranking can be used as a basis to infer (from the 1975 results) the approximate orientation of the public.

Tables 41 and 42 present the results of the 1975 survey of elite attitudes. Of the total sample, 64 percent felt that foreign investment was "very important" and 24 percent felt it was "fairly important." In terms of perception of the effects of foreign investment on Colombia, 60 percent of the respondents believed it to be "more beneficial" and 35 percent thought it was "more harmful" to the country. These ratings varied considerably depending upon the elite groups being sampled, with business executives, military officers, and media leaders giving positive appraisals of foreign investment's effects (81 percent, 78 percent, and 72 percent, respectively), and university students, labor leaders, and university professors giving the highest harmful appraisal of DFI (61 percent, 53 percent, and 43 percent, respectively). Given the placement of the general public sample in the 1971 poll, one can extrapolate about 72-81 percent of the general public giving foreign investment a "beneficial" rating and 14-24 percent giving it a "harmful" rating.

Table 42 presents a summary of elite group attitudes towards government policy towards foreign investment. For the entire sample 58 percent of the respondents felt that the government policy should discourage it. Those groups most in favor of encouraging foreign investment were business executives (77 percent), military officers (72 percent), government officials (64 percent), media leaders (62 percent), and clergy (61 percent). Those groups most in favor of discouraging foreign investment were university students (58 percent), labor leaders (56 percent), university professors (38 percent), and media leaders (34 percent), An extrapolation of the general public's attitudes (based on the rankings in the 1971 poll) showed that about 62-77 percent were in favor of encouraging foreign investment and about 21-34 percent wanted to discourage foreign investment.

The attitudes of both the elite groups and the general public strongly preferred a government policy of encouraging new foreign investments and discouraging the acquisitions of existing Colombian firms by foreign investors. Of the entire elite sample, 19 percent wanted a government policy that moderately encouraged these firms, and only 25 percent supported any type of government policy which discouraged new foreign investments (see Table 42). Extrapolations of the attitudes of the general public find approximately 69-75 percent wanting government policies that encourage new foreign firms to enter the country.

The opinions of the elite groups were strongly opposed to encouraging acquisitions of Colombian firms by foreign investors. Only 9 percent of the elite sample favored a government policy of encouraging these acquisitions, while 82 percent of the elite sample favored policies that would discourage these acquisitions. An extrapolation of the general public's attitudes showed that approximately 80-83 percent wanted government policies that discouraged foreign purchases of existing Colombian firms.

TABLE 41
OVERALL IMPORTANCE AND DESIRABILITY OF FOREIGN INVESTMENT

| Total No. of Cases (800) | Bus. Execs. (100) | Media Ldrs (100) | Clergy (100) | Gov't Off'ls (100) | Mil Off'rs (100) | Labor Ldrs (100) | Univ. Profs. (100) | Univ. Stud (100) | Total (800) |
|---|---|---|---|---|---|---|---|---|---|
| Importance of Foreign Investment | | | | | | | | | |
| Very Important | 76% | 75% | 65% | 63% | 80% | 50% | 62% | 42% | 64% |
| Fairly Important | 18 | 17 | 27 | 24 | 14 | 29 | 25 | 34 | 24 |
| A Little Important | 4 | 5 | 3 | 4 | 3 | 8 | 4 | 10 | 5 |
| Not at all Important | 1 | 1 | 3 | 5 | 3 | 12 | 8 | 14 | 6 |
| Don't know | 1 | 2 | 1 | 4 | - | 1 | 1 | - | 1 |
| Totals | 100% | 100% | 100% | 100% | 100% | 100% | 100% | 100% | 100% |
| Desirability of Foreign Investment | | | | | | | | | |
| More Beneficial | 81% | 72% | 55% | 63% | 78% | 42% | 53% | 33% | 60% |
| More Harmful | 14 | 24 | 35 | 28 | 19 | 53 | 43 | 61 | 35 |
| Has no Effect (Voluntary) | 4 | 1 | 2 | 4 | 1 | 5 | 1 | 6 | 3 |
| Don't know | 1 | 3 | 8 | 5 | 2 | - | 3 | - | 3 |
| Totals | 100% | 100% | 100% | 100% | 100% | 100% | 100% | 100% | 100% |

SOURCE: (USIA, 1977: 27)

TABLE 42
PREFERRED GOVERNMENT POLICY TOWARD FOREIGN INVESTMENT

| Total No. of Cases (800) | Bus. Execs. (100) | Media Ldrs (100) | Clergy (100) | Gov't Off'ls (100) | Mil. Off'rs (100) | Labor Ldrs (100) | Univ. Profs. (100) | Univ. Stud (100) | Total (800) |
|---|---|---|---|---|---|---|---|---|---|
| General Policy Towards Foreign Investment: | | | | | | | | | |
| Encourage | 77% | 62% | 61% | 64% | 72% | 38% | 53% | 33% | 58% |
| Encourage, with controls (Voluntary) | 1 | 1 | 3 | 2 | 3 | 1 | 6 | 2 | 2 |
| Discourage | 21 | 34 | 26 | 30 | 22 | 56 | 38 | 58 | 36 |
| Don't know | – | 3 | 10 | 4 | 3 | 5 | 2 | 7 | 4 |
| Totals | 99% | 100% | 100% | 100% | 100% | 100% | 99% | 100% | 100% |
| Policy Toward New Firms: | | | | | | | | | |
| Strongly Encourage | 24% | 18% | 15% | 31% | 31% | 9% | 18% | 6% | 19% |
| Moderately Encourage | 51 | 51 | 54 | 40 | 49 | 38 | 42 | 40 | 46 |
| Impartial | 6 | 12 | 10 | 9 | 11 | 11 | 6 | 12 | 10 |
| Moderately Discourage | 13 | 9 | 10 | 7 | 4 | 18 | 21 | 19 | 13 |
| Strongly Discourage | 6 | 9 | 4 | 13 | 4 | 24 | 12 | 23 | 12 |
| Don't Know | – | 1 | 7 | – | 1 | – | 1 | – | 1 |
| Totals | 100% | 100% | 100% | 100% | 100% | 100% | 100% | 100% | 100% |

SOURCE: (USIA, 1977: 30–1)

TABLE 42 (continued)
PREFERRED GOVERNMENT POLICY TOWARD FOREIGN INVESTMENT

| Policy Toward Takeovers: | | | | | | | | | |
|---|---|---|---|---|---|---|---|---|---|
| Strongly Encourage | 2% | 2% | 6% | 5% | 4% | 3% | 2% | 4% | 4% |
| Moderately Encourage | 7 | 3 | 6 | 4 | 6 | 3 | 7 | 5 | 5 |
| Impartial | 11 | 11 | 6 | 3 | 12 | 9 | 11 | 3 | 8 |
| Moderately Discourage | 18 | 15 | 15 | 14 | 25 | 14 | 19 | 26 | 18 |
| Strongly Discourage | 62 | 68 | 61 | 74 | 53 | 70 | 59 | 61 | 64 |
| Don't Know | – | 1 | 6 | – | – | 1 | 2 | 1 | 1 |
| Totals | 100% | 100% | 100% | 100% | 100% | 100% | 100% | 100% | 100% |

SOURCE: (USIA, 1977: 30–1)

With the exception of the issue of foreign acquisitions of Colombian companies, there were substantial differences of opinion among the different elite groups. Generally, the military officers and business executives were most supportive of policies that encouraged DFI and of interpreting a positive role for foreign investment in the country. University students, labor leaders, and university professors were more likely to view the role of foreign investment as harmful and to support government policies discouraging foreign investment. The combined attitudes of the elite groups showed a high acceptance of foreign investment (see Table 42).

These attitudes towards foreign investment can be interpreted in many different ways. One could interpret the attitudes as a vox populi prescribing an end to policies of domestication. Here one could argue that, since most of the general public and of the elite groups in Colombia view foreign investment favorably, then they benefit in a nonmaterial way from the presence of DFI. Therefore, the government should not try to eliminate DFI. One could also interpret these attitudes as a symptom of cultural conquest, arguing that Colombians have already internalized values and attitudes that have been imposed upon them through the penetration of foreign investment. (See the third section of this chapter for a further elaboration on this idea). If this were true then a policy of domestication might be able to start a renationalization of attitudes and culture.

Both of these interpretations oversimplify elite and public opinion. These opinions are complex and mutable phenomena which affect, and are affected by, many other factors. For example, there is evidence that the attitudes of elite groups towards DFI changed between 1971 ans 1975, a time during which domestication policies were being debated in Colombia. Comparing the results of its 1971 and 1975 polls, the USIA found that the percentage of respondents who wanted to encourage foreign investment declined from 76 percent in 1971 to 68 percent in 1975. In addition, those who considered "foreign domination" a disadvantage attributable to foreign investment increased from 14 percent in 1971 to 34 percent in 1975. Those who considered the spurring of economic development to be aided by foreign investment declined from 55 percent to 40 percent during the period, and those who considered increased employment an advantage attributable to foreign investment declined from 59 percent to 39 percent between 1971 and 1975 (USIA, 1977: 9). The polls used different samples in different proportions, so they are not completely comparable. In its listing of the 1975 poll results, the USIA did not consider university students. It did this in order to get greater comparability with the 1971 poll, in which university students and professors were a part of the same sample group. Since the students (the strongest anti-DFI group) were omitted from the 1975 sample, even more support is given to the suggested gradual decline of support for DFI in Colombia.

From the evidence available, one can make no certain

projections of the likely effects of domestication upon elite or public opinion. There is evidence that attitudes towards foreign investment in Colombia change, and there is some indication that the increased visibility of foreign investment is associated with more negative evaluations of foreign investment. However, attitudes (of the general public and of elite groups) of Colombians towards foreign investment are too complex and too mutable to make any confident predictions about the effects of domestication.

## B. Managerial Attitudes and Domestication

Another area in which domestication could affect attitudes is by changing the attitudes of managers of domesticated companies. In this section I will argue that domestication will alter the nationality of managers by increasing the percentage of Colombian managers as they take over jobs previously held by foreign managers. I will further argue that there is a tendancy for managers' attitudes to vary, depending on nationality. Thus, the likely effects of domestication on managers' attitudes can be studied (in part) by comparing the attitudes of Colombian managers with those of managers in the major countries with DFI in Colombia (i.e., the U.S., Canada, Switzerland, France, West Germany, Venzuela, and the United Kingdom). To the extent that these attitudes are similar, domestication can be said to have no effect on managers' attitudes. To the extent that they differ, domestication can be stated to change attitudes away from those held by investing-country managers and towards those held by Colombian managers.

First, it seems certain that domestication will transfer effective decision-making in firms from foreigners to national citizens. Of the existing plants in Colombia, foreign plants use a much higher proportion of foreign managers/total managers (13.4 percent) than do domestic plants (7.7 percent). (Adapted from Table 25) Even when foreign plants employ national managers, major decisions of the plant are made not by the local manager but by executives in the investing-country. For example, a survey of U.S. multinational corporations found that many of them (72 percent) give their foreign subsidiaries low autonomy with regard to decisions on new investments (Pohlman, 1976: 16). It appears likely, therefore, that domestication will result in effective decision-making power of Colombian managers increasing and that of managers from investing-countries decreasing.

There is a substantial amount of evidence to indicate that the nationality of managers and employees has a great deal of effect upon their attitudes. One of the first major cross-cultural studies of managers was conducted by Haire, Ghiselli and Porter (1966), who interviewed 3,741 managers in fourteen different countries. They demonstrated that nationality was an important factor influencing the attitudes of these managers, concluding that "...of all the differences among managers, 25 to 30 percent of the variation is associated with national origin. There are differences between countries, and the differences are real and substantial" (p. 10). They also found that, although there were major differences based on nationality, some nationalities had more similar attitudes than others, and could be grouped into what they called "cultural clusters" (p.180).

Sirota and Greenwood (1971) studied the attitudes of 13,000 IBM employees in twenty-five different countries with regard to their work goals. They found substantial differences based on nationality, and they also found the existence of cultural aggregates of countries (p. 59). Ronen and Kraut (1977) used computer mapping to draw up a composit of cross-national clusters using the data from Haire, Ghiselli amd Porter, from Sirota and Greenwood, and from another study of technical employees in fifteen European countries. The resulting map showed five major cultural aggregates as well as a few independent countries which did not fit into any aggregate. Table 43 shows these aggregates.

TABLE 43
CULTURAL AGGREGATES

| ANGLO-AMERICAN | LATIN-EUROPEAN | CENTRAL-EUROPEAN |
|---|---|---|
| United States | Portugal | Switzerland |
| United Kingdom | Spain | Germany |
| Canada | Belgium | Austria |
| Ireland | Italy | |
| South Africa | France | |
| New Zealand | | |
| Australia | | |
| LATIN AMERICAN | NORDIC | INDEPENDENT |
| Colombia | Norway | Brazil |
| Peru | Finland | Japan |
| Mexico | Denmark | India |
| Chile | Sweden | Israel |
| Argentina | | |
| Venezuela | | |

SOURCE: (Ronen & Kraut, 1977: 94)

This chart gives some evidence that the attitudes of Colombian managers tend to cluster together with those from other Latin American countries (except for Brazil). As the chart also shows, most of the countries with direct foreign investment in Colombia fit into different cultural aggregates than does Colombia. In the following pages I will be comparing attitudes of a sample of "Latin American" managers with the attitudes of managers from other countries (most notably, the U.S.). I will

TABLE 44
SALARY INCREASES RECOMMENDED BY NATIONALITY OF MANAGERS
(as percentage of that recommended for an average worker)

| | Colombia | Latin America | United States | France | Nether-lands | Germany/ Austria | Britain | Scandan-avia |
|---|---|---|---|---|---|---|---|---|
| N Managers | 24 | 193 | 387 | 119 | 444 | 289 | 1,728 | 207 |
| Average Worker | 100% | 100% | 100% | 100% | 100% | 100% | 100% | 100% |
| High Merit Worker | 163% | 161 | 161 | 179 | 154 | 165 | 164 | 152 |
| Low Merit Worker | 93% | 93 | 74 | 82 | 80 | 84 | 82 | 82 |
| Job Conditions: | | | | | | | | |
| No Security | 94% | 105 | 109 | 120 | 113 | 123 | 121 | 112 |
| No Opportunity | 106% | 103 | 103 | 108 | 104 | 107 | 106 | 103 |
| Bad Working Conditions | 143% | 128 | 121 | 130 | 122 | 130 | 128 | 123 |
| Low Prestige | 113% | 111 | 112 | 128 | 116 | 123 | 120 | 113 |
| Unfriendly Co-workers | 120% | 122 | 116 | 128 | 123 | 126 | 126 | 123 |
| Boring Job | 127% | 124 | 116 | 137 | 122 | 132 | 129 | 123 |
| Competitive Offer | 108% | 109 | 112 | 126 | 118 | 115 | 120 | 108 |

SOURCES: (Bass & Burger, 1979: 106; Bass & Ryterband, 1979: 367)
NOTE: Latin American sample includes managers from Colombia, Venezuela, Mexico and Brazil.

be using the attitudes of Latin American managers as an indicator for the attitudes of Colombian managers. This constitutes an ecological fallacy to the extent that I am ascertaining attitudes of managers from throughout Latin America and inferring them to be accurate descriptions of a single Latin American country: Colombia. However, there are two reasons why the Latin American sample is an accurate projection of Colombian managers' attitudes. First, Colombian managers comprised a part of the Latin American sample. Second, there are many similarities between the attitudes of Colombian managers and those of Latin American managers in general. Table 44 presents a comparison of a sample of Colombian managers with a larger sample of Latin American managers and with managers from several other countries. The issues themselves are not as important as the facts that Colombian managers' attitudes are similar to those of Latin American managers, and that in almost every case Colombian managers' attitudes were closer to those of the Latin American managers than to the attitudes of U.S. managers.

TABLE 45
PERCENTAGE OF MANAGERS RANKING THE LIFE GOAL OF SERVICE AMONG TOP THREE IN IMPORTANCE

| | Top Three | N | Mean Ranking* | N |
|---|---|---|---|---|
| Latin America | 26% | 119 | 5.81 | 142 |
| United States | 18% | 227 | 6.32 | 272 |
| France | 30% | 103 | 5.89 | 154 |
| Netherlands | 18% | 119 | 5.80 | 441 |
| Germany/Austria | 13% | 142 | 6.95 | 284 |
| Britain | 21% | 426 | 5.88 | 618 |
| Scandanavia | 31% | 160 | 5.44 | 253 |

SOURCE: (Bass & Burger, 1979: 62 & 64)
NOTE: Service is defined as "to contribute to the satisfaction of others; to be helpful to others who need it." (Bass & Burger, 1979: 56.)
*Mean ranking out of eleven variables, with 1.00 being most important life goal of the manager and 11.00 being the least important.

As Table 45 shows, there are some differences between the attitudes of Latin American managers and those of managers from countries with DFI in Colombia. The table shows a comparison of the life-goals of managers. In this exercise, managers from several countries were asks to rank eleven life-goals. Of the eleven goals, only one--service--seemed to be an indicator of social responsibility, of the belief that the manager had an obligation to aid society and not just to serve the corporation or to benefit him or herself. This life-goal was defined as contributing "to the satisfaction of others; to be helpful to others who need it" (Bass & Burger, 1979: 56). In ranking the eleven life-goals, 26 percent of the Latin American managers listed "service" among the top three goals, compared to only 18 percent of U.S. and Dutch managers, 13 percent of German and Austrian managers, and 21 percent of British managers. Scandanavian and French managers were slightly more likely to rank this goal among the top three.

Separate studies of individual Latin American countries show that Colombian executives tend to give more importance to this life-goal than managers from other Latin American countries. Executives from Colombia, Argentina, and Chile were asked to rank the satisfactions that they seek in their role as manager. "Service," defined as "the opportunity to help people," was ranked along with six other goals (see Table 46). Over 40% of the Colombians ranked service as the primary satisfaction of the entrepreneur, compared to only 23 percent for the Argentine sample and 33 percent of the Chilean sample. This reinforces the idea that Colombian managers view service as a higher goal than their colleagues in the U.S. and Western Europe or even in the rest of Latin America.

TABLE 46
SATISFACTIONS SOUGHT BY THE ENTREPRENEUR

| | Colombia | | | Argentina | Chile |
|---|---|---|---|---|---|
| | 1st | 2nd | 3rd | 1st Only | 1st Only |
| Opportunity to Help People | 41% | 23% | 15% | 23% | 33% |
| Personal Independence | 23% | 16% | 20% | 23% | 11% |
| Economic Security | 23% | 41% | 15% | 46% | 33% |
| Opportunity to Command | 3% | 2% | 2% | 0% | 6% |
| Social Prestige | 0% | 5% | 20% | 0% | 15% |
| Risk | 0% | 8% | 3% | 6% | 2% |
| Other | 10% | 5% | 16% | 0% | 0% |
| No Answer | 0% | 0% | 13% | 4% | 0% |
| | 100% | 100% | 100% | 100% | 100% |

SOURCES: (Cardoso, 1970: 110; Lipman, 1969: 91)

This raises the possibility that, following the implementation of a policy of domestication in Colombia, decision-making authority in the economy would move to Colombian managers, who tend to see their managerial role as including some responsibility to society at large. This raises the question of the extent to which these different attitudes of managers are actually translated into practice in the management of the firm. To what degree would these different attitudes affect the actual operations of the firms that these managers control?

A partial answer to this question can be found in Table 47. The table shows the attitudes of managers from various countries when faced with five hypothetical cases. In each case the managers were asked to choose between two alternatives: to spend money on projects such as eliminating safety hazards or improving low-quality products, or to refuse to spend the money. In each case the refusal to spend the money was seen as the more pragmatic decision and the only one in keeping with the maximization of company profits. The decision to spend the money can be seen as an indication that the manager considers the well-being of the workers and of the general public to be important considerations. In each case, the nationality of managers was related to significantly different responses (at the .01 level for all five questions). Bass and Burger (1979) note that "with senior U.S. managers trained in cost-benefit analysis and oriented towards profit maximization as the objective of the firm, discussions...led to disapproval of all of the expenditures"(pp.98-102). This is a study of managers working in their own countries (i.e., U.S. managers working in the U.S., Latin American managers working in Latin America) and not U.S. managers working in Latin America. It is assumed that managers of U.S. subsidiaries in Colombia have attitudes similar to U.S. managers working in the U.S.

Of the five issues studied, two (safety and strike settlement) showed no marked differences between the attitudes of Latin American managers and non-Latin American managers. On one issue (product quality) Latin American managers were less willing to spend than U.S. managers but more willing to spent than the average of the non-Latin American managers. On two issues (morale and controlling pollution) Latin American managers were substantially more willing to spend than either U.S. managers or all of the non-Latin American managers.

On the basis of these results, one can draw inferences about the likely effects of domestication. On the issues of safety, strike settlement, and product quality, the effects of domestication upon managerial attitudes would depend entirely upon the nationality of the firms being domesticated and in most cases would be negligible. On the issues of morale and pollution control, however, it seems likely that domestication in Colombia would bring into decision-making positions managers who have a greater concern for the well-being of their employees and of the population in general. To the extent that this is true, it can be inferred that the domestication of foreign manufacturing plants in Colombia would benefit the well-being of the plant's employees and of the general public.

There is some evidence to indicate that the attitudes of managers are influenced not only by the manager's nationality but also by whether the manager works for a domestically-owned company or the foreign subsidiary of a multinational corporation. Petras and Cook (1973) found conflicting evidence on this. In their study of the attitudes of Argentine executives who worked

TABLE 47
WILLINGNESS TO SPEND MONEY FOR FIVE NEEDS
(BY NATIONALITY OF MANAGER)

| | N Managers | Safety(a) | Settle Strike(b) | Morale(c) | Product Quality(d) | Control Pollution(e) |
|---|---|---|---|---|---|---|
| Latin America | 256 | 66% | 66% | 83% | 79% | 71% |
| United States | 344 | 67% | 64% | 70% | 84% | 65% |
| France | 370 | 65% | 63% | 78% | 60% | 38% |
| Netherlands | 592 | 76% | 57% | 70% | 86% | 45% |
| Germany/Austria | 292 | 67% | 74% | 72% | 77% | 48% |
| Britain | 1,348 | 60% | 68% | 62% | 75% | 35% |
| Scandanavia | 336 | 73% | 62% | 75% | 76% | 44% |
| Mean of Non Latin-Americans | | 68% | 65% | 71% | 76% | 46% |

SOURCE: (Bass & Burger, 1979: 102)
NOTES: The numbers represent the percentsge of managers who were willing to make the expenditures. All responses listed are significant at the .01 level. The Latin American sample includes Colombia, Mexico, Venezuela, and Brazil.

(a)Percentage willing to spend $225,000 to eliminate a safety hazard or accept a 50-50 probability of a serious injury or death per year (p. 97).

(b)Percentage willing to spend $750,000 to settle wage negotiations to avoid risking a long, costly strike.

(c)Percentage willing to spend $200,000 on personnel selection, development, and counseling.

(d)Percentage willing to spend $375,000 on improving a low-quality product rather than $75,000 on special advertising to improve its sales.

(e)Percentage willing to spend $150,000 to modify a plant polluting a stream or accept likely legal costs of $25,000 annually to let matters ride.

for national and foreign businesses in Argentina, they found only slight differences in opinions regarding foreign economic penetration (pp. 163-5). When they studied the type of political institutions preferred by the two groups of executives, they found substantial differences, with executives of national companies preferring institutions of parliamentary democracy and those in foreign companies preferring the Brazilian model of authoritarian-corporatist government (p. 190). Supplementing this is Russett and Hanson's (1975) survey of the attitudes of 567 high-level vice presidents of large U.S. industrial and financial companies. Respondents were asked to rank the kinds of policies followed by LDC governments that would best coincide with U.S. interests. The highest priority was given to "a stable government capable of preserving internal order." (p.83)

Smetanka's study of the attitudes of Canadian executives in national companies and foreign subsidiaries also found important differences between the two, leading him to conclude that:

> ...host-country executives of foreign-owned subsidiaries can be expected to be more oriented to the international system than to their own nation-state as a result of their transnational business contacts and international work responsibilities. They can be expected to identify more with businessmen from other countries who are involved in the concerns and interests of international business than with their fellow nationals in domestic industries and to perceive that their own personal, economic security is dependent more on the course of international, relative to national, events and developments. Thus, they have a personal stake in economic and political arrangements which render such events comprehensible and predictable. Multinational managers, therefore, can be expected to support an 'open' international economic system and/or more formal political arrangements related to the harmonization of policies between countries. They can also be expected to develop a sense of international community more so than domestic managers whose business roles limit opportunities for the discovery of similar concerns and interests between their own and other societies (Smetanka, 1977: 9).

These differences in the attitudes of managers of the same nationality but employed by foreign-subsidiaries (as opposed to domestic companies) could have contradictory results upon domestication in Colombia (assuming that nationality of ownership of firms has effects in Colombia that are similar to those found to exist in Argentina or Canada). To the extent that newly domesticated firms in Colombia would employ as managers the same Colombians who had previously worked for the firm (when it was foreign-owned), domestication would probably not alter the attitudes of these managers, who would still be more internationally oriented that their counterparts in domestic firms. To the extern that the Colombian managers of domesticated firms would maintain their international identification, domestication would have no appreciable effect in the short run.

In the long run, the altered ownership structure of domesticated firms might alter the attitudes of existing Colombian managers as well as altering the attitudes of new Colombian managers. Smetanka (1977) has argued that:

> Perhaps...the long-term challenge MNCs present to the nation-state is not so much the frustration of sovereignty as the gradual 'de-nationalization' of important segments of the business community from identification with and involvement in the national development process (p.31).

One possible result of a policy of domestication is that it might begin a renationalization of the identification of these managers. The identification of managers with the nation is not necessarily a benefit to national well-being, but it does raise the possibility that the decisions that they make will be made with a greater awareness of their impact upon the national development process, rather than the previous awareness of the international corporate framework.

The study of attitudes is vital to understanding the potential effects of domestication, since attitudes make up an important non-material effect of domestication. This research on attitudes is made difficult because people's perceptions and orientations are complex and mutable. There can be no certainty about the existence, much less the direction, of change in people's attitudes as a result of domestication. From the evidence available, certain changes in attitudes seem more likely than others. With regard to the very important issue of the attitudes of the general and elite publics in Colombia, a policy of domestication seems likely to increase people's desire to restrict foreign investment. Domestication also seems likely to increase the degree to which the general and elite publics assess negatively the impact of foreign investment. Domestication policies are also likely to alter the attitudes of the managers of companies in Colombia. It seems likely that domestication will increase the effective control of Colombian managers, who tend to perceive their role as including some obligation to society in general. This perception may often result in policy decisions (e.g., on pollution control) that give less importance to the firm's impact upon its workers and on the general public. It also seems likely that domestication will increase the identification that managers feel with the nation and reduce their identification with managers in other countries. To the degree that this happens, the decisions of these managers are likely to increase national autonomy.

Domestication and National Autonomy

> ...in order to develop, a society must remain true to itself, draw its strength from its own culture and ways of thought and action, and set itself objectives consonant with its values and felt needs... (Salinas & Paldan, 1979: 82).

This statement by the Director-General of UNESCO will serve as another area in which domestication can have an impact on a developing country: the possibility that domestication can alter the external domination of the culture, economy, or polity of the country. To the degree that domestication increases national autonomy and makes the country more "true to itself," the country can be said to benefit. To the extent that it reduces national autonomy, domestication can be said to harm tha country.

Foreign investment has been accused of creating and fostering a kind of social and cultural domination in developing countries in which the values that come to dominate in the developing countries are transmitted from abroad through such means as product choice and advertising (Sauvant, 1979). This is a type of cultural invasion similar to that described by Paulo Freire (n.d.):

> Cultural conquest leads to the cultural inauthenticity of those who are invaded; they begin to respond to the values, the standards, and the goals of the invaders....In cultural invasion it is essential that those who are invaded come to see their reality with the outlook of the invaders rather that their own....
>
> For cultural invasion to succeed, it is essential that those invaded become convinced of their intrinsic inferiority.... if those who are invaded consider themselves inferior, they must necessarily recognize the superiority of the invaders. The values of the latter become the pattern of the former. The more invasion is accentuated and those invaded are alienated from the spirit of their own culture and from themselves, the more the latter want to be like the invaders: to walk like them, dress like them, talk like them (pp. 150-1).

In studying domestication in Colombia and its effects upon national autonomy, three questions arise. First, does external cultural domestication (i.e., a lack of national autonomy) currently exist in Colombia? Second, is direct foreign investment responsible for creating or reinforcing this domination? Third, what likely effects will domestication have upon national autonomy in the long run and the short run?

There is evidence that many of the dominant values within Colombia originate from outside. Several noted scholars and students of the Colombian society have commented upon this external cultural domination. Alfonzo Lopez Michelson, President of Colombia from 1974-1978, criticized the country's upper class in the 1960s for being "oriented toward foreign standards" (Dix, 1971: 259). Robert Dix, a well-known and respected student of Colombian politics, reiterated this interpretation when he wrote of the tendancy of the ruling oligarchy in Colombia to

> scorn the autochthonous and to look abroad for everything from its fashions in clothing and its literary tastes and themes, to its political ideologies. There is a certain propensity...for members of the Colombian upper class to regard themselves as part of a cosmopolitan elite of 'civilization' and culture over against the 'barbarism' and lack of culture of the lower-class...members of their own society. Such 'foreignizing' attitudes cut the elite off from the real roots of Colombian nationality and to that degree incapacitate it to lead the people of its own country in creating a truly national community (p.55).

Writing about the effects of cultural domination in the Philippines, Constantino (1978) noted the "spiritual emptiness of the people" and went on to describe the effects of the domination in the following terms:

> We have been indulging in an orgy of blind imitation of foreign education, art, culture, and even manners and morals... (p.32).
>
> Another manifestation of our inferiority complex is our disparagement of ourselves, our ideas and achievements, and our products. We are so certain of our inferiority vis-a-vis the Western world that we automatically prefer anything labelled 'not made in the Philippines' (p.141).

In his study of Colombian society, Dix (1971) noted the same characteristics, stating:

> It is also true that there tends to be a certain deprecation of the national self among Colombians at all social levels. Derived in part from the 'foreignizing' ways of the elite itself, in part, perhaps, from the absence of a visable national goal or external enemy, it expresses itself in many ways: a talking-down of one's own country; a hardly disguised scorn for one's own fellow nationals; the hope that one might somehow escape one's own country; the imitation of foreign ways and foreign ideas (p.404).

This observation was also made by Lipman (1969) in his study of Colombian society. He noted that:

> a tendancy exists on the part of the Colombians to award higher prestige to foreigners, as a result of a type of national inferiority feeling--a feeling of ambivalence toward themselves as a nation and their achievements as compared to other nations. Thus, existing alongside a nationalistic feeling of pride is a self-image as an underdeveloped or backward nation; articles manufactured in other countries are often considered superior to Colombian-made products, and carry-over of this ambivalent feeling seems to include people, as well (p.43).

This interpretation is supported by a survey done by Lipman and Havens of the attitudes of Colombians towards their own country. Using a random sample of one hundred urban lower-class Colombians, they asked the respondants to agree or disagree with the following question: "All countries have their rights and wrongs, but Colombia is almost always wrong." Only 11 percent of the sample disagreed with the statement (p. 128).

This feeling of national inferiority also carries over into preference for foreign products rather than national ones in Colombia. Schmidt (1971) noted that "for many years a high level of prestige was associated with the ownership of a pair of genuine American blue jeans." Part of this could be explained by the higher quality of American-made products, but Schmidt also gives evidence of Colombians buying a Colombian brand of jeans and then purchasing labels for "Levi's" or "Wrangler" in order "to transform a Colombian garment into a high-prestige American product." Schmidt's un-random sample of consumer attitudes in Colombia supports the impressionistic interpretations of preferences for foreign products. Of his sample, 62 percent ranked Colombian goods as "undesirable," only 18 percent rated them as "desirable," and 20 percent were inconclusive (pp. 3-5). It is still not clear, however, whether these results are the result of cultural domination by foreign investors.

In response to the question on the existence of external domination, there is evidence to support the view that such domination currently exists in Colombia. The second question asked whether direct foreign investment was responsible for creating or reinforcing this external cultural domination. Except for assertions to the effect that DFI did or did not cause this cultural domination, there is scanty evidence on the subject. Schmidt's rather haphazard sample provides some impressionistic evidence of this, since he did divide his respondents according to age group. Chapter 3 documented the rapid rise of manufacturing foreign investment in Colombia from the mid-1940s through the early 1970s. This rapid rise of manufacturing DFI undoubtedly brought with it the advertising of foreign products that now characterizes Colombian marketing. If this manufacturing DFI and its advertising were responsible for the perceived superiority of foreign products and inferiority of Colombian ones, then one might expect people born and socialized in the post-World War II period to feel greater national inferiority than those who were born and socialized earlier. The sketchy evidence available from Schmidt's sample does not support this conclusion (see Table 48). As the table indicates, people born and socialized in the period of greater involvement of manufacturing DFI held attitudes that were virtually identical with those of citizens born and socialized during a time of minimal involvement of direct foreign investment in manufacturing. It seems that the problem of cultural domination in Colombia is too complex to be explained solely in terms of direct foreign investment.

The third question that arises is what effect domestication will have on national autonomy and cultural domination. Regardless of what caused the feelings of inferiority that Colombians have towards themselves and the goods they produce, what effects will domestication have on those attitudes as they exist today? The implementation of a policy of domestication cannot erase the past, but it can have effects upon the present and future. What kind of effect will it have? One effect domestication could have is in transferring control over the economy to firms that have a different degree of dependence upon external personnel and technology than those firms currently producing. Since domestication would involve transferring control from foreign to domestic firms, it is important to know whether foreign firms currently in the economy have a different dependence upon foreign personnel and technology than do domestic firms; and, if so, how are they different. Tables 49 through 51 present a sketchy comparison of paired foreign and domestic firms in Colombia. Most of the differences are not statistically significant due to the small size of the sample, but the evidence presentsd can be taken as generally indicative of possible effects of domestication on national autonomy.

TABLE 48
OPINIONS ABOUT COLOMBIAN PRODUCTS

| Year of Birth | Percent of Respondents Who Found Colombian Products Desirable | Undesirable | Inconclusive |
|---|---|---|---|
| 1919–1938 | 19% | 62% | 19% |
| 1939– | 17% | 63% | 21% |

SOURCE: (Schmidt, 1971: 5).
NOTE: Interviews were conducted in 1968, so it seems unlikely that anyone born after 1960 was interviewed. It should be reiterated here that this table presents very inexact figures. Schmidt did not disclose such basic aspects as the number of

respondents, so the table should be taken as only a general indication of opinion.

As the tables show, domestic firms are less likely to depend on foreign technology and skilled personnel (engineers and administrators). Domestic firms were more likely to develop their technology locally and to use national skilled personnel. This seems to indicate that domestic firms can respond more to national values and situations, thus increasing national autonomy. The average domestic firm used far fewer U.S. patents than the average foreign firm (Table 49). They spent more on research and development than foreign firms did, built more of their own machinery, introduced more patents, and spent more engineers' man-hours/week in developing new products (Table 50). Domestic firms were more likely to use Colombian engineers and administrators, both within the firm and as outside consultants (Table 51). Also, domestic firms were more likely to conduct their research and development within the country, either inside the firm or in local research institutions (Table 49). Foreign firms showed a greater dependence upon foreign sources of technology, while domestic firms seem unable to develop more of their technology locally, adapting to local situations. Reuber notes in his survey of foreign firms that they are more likely to bring their technology into developing countries with very little adaptation to meet local circumstances:

> In 57 out of 78 cases in our survey the investing (foreign) firm introduced its production technology intact and in an additional 10 cases it was introduced in an adapted form. In the area of quality control, the investing firm introduced its standard system without adaptation in 48 out of 59 cases and with adaptation in 9 instances (Reuber, 1974: 132).

Mytalka's (1978) study of technological self-sufficiency of chemicals and metal-working firms in Colombia, Ecuador and Peru found that domestic firms were more likely to feel that they could introduce new products, and less likely to license their technology from other firms, than were foreign firms. The firms were asked if they planned to introduce new products if they could develop new product technology: 44 percent of the domestic firms responded affirmatively, compared to only 6 percent of the foreign and state-owned companies. In addition, only 39 percent of domestic companies licensed their technology, compared to 82 percent of majority-foreign and 75 percent of mixed-foreign companies (pp.117-8). Mytelka concluded that, in sectors with less complex technology,

> we find that it is precisely the national firms which overwhelmingly generate their own technology while the foreign and mixed private firms license technology whose simplicity and stability would imply far greater

possibilities for self-reliant technological development (pp.117-8).

The importing of technology by foreign firms raises a danger to national autonomy. To a large degree, the imported technology is designed to produce goods that respond to circumstances outside of the country, generally in more affluent markets. Domestic firms are perhaps more likely to respond to national needs and circumstances because they develop more of their technology domestically. How does all this relate to domestication? To the extent that domestication will transfer effective control over the economy to domestic firms from foreign ones, it seems likely that there would be a reduction in the use of foreign technology and foreign skilled personnel. It also appears likely that there would be an increase in the domestic development of technology and the use of domestic administrators and engineers. These are all short-run consequences of domestication, and they have no necessary effect upon national autonomy.

TABLE 49
TECHNOLOGICAL DEPENDENCE OF FOREIGN AND DOMESTIC PLANTS IN COLOMBIA
(Study of Paired Firms)

| | Average Domestic Firms | Average Foreign Firms |
|---|---|---|
| U.S. Patents Being Used 1974: | 0.71 | 6.43 |
| Foreign, Non-U.S. Patents Being Used 1974: | 0.24 | 0.12 |
| U.S. Licenses Being Used 1974: | 0.48 | 0.40 |
| Foreign, Non-U.S. Licenses Being Used, 1974: | 0.04 | 0.12 |
| U.S. Technical Assistance Contracts Being Used, 1974: | 0.12 | 0.20 |
| Foreign, Non-U.S. Technical Assistance Contracts Being Used, 1974: | 0.20 | 0.04 |
| Percentages of R&D Expenditures In Local Private Institutions: | 1.76% | 0% |
| Percentages of R&D Expenditures in Local Government Institutions: | 1.57% | 0.48% |
| Percentage of R&D Expenditures Inside the Firm: | 81.76% | 73.57% |

SOURCE: (DeCarvalho, 1977: 204, 208).

TABLE 50
LOCAL INNOVATION BY DOMESTIC AND FOREIGN FIRMS IN COLOMBIA
(Study of Paired Firms)

| | Average Domestic Firm | Average Foreign Firm |
|---|---|---|
| R & D Expenditures/Sales: | | |
| 1974 | 0.4% | 0.2% |
| 1970–74 | 0.5% | 0.2% |
| Firms Devoting Formal Attention to the Development of New Products: | | |
| Before 1972 | 32.0% | 24.0% |
| Since 1972 | 73.1% | 73.1% |
| Firms Introducing Changes in Process: | | |
| Since 1972 | 73.1% | 69.2% |
| Percent of Sales of New Products: | 11.0% | 8.4% |
| Engineers Man-Hours/Week for Development of New Products: | 61.8 | 27.7 |
| Firms Building and Designing Their Own Machinery: | 80.8% | 76.9% |
| Percentage of the Value of Machinery Produced by Firm: | 13.6% | 11.8% |
| Percentage of Firms Developing Their Own Patents Since 1970: | 50% | 19% |
| Patents Developed and Registered | | |
| Since 1970: | 2.69 | .96 |
| 1960–1970 | 2.73 | .89 |

SOURCES: (DeCarvalho, 1977: 200–213; Ingles and Fairchild, 1977:68–69).

TABLE 51
USE OF DOMESTIC AND FOREIGN ADMINISTRATORS AND ENGINEERS
(Study of Paired Firms in Colombia)

| | Average Domestic Firm | Average Foreign Firm |
|---|---|---|
| National Engineers/Total Engineers, 1974: | 97.3% | 92.3% |
| 1970-1974 | 94.4% | 91.5% |
| National Administrators/ Total Administrators | | |
| 1974: | 97.1% | 88.2% |
| 1970-74 | 96.6% | 88.7% |
| National Administrators, 1974: | 11.7 | 8.6 |
| Foreign Administrators, 1974:* | .2 | .9 |
| Firms Using an Outside Engineer as a Consultant: | | |
| U.S. Engineer | 30.8% | 57.7% |
| Foreign, non-U.S. Engineer | 3.9% | 7.7% |
| Domestic Engineer | 23.1% | 11.5% |

SOURCE: (DeCarvalho, 1977: 208, 230).
*Significant at .05 level.

If the national administrators and engineers, and the technology that they produce, do not respond to the needs and circumstances of the country, then national autonomy may be unaffected in the long run. However, domestication carries with it the possibility of creating in the long run a national culture that is more autonomous, that responds to needs arising from within the country rather than those from without. There is no guarantee that domestication will have this effect. To a large degree, the long range effects of domestication upon national autonomy depend upon which Colombians assume effective control over the economy when foreign investment declines.

## Domestication and the Colombian Power Structure

Another possible nonmaterial effect of domestication is the role it would play in altering the distribution of power within Colombia. Well-respected scholars of Colombian society have long noted that a limited number of families are the center of economic, social and political power in the country (Dix, 1971: 42-73 and Blutstein, 1977: 107-23). Robert Dix has argued that to refer to Colombian society with

> the term oligarchy is justifiable...to the extent that the Colombian elite is substantially a self-perpetuating minority in control of the key power resources of the society, without any real accountability to the rest of the community (p.43).

Blutstein (1977) explains how this concentration extende across the major institutions in the society. He states that this concentration of power

> links influential individuals and institutions in such a way that an important university, a commercial bank, an investment bank, an association of industries, and agricultural interests may all be coordinated and controlled by a few men (p. 108).

This concentration of control extends into the economy. Weisner Duran (n.d.) provides evidence of the concentration of personal control over companies listed on the Bogota stock exchange. Silva Colmenares (1977) writes about the existence of a few very powerful economic groups in the country. Sorpa (1976: 413-6) also notes the existence of a handful of these groups which base their power on the ownership of a combination of banks, insurance companies, finance companies, and manufacturing firms. Among these groups he lists the Suramerica Group, the Bogota Group, the Grancolombia Group, the Santo Domingo Group, and the Cafetero Group. The groups are not completely distinct from one another. There is a good deal of overlapping among the different financial groups.

Domestication could effect this concentration of power in Colombia. To the extent that foreign firms now operating in Colombia create alternate centers of economic (and possibly political) power, these firms could benefit the citizenry of the country by providing a greater access to economic and social mobility. This would benefit the majority of the country's population who are not a part of the existing oligarchy. If foreign firms do constitute such alternate centers of power, then a policy of domestication is likely to place the formerly foreign firms into the hands of this oligarchy. This would increase the control that this oligarchy now has over Colombian society. To the extent that domestication would thus be phasing-out foreign control over firms and phasing-in an even stronger control by the domestic oligarchy, it would be worsening the already severe concentration of power in the country.

However, this analysis depends upon whether foreign firms do, in fact, constitute alternate centers of power. The central issue is the degree to which foreign firms in Colombia are currently independent of the domestic oligarchy. In order to investigate this issue, a study was made of the interlocking directorates of foreign firms in Colombia to see if these firms were linked to domestic firms, which were a part of the economic power groups. The checking of interlocking directorates assumes that a single individual's presence on the boards of directors of more than one firm represents more than a coincidence. Rather, it is assumed to represent a connection between the companies involved and to suggest that these companies may not be operating in an independent fashion. In order to check these interlocking directorates in Colombia, information was obtained on the memberships of the boards of directors of thirteen manufacturing companies which were listed on the Bogota stock exchange in 1977 and which had some degree of foreign ownership. These thirteen foreign firms were checked to see to what degree they had interlocking directorates with national manufacturing, financial, banking, insurance, and service industries. As a comparison, the remaining sixty-three domestic manufacturing companies listed in the 1977 Bogota stock exchange were also checked for their interlocking directorates. The interlocking directorates of the thirteen foreign manufacturing firms were compared with the sixty-three domestic manufacturing companies to determine whether foreign firms actually had fewer ties with the existing economic power centers (as was hypothesized on the last page).

According to Matter (1977), these seventy-six firms accounted for thirty-one of the largest one hundred manufacturing companies operating in Colombia in 1968. It can be argued that the thirteen foreign firms issue stock in Colombia and, therefore, are not representative of the other foreign manufacturing firms in the country. It can also be argued that interlocking directorates do not represent an effective connection between the companies involved and that many of the board members of foreign manufacturing companies are merely figureheads used to provide a national facade for foreign companies. I am assuming that these are not the case. There is no way of determining whether the thirteen firms in this sample are unrepresentative, given the data that I have available. Interlocking directorates are one of the few means available for measuring connections between firms.

The results appear in Table 52 and Table 53. Table 52 shows the interlocking directorates of the thirteen foreign manufacturing firms. These firms had 142 interlocking directorates, 24 of which were with other foreign manufacturing firms, and 118 of which were with domestic companies. There was variation among the thirteen firms in terms of their linkages with other companies. Carton de Colombia (a paper company) had only 2 interlocking directorates, and one of those was with another foreign company. Celanese Colombiana, on the other hand, had 26 interlocking directorates with three foreign manufacturing companies and nine different domestic companies.

Table 53 presents a comparison of the interlocking directorates of foreign firms with those of sixty-three domestic manufacturing companies in Colombia. As the table shows, foreign

TABLE 52
INTERLOCKING DIRECTORATES OF THIRTEEN FOREIGN FIRMS IN COLOMBIA

| Interlocks with National Companies | Interlocks with Other Foreign Manufacturing Companies |
|---|---|
| **1. Abonos Colombianos** | |
| Caucho Eterna (1) | Celanese Colombiana (3) |
| Banco de Bogota (3) | Hilanderias del Fonce (2) |
| Mineros Colombianos (1) | |
| Colcurtidos (1) | |
| Proficol (1) | |
| Paz del Rio (1) | |
| Colseguros (1) | |
| Ahorros Bolivar (1) | |
| Alicachin (1) | |
| **2. Carton de Colombia** | |
| Ospinas y Cia. (1) | Cementos Boyaca (1) |
| **3. Celanese Colombiana** | |
| Avianca (2) | Eternit Atlantico (1) |
| Colcurtidos (2) | Abonos Colombianos (3) |
| Cemento Samper (6) | Hilanderias del Fonce (1) |
| Banco de Bogota (3) | |
| Bavaria (1) | |
| Ahorros de Bolivar (4) | |
| Central de Mezclas (1) | |
| Manufacturas de Cemento (1) | |
| Talleras Centrales (1) | |
| **4. Cementos Boyaca** | |
| Colseguros (2) | Industrias Apolo (1) |
| Banco de Bogota (2) | Eternit Atlantico (1) |
| Ospinas y Cia. (2) | Eternit Colombiana (2) |
| Manufacturas de Cemento (1) | Carton de Colombia (1) |

| Interlocks with National Companies | Interlocks with Other Foreign Manufacturing Companies |
|---|---|
| **5. Chrysler "Colmoteres"** | |
| Ospinas y Cia. (2) | |
| Caracol (2) | |
| Banco de Comercio (1) | |
| **6. Colombit** | |
| Ladrillera Santa Fe (1) | |
| Tejidos Unica (1) | |
| Celema (1) | |
| Cementos Caldas (2) | |
| Corporacion Financiera de Caldas (3) | |
| Derivados del Azufre (2) | |
| Banco del Comercio (1) | |
| **7. Eternit Atlantico** | |
| Banco Sandander (1) | Cementos Boyaca (1) |
| Colcurtidos (1) | Celanese Colombians (1) |
| Manufacturas de Cemento (2) | |
| Siderurgica del Muna (1) | |
| Cemento Samper (1) | |
| Union Industrial (1) | |
| Colseguros (1) | |
| Colgas (1) | |
| Propiedad Raiz (1) | |
| Banco de Bogota (1) | |
| Ahorros Bolivar (1) | |
| Corporacion Financiera del Norte (1) | |
| **8. Eternit Colombiana** | |
| Industria Harinera (1) | Cementos Boyaca (2) |
| Paz del Rio (2) | Industrias Apolo (1) |
| Banco Tequendama (1) | |
| Talleras Centrales (1) | |
| Manuelita (1) | |
| Corporacion Financiera de Caldas (1) | |
| Banco de Bogota (3) | |
| Colseguros (2) | |
| Cementos del Valle (1) | |
| Ospinas y Cia. (1) | |

| Interlocks with National Companies | Interlocks with Other Foreign Manufacturing Companies |
|---|---|
| **9. Eternit Pacifico** | |
| Manuelita (1) | |
| Cementos del Valle (2) | |
| Garantia A. Dishington (1) | |
| **10. Hilanderias del Fonce** | |
| Bavaria (1) | Abonos Colombianos (2) |
| Banco de Santander (1) | Celanese Colombiana (1) |
| Bavaria (1) | |
| Urbanizodora David Puyana (1) | |
| Corporacion Naconal de Cigarillos (2) | |
| **11. Industrias Apolo** | |
| Cemento Argos (1) | Banco del Comercio (1) |
| Banco Central Antioqueno (1) | Tejicondor (1) |
| Colseguros (1) | Eternit Colombiana (1) |
| Noel (1) | Cementos Boyaca (1) |
| Panos Vicuna Santa Fe (1) | |
| Banco Industrial Colombiano (1) | |
| Corporacion Financiera de Medellin (1) | |
| Metalica de Palmira (1) | |
| Banco de Bogota (1) | |
| Fabricato (1) | |
| **12. Tejicondor** | |
| Coltabaco (1) | Industrias Apolo (2) |
| Coltejer (1) | |
| Everfit (1) | |
| Banco Central Hipotecaria (1) | |
| Banco Industrial Colombiano (1) | |
| **13. Uniroyal Croydon** | |
| Banco del Occidente (1) | |
| Siderurgica del Pacifico (1) | |
| Procesadora de Leches (1) | |

SOURCES: (Bolsa de Bogota, 1977; Aldana et al., 1977: 150-158; Silva Colmenares, 1977: 326-342).

NOTE: Interlocking directorates existed when the same individual was on the board of directors of more than one company listed by the stock exchange. The study checked the interlocking directorates of foreign and domestic manufacturing companies and with other companies in the sectors of banking, finance, insurance, and services.

firms are tied closely to one another and to national firms in Colombia. Foreign firms had more interlocking directorates per firm with each other (1.8) and with domestic companies (9.1) than did domestic manufacturing firms (0.9 and 6.8, respectively). The evidence available from this sample suggests that foreign firms, instead of creating alternate centers of economic power, are already associated with the major economic power groups in Colombia. According to Silva Colmenares (1977: 317-34) and Bolsa de Bogota (1977), the Bogota group had partial ownership of six of the thirteen foreign firms listed. In addition, it had five interlocking directorates with a sixth foreign firm. The Suramerica group had partial ownership of three of the foreign firms and four interlocking directorates with three others. The Santo Domingo group had six interlocking directorates with three of the foreign firms. The Cafetero group had six interlocking directorates with two of the foreign manufacturing firms. This would also explain why the domestic associations of industries and banks were opposed to the government's domestication policies (Sherman, 1973: 112).

TABLE 53
INTERLOCKING DIRECTORATES

| | Foreign Manufacturing Companies | Domestic Manufacturing Companies |
|---|---|---|
| Number of Companies | 13 | 63 |
| Interlocks with All Other Companies | 142 | 484 |
| (Interlocks/Company) | 10.9 | 7.7 |
| Interlocks with Thirteen Foreign Companies | 24 | 54 |
| (Interlocks/Company) | 1.8 | 0.9 |
| Interlocks with Domestic Companies | 118 | 430 |
| (Interlocks/Company) | 9.1 | 6.8 |

SOURCES: See Table 52.

The issue raised in this section was whether domestication will lead to greater concentration of economic, social, and political power in Colombia. It was shown that a small oligarchy dominated the Colombian society, and that this concentration of power existed in the economy as well. It was hypothesized that, if foreign firms were less tied to the domestic power groups than were foreign firms, then domestication might result in an even greater concentration of economic power in that country. The evidence on interlocking directorates indicates that foreign firms are already strongly associated with these domestic power groups. It seems likely that domestication will not intensify concentration of economic power in Colombia. Nor is domestication likely to diffuse the concentration of economic power in Colombia.

The Colombian economy is likely to be dominated by the same oligarchy that now controls it, and this concentration of power is a very important aspect of Colombian society today. With regard to this issue, domestication is not likely to benefit or harm the well-being of the Colombian citizenry. Rather, domestication is irrelevant to the issue of concentration of power in Colombia. By focusing solely upon the foreignness versus the domesticness of a firm, it draws attention away from the fact that the groups that currently dominate the Colombian society are both foreign and domestic. Foreign manufacturing firms are already a part of the Colombian economic oligarchy, and domestication is not likely to change that. Domestication may alter the nationality of ownership of firms currently operating in the country, but it is unlikely to change the concentration of control within the economy.

## Conclusion

This chapter has looked at three areas in which domestication could affect the Colombian citizenry in a nonmaterial sense: attitudes, national autonomy, and the socioeconomic power structure. With regard to attitudes, it was found that there would be no clear-cut effects of domestication upon the attitudes of the general public or of elite publics. Managerial attitudes, on the other hand, seem likely to be affected by a policy of domestication. Domestication most likely would increase the identification that managers feel towards the nation and increase the degree to which managers see their role as including some obligation to society (and not just towards the firm).

In studying the effects of domestication upon national autonomy, it was found that Colombian culture is to a large degree dominated externally, causing Colombians to view themselves as inferior to other societies and to seek their values and tastes from abroad. Domestication is not likely to end this lack of national autonomy in the short run. It does seen likely to increase the degree to which firms in the economy generate their technology domestically, responding to local needs and circumstances. In the long run, this local development of technology brings with it the possibility of greater national autonomy. The chapter also studied the possible effects of domestication upon the domestic power structure of Colombia, in which socioeconomic domination of the country is in the hands of a small elite. It was found that foreign and domestic firms are tied together closely in the Colombian economy, and it thus seems unlikely that domestication will have any effect on the level of concentration of control over the Colombian economy.

# CHAPTER 9

# CONCLUSION

What does this study tell us about foreign and domestic investment in Colombia? First, there are some differences between foreign and domestic investment, and these differences create the likelihood that a Colombian economy that allows direct foreign investment will have different characteristics from one that restricts investment to private domestic owners. Second, there are some effects of investment (e.g., the concentration of industrial power) that are not related to the nationality of ownership. In such cases, policies that focus on the nationality of ownership are unlikely to achieve desired goals.

Based on the evidence contained in the earlier chapters, one can make the following projections about the probable short-run effects of domestication on the industrial sector in Colombia::

--productivity of both labor and capital would decline, most likely giving rise to lower rates of growth in manufacturing output.

--the distribution of income among industrial workers and among the different regions of the country would become more equal.

--industrial wages would decline.

--the exports and imports of the industrial sector would decline.

--the overall balance of payments effects of the industrial sector would improve.

--attitudes among managers would probably change, making their views and perhaps their actions more responsible socially.

--there would be greater employment of national skilled personnel.

--there would be more domestic innovation and less dependence on foreign technology.

--the concentration of economic power in the industrial sector would not change.

## Limitations of the Study

The major limitations of this study stem from its historical, geographic, and conceptual specificity. In short, its focus is narrow. It uses as a case study one country--Colombia--whose uniqueness makes difficult any generalization to other developing countries. It compares foreign and domestic investment in only one part of the country--the factory manufacturing sector. Implicit in the study is the assumption that this sector is important for Colombia's development. It can be argued that other sectors of the economy (especially agriculture and cottage-industries) have a bigger impact on the country. Both of those sectors have virtually no foreign investment.

The most important limitation of the study is that it compares foreign and domestic investment in Colombia at only one time. The results that were obtained were a snapshot (or still life) of foreign and domestic investment as they stood at that time, with little indication of whether or how they were changing. Such a method contributes to the view that foreign and domestic investment are unchanged and unchanging phenomena. This approach is unable to see how they have changed, and how they have changed one another. It is unable, for example, to determine if the presence of DFI in Colombia has altered the economic structure of the country over time.

Another limitation arises out of this methodology: it is unable to address the counterfactual alternative. It is not capable of assessing what the Colombian economy would currently look like if foreign firms had never entered the country.

## Policy Implications

It is possible that the differences between foreign and domestic firms in Colombia are due to factors that are only indirectly related to nationality. For example, there is some evidence that the greater size of foreign plants and the specific products which they produce account for some of the differences observed in this study. To the extent that this is true, policies of domestication are misdirected. A more effective approach would be to adopt policies which address directly those factors (e.g., size and product manufactured) that account for the differences in bahavior, or to take an even more direct approach and implement policies that focus specifically on behavior. Both of these policies might be more effective in bringing about changes in behavior than would domestication, which deals with the behavior of firms through the indirect means of the nationality of ownership. Perhaps the difficulty is that we expect the behavior of foreign and domestic firms to correspond to some universal law that does not exist. Maybe there are no universal patterns, and the relative effects of foreign and domestic firms have more to do with the historical development and social fabric of the country involved than to the foreignness or domesticness of the company. However, the fact remains that there are differences in firms' behavior that are based on nationality, and changes in the nationality of ownership are likely to bring substantial short-run changes in the industrial sector.

In the long run the implementation of a policy of domestication will likely effect possibilities for more profound change. Inasmuch as domestication transfers some control over the economy from foreign actors (i.e., direct foreign investors) to national ones (i.e., private domestic investors and the national government), it will increase national autonomy. More and more of the decisions affecting the society would be made by domestic citizens, opening a whole new array of possibilities for national development. As Peter Evans (1970) has written:

> Moving toward greater autonomy is essentially choosing to orient economic decisions around the political constituency of the nation-state rather than to allow the locus of decision-making to gravitate toward private, profit-making corporations based in rich countries. There is good reason to believe this policy an economically rational choice, but it provides no ready-made solutions to the problems of poor countries. It is rather the selection of a new paradigm, a new framework in which to seek solutions (p.342).

The domestication policy provides a new conceptual approach through which to organize economic decision-making. This approach views direct foreign investment and the penetration of multinational corporations as obstacles to development in Colombia. Therefore, it seeks seeks to eliminate these corporations and to transfer their control over the economy to private domestic businesses, whose decision-making centers generally around the national market. The success of this framework depends upon whether the private domestic businesses, either on their own or as a result of government pressure, can become more dynamic elements in national development. Past experience offers little basis for optimism, and an analysis of the present situation suggests that significant changes in the Colombian society are not likely. Power would most likely remain in the hands of an entrenched national elite who have given little indication of a willingness or ability to change.

However, domestication does bring with it the possibility for significant change. The existing concentration of economic and political power in Colombia is not an immutable aspect of that society. It was created by human action and it can be changed by similar action. Domestication would open the possibility for such change because it would give to the national government the potential to have greater control over the institutions of economic decision-making (i.e., domestic businesses). Foreign businesses have the ability to evade the control of national governments by transferring resources internationally. Domestic business has less abiltity to do this.

This raises the possibility of substantial changes taking place in the Colombian economy if there are major changes in government policy. Such changes have been virtually impossible in the past. With the implementation of domestic such changes would be possible but unlikely.

# APPENDIX A

## DIRECT FOREIGN INVESTMENT IN COLOMBIA

The data that are available on direct foreign investment in Colombia are not totally compatible with one another. The two primary sources from which most of these data are taken are the Oficina de Cambios (Exchange Office) of the Banco de la Republica (Central Bank) in Colombia and the Department of Commerce of the United States. The Oficina de Cambios provides information on registered DFI in Colombia, excluding the petroleum sector. Data are available from the period from 1917-1976. However, figures from 1917 through 1966 are estimates and are of questionable reliability because it was not until 1967 that the Colombian government enforced the registration of foreign investment as well as control over imports and exports of capital by foreign firms. The 1917-1966 data refer to the investments of those companies which still remained in the country in 1967. Foreign companies that went bankrupt or were bought out before 1967 are not included.

Oficina de Cambios data from 1967 to 1976 are much more accurate, but they suffer from another problem: these data are readjusted almost every year (so that the figure for total registered DFI in Colombia in 1967 is reported differently in 1972 publications than it is in 1977 publications). To minimize this problem, I have tried to select what appear to be the most consistent and reliable figures. However, it was impossible to do this without inconsistencies appearing. A second problem with the Oficina de Cambios figures is that they exclude DFI in petroleum. Because the U.S. Department of Commerce figures do include petroleum in DFI in Colombia, they provide a useful supplement to the Oficina de Cambios data.

Information is available from the U.S. Department of Commerce on the "book value" of U.S. direct foreign investment in Colombia. For recent years, information is also available on the sales of majority-owned foreign affiliates of U.S. companies. Unfortunately, these data rely on information that is submitted to the Department of Commerce by individual firms, and its reliability is questionable. In addition, pre-1950 figures are estimates.

The "book value" for U.S. DFI in Colombia is invariably larger than the "registered" U.S. DFI figure in the Oficina de Cambios. Part of this difference may be reconciled by realizing that much U.S. direct foreign investment in Colombia is invested by U.S. companies operating out of third countries (particularly in the Caribbean). The Department of Commerce might consider such investment as coming from the U.S., while the Oficina de

Cambios might consider it Panamanian or Bahamian investment. In addition, the "book value" figure looks at the companies' assessed value of plant and equipment, while the Oficina de Cambios figure looks only at the entry of foreign capital and approved reinvestments.

Several things should be kept in mind when looking at the following tables. First, the Department of Commerce figures tend to overvalue U.S. DFI relative to how they would be registered in Colombia. Second, the Oficina de Cambios figures exclude petroleum investments, which for most of this century have been the major sector for DFI in Colombia. Finally, the Oficina de Cambios figures tend to undervalue DFI during the 1917-1966 period because they took as their universe those firms existing in 1967.

The following data on U.S. direct foreign investment in Colombia between 1897 and 1967 come from Conrad Matter's Inversiones Extranjeras en la Economia Colombiana, pages 119-120. All other U.S. data comes from the U.S. Department of Commerce's Survey of Current Business: 1968 data come from page 28 of the October 1969 issue. 1969 and 1970 data from pages 32-35 of the October 1971 issue, 1971 and 1972 data from pages 26-29 of the September 1973 issue, 1973 and 1974 data from pages 52-53 of the October 1975 issue, 1975 data from page 49 of the August 1976 issue, 1976 data from page 45 of the August 1977 issue, and 1977 data from page 28 of the August 1978 issue. All other figures in this appendix show the registered nonpetroleum direct foreign investment in Colombia. Data from 1917 through 1970 were adapted from the Colombian Departamento Administrativo Nacional de Estadistica's Boletin Mensual de Estadistica of June 1971, pages 70-71 and 79-81. Post-1970 data come from the Colombian Banco de la Republica's "Registro de Inversiones Extranjeras en Colombia," 1973-1977.

TABLE 54
UNITED STATED DIRECT FOREIGN INVESTMENT IN COLOMBIA, 1897-1977 (Book value in millions of $)

| Year | Total | Manufacturing | Petroleum |
|---|---|---|---|
| 1897 | 9 | 0 | 0 |
| 1908 | 11 | 0 | 0 |
| 1914 | 24 | 0 | 0 |
| 1919 | 45 | 0 | 5 (11.1%) |
| 1924 | 84 | 0 | 0 |
| 1929 | 124 | 4 (3.2%) | 56 (45.2%) |
| 1936 | 107 | 0 | 60 (54.1%) |
| 1940 | 112 | 1 (0.9%) | 75 (67.0%) |
| 1943 | 117 | 4 (3.4%) | 77 (65.8%) |
| 1946 | 189 | 12 (6.3%) | 126 (66.7%) |
| 1950 | 193 | 25 (13.0%) | 112 (58.0%) |
| 1955 | 336 | 58 (17.3%) | 178 (53.0%) |
| 1960 | 425 | 92 (21.6%) | 233 (54.8%) |
| 1963 | 464 | 120 (25.9%) | 246 (53.0%) |
| 1966 | 571 | 190 (33.3%) | 277 (48.5%) |
| 1967 | 597 | 192 (32.2%) | 294 (49.2%) |
| 1968 | 629 | 193 (30.7%) | 324 (51.5%) |
| 1969 | 684 | 220 (32.2%) | 342 (50.0%) |
| 1970 | 691 | 229 (33.1%) | 334 (48.3%) |
| 1971 | 744 | 256 (34.4%) | 345 (46.6%) |
| 1972 | 739 | 262 (35.5%) | 327 (44.2%) |
| 1973 | 608 | 325 (53.5%) | 76 (12.5%) |
| 1974 | 629 | 375 (59.6%) | 58 (9.2%) |
| 1975 | 648 | 380 (58.6%0 | 62 (9.6%) |
| 1976 | 653 | 387 (59.3%) | 56 (8.6%) |
| 1977 | 706 | 436 (61.8%) | 71 (10.1%) |

TABLE 55
CUMULATIVE NONPETROLEUM REGISTERED DIRECT FOREIGN INVESTMENT IN COLOMBIA
(millions of U.S. $)

| Year | Total | Commerce | Finance | Mining | Manufacturing |
|---|---|---|---|---|---|
| 1917 | 2.99 | 2.99 | --- | --- | |
| 1920 | 7.29 | 2.99 | 4.30 | --- | |
| 1924 | 13.19 | 2.99 | 10.20 | --- | |
| 1925 | 17.50 | 2.99 | 14.51 | --- | |
| 1926 | 20.20 | 2.99 | 14.51 | 2.70 | |
| 1927 | 33.62 | 2.99 | 15.30 | 2.70 | 12.63 |
| 1928 | 35.53 | 2.99 | 15.30 | 2.70 | 14.54 |
| 1929 | 35.71 | 3.17 | 15.30 | 2.70 | 14.54 |
| 1930 | 44.15 | 3.54 | 15.30 | 2.70 | 14.54 |
| 1932 | 46.43 | 3.54 | 15.30 | 2.70 | 16.82 |
| 1934 | 46.99 | 3.54 | 15.30 | 2.70 | 17.38 |
| 1935 | 47.26 | 3.59 | 15.30 | 2.70 | 17.39 |
| 1936 | 51.94 | 3.59 | 15.30 | 7.38 | 17.39 |
| 1938 | 57.66 | 3.59 | 15.30 | 7.38 | 23.11 |
| 1940 | 58.51 | 3.59 | 15.30 | 7.38 | 23.96 |
| 1941 | 67.82 | 3.59 | 15.30 | 7.38 | 32.76 |
| 1943 | 75.15 | 3.59 | 15.30 | 7.38 | 36.54 |
| 1944 | 114.99 | 3.59 | 15.30 | 7.38 | 79.93 |
| 1945 | 123.29 | 3.59 | 15.30 | 7.38 | 88.23 |
| 1946 | 126.52 | 3.59 | 15.30 | 7.38 | 91.46 |
| 1947 | 131.73 | 4.27 | 15.30 | 7.38 | 95.99 |
| 1948 | 142.01 | 4.27 | 20.11 | 7.38 | 101.46 |
| 1949 | 146.29 | 4.27 | 20.11 | 7.38 | 105.74 |
| 1950 | 202.67 | 34.84 | 20.11 | 7.38 | 131.55 |
| 1951 | 210.14 | 39.79 | 20.72 | 7.38 | 133.44 |
| 1952 | 215.71 | 40.55 | 21.42 | 7.38 | 138.67 |
| 1953 | 223.25 | 41.77 | 21.42 | 7.38 | 141.37 |
| 1954 | 236.71 | 42.83 | 25.01 | 7.38 | 143.37 |
| 1955 | 237.22 | 42.93 | 25.01 | 7.38 | 143.62 |
| 1956 | 240.27 | 43.17 | 25.07 | 7.38 | 145.45 |
| 1957 | 265.21 | 43.56 | 25.10 | 7.38 | 169.54 |
| 1958 | 282.15 | 43.65 | 25.10 | 7.38 | 181.49 |
| 1959 | 288.48 | 44.37 | 25.11 | 7.38 | 185.59 |
| 1960 | 314.05 | 44.38 | 30.85 | 7.38 | 200.67 |
| 1961 | 338.94 | 44.49 | 35.11 | 7.89 | 220.07 |
| 1962 | 359.44 | 45.42 | 35.62 | 7.89 | 226.17 |
| 1963 | 367.48 | 46.96 | 38.88 | 7.89 | 228.71 |
| 1964 | 383.66 | 47.30 | 38.95 | 7.89 | 243.23 |
| 1965 | 390.27 | 48.13 | 40.04 | 7.89 | 244.94 |

TABLE 55 (continued)

| Year | Total | Commerce | Finance | Mining | Manufacturing |
|---|---|---|---|---|---|
| 1966 | 393.29 | 48.34 | 40.59 | 7.89 | 246.83 |
| 1967 | 411.66 | 48.50 | 50.38 | 9.32 | 252.83 |
| 1968 | 424.97 | 48.84 | 52.48 | 9.32 | 259.60 |
| 1969 | 443.34 | 49.45 | 56.87 | 9.32 | 263.69 |
| 1970 | 450.98 | 49.46 | 57.90 | 9.39 | 267.71 |
| 1971 | 501.51 | 53.39 | 68.61 | 13.32 | 346.00 |
| 1972 | 540.11 | 56.03 | 76.11 | 13.35 | 373.30 |
| 1973 | 560.45 | 57.01 | 83.36 | 13.35 | 383.39 |
| 1974 | 584.47 | 59.00 | 92.78 | 14.36 | 395.46 |
| 1975 | 632.94 | 65.38 | 100.43 | 14.93 | 427.43 |
| 1976 | 685.56 | 65.17 | 104.51 | 26.43 | 453.89 |

TABLE 56

REGISTERED NONPETROLEUM FOREIGN INVESTMENT IN COLOMBIA; BY COUNTRY OF ORIGIN

(millions of U.S.$)

| Country or Region | 1966 | 1967 | 1967 | 1969 | 1970 | 1971 | 1972 | 1973 | 1974 | 1975 | 1976 |
|---|---|---|---|---|---|---|---|---|---|---|---|
| North America | | | | | | 322.2 | 338.4 | 345.0 | 355.2 | 369.8 | 388.4 |
| United States | 277.5 | 293.4 | 298.9 | 307.6 | 309.7 | 258.8 | 274.2 | 280.4 | 290.6 | 304.4 | 338.7 |
| Canada | | | | | | 63.5 | 64.2 | 64.6 | 64.3 | 65.4 | 49.6 |
| Central America | 45.5 | 46.2 | 49.5 | 50.5 | 51.4 | 72.4 | 80.9 | 85.5 | 89.1 | 96.8 | 99.1 |
| Panama | | | | | | 36.8 | 41.5 | 44.7 | 47.0 | 53.8 | 55.7 |
| Bahamas | | | | | | 9.0 | 9.3 | 9.3 | 9.5 | 10.0 | 10.6 |
| Curcao | | | | | | 15.5 | 17.7 | 18.7 | 19.9 | 20.3 | 20.9 |
| South America | | | | | | 14.3 | 14.5 | 15.0 | 15.2 | 28.2 | 42.7 |
| Venezuela | | | | | | 8.8 | 8.9 | 8.9 | 9.1 | 19.3 | 21.4 |
| Europe | 60.8 | 62.5 | 66.3 | 71.1 | 75.4 | 91.5 | 103.3 | 111.9 | 120.3 | 133.3 | 148.7 |
| France | | | | | | 16.3 | 19.2 | 24.4 | 25.5 | 27.1 | 26.8 |
| Netherlands | | | | | | 16.5 | 17.8 | 18.0 | 18.4 | 21.7 | 24.3 |
| Switzerland | | | | | | 17.2 | 20.4 | 21.3 | 25.7 | 28.8 | 33.2 |
| Germany (FRG) | | | | | | 12.4 | 13.4 | 13.8 | 14.7 | 16.1 | 20.1 |
| United Kingdom | | | | | | 11.3 | 11.7 | 12.6 | 13.5 | 13.7 | 14.1 |
| Other | 9.3 | 9.4 | 10.1 | 14.0 | 14.3 | 1.1 | 3.0 | 3.0 | 4.6 | 4.8 | 6.8 |
| Japan | | | | | | 0.5 | 2.1 | 2.1 | 3.7 | 3.8 | 5.8 |
| Total | 393.2 | 411.6 | 424.9 | 443.3 | 450.9 | 501.5 | 540.1 | 460.4 | 484.5 | 632.9 | 685.6 |

TABLE 57

REGISTERED NONPETROLEUM DIRECT FOREIGN INVESTMENT IN COLOMBIA; BY SECTOR

(millions of U.S. $)

| Sector | 1966 | 1967 | 1968 | 1969 | 1970 | 1971 | 1972 | 1973 | 1974 | 1975 | 1976 |
|---|---|---|---|---|---|---|---|---|---|---|---|
| Agriculture | 2.6 | 2.9 | 3.2 | 3.5 | 3.8 | 4.2 | 4.9 | 5.5 | 5.9 | 6.5 | 7.4 |
| Mining | 7.9 | 9.3 | 9.3 | 9.3 | 9.4 | 13.4 | 13.4 | 13.4 | 14.4 | 14.9 | 26.4 |
| Manufacturing | 246.8 | 252.8 | 259.6 | 263.7 | 267.7 | 346.0 | 373.3 | 383.4 | 395.5 | 427.4 | 453.9 |
| Utilities | * | * | * | * | * | 0.9 | 0.9 | 0.9 | 0.9 | 0.9 | 0.9 |
| Construction | 2.5 | 2.6 | 2.9 | 3.1 | 3.1 | 1.9 | 2.0 | 2.0 | 2.0 | 3.1 | 2.2 |
| Commerce | 48.3 | 48.5 | 48.8 | 49.4 | 49.5 | 53.6 | 56.0 | 57.0 | 59.0 | 65.4 | 65.2 |
| Transportation $ Communications | * | * | * | * | * | 10.9 | 11.3 | 11.3 | 11.3 | 11.3 | 22.1 |
| Finance & Insurance | 40.6 | 50.4 | 52.5 | 56.9 | 57.9 | 68.6 | 76.1 | 84.4 | 92.8 | 100.4 | 104.5 |
| Services | 14.4 | 14.5 | 15.7 | 16.2 | 16.7 | 0.6 | 0.6 | 0.6 | 0.6 | 0.8 | 0.8 |
| Miscellaneous | 30.1 | 30.6 | 32.9 | 41.2 | 42.8 | 1.4 | 1.7 | 2.1 | 2.2 | 2.2 | 2.2 |
| Total | 393.2 | 411.6 | 424.9 | 443.9 | 450.9 | 501.5 | 540.1 | 560.5 | 584.5 | 632.9 | 685.6 |

* Included under miscellaneous.

# APPENDIX B

## FOREIGN, DOMESTIC, AND NATIONAL PLANTS IN COLOMBIA

This appendix provides data on three particularly overlapping sets of manufacturing plants in Colombia. These include a set of all factory manufacturing plants operating in Colombia in 1974 (Set N), a set of 421 manufacturing plants with some amount of direct foreign investment (Set F), and a set of all national factory manufacturing plants excluding those with direct foreign investment (Set D). These plants were grouped into twenty-seven industries according to the International Uniform Industrial Classification System. Table 58 provides description of these industries. It was obtained from the Colombian Departamento Administrativo Nacional de Estadistica's (DANE) Boletin Mensual de Estadistica, October 1976, pages 146-147.

Data on the number, production, value added, employment, and total remuneration of national plants were obtained from DANE's Industria Manufacturera 1974, pages 12-21. Data on the remuneration per capita of foreign and national plants in 1972 were obtained from DANE's Boletin Mensual de Estadistica, September 1976, pages 209-210. Data on the 1973 average per capita remuneration of foreign and national plants were obtained from pages 195-196 of the same source. Data on the number of foreign plants were obtained from pages 138-139 of that source, and data on the gross production and value added of foreign plants in 1974 were obtained from pages 158-159 of that source. Data on the employment by foreign plants are from pages 165-166 of that source.

Data on the 1972 remuneration /personnel, per capita remuneration/per capita value added, fixed assets/personnel, value added/personnel, production/personnel, value added/production, production/plant, and value added/plant for both national and foreign plants were obtained from DANE's Boletin Mensual de Estadistica, October 1976, pages 145-148. Data on the manufactured direct exports of foreign and national plants were obtained from page 110 of this source. Data on the total use of raw materials and use of foreign raw materials were obtained from pages 150-151 of this source. Data on the 1974 value added/personnel, production/personnel, value added/production, production/plant, and value added/plant for both foreign and national plants were adapted from the other tables in this appendix. All the data on domestic plants (Set D) were obtained by subtracting Set F from Set N.

TABLE 58
INTERNATIONAL UNIFORM INDUSTRIAL CLASSIFICATION SYSTEM

| | |
|---|---|
| 31 | Food, Beverage, and Tobacco Products |
| 311-312 | Manufacture of Food Products (except beverages) |
| 313 | Beverage Industries |
| 314 | Tobacco Industries |
| | |
| 32 | Textiles, Apparel, & Leather Industries |
| 321 | Manufacture of Textiles |
| 322 | Manufacture of Apparel (except footwear) |
| 323 | Leather and Leather products (except footwear) |
| 324 | Footwear |
| | |
| 33 | Wood and Wood Products |
| 331 | Wood & Products, Cork |
| 332 | Furniture & Accessories |
| | |
| 34 | Manufacture of Paper & Products, Printing & Publishing |
| 341 | Paper & Products |
| 342 | Printing, Publishing, & Related Industries |
| | |
| 35 | Manufacture of Chemical Products |
| 351 | Manufcture of Industrial Chemicals |
| 352 | Manufacture of Other Chemical Products |
| 353 | Petroleum Refineries |
| 354 | Manufacture of Petroleum & Carbon Derivatives |
| 355 | Manufacture of Rubber Products |
| 365 | Manufacture of Plastic Products |
| | |
| 36 | Manufacture of Non-metallic Minerals |
| 361 | Manufacture of Clay & Porcelain Objects |
| 362 | Manufacture of Glass & Glass Products |
| 369 | Manufacture of Other Non-metallic Minerals |
| | |
| 37 | Basic Metals |
| 371 | Basic Iron & Steel Industries |
| 372 | Basic Nonferrous Metals Industries |
| | |
| 38 | Manufacture of Metal Products, Machinery, & Equipment |
| 381 | Manufacture of Metal Products |
| 382 | Construction of Nonelectrical Machinery |
| 383 | Construction of Electrical Machinery & Accessories |
| 384 | Construction of Transportation Equipment & Material |
| 385 | Gauges, Photographical Apparatus, & Optical Equipment |
| | |
| 39 | Other Manufacturing Industries |
| 391 | Other Manufacturing Industries |

TABLE 59
NATIONAL MANUFACTURING INDUSTRIES: SET N

| Industry | # of Plants | Gross Production 1974 (millions of pesos) | Value Added 1974 (millions of pesos) | Employment 1974 | Total Remuneration, 1974 (millions of pesos) |
|---|---|---|---|---|---|
| Total | 6,066 | 166,857 | 67,280 | 448,174 | 20,391 |
| 311-2 | 1,113 | 37,377 | 9,081 | 60,663 | 2,318 |
| 313 | 122 | 12,100 | 7,830 | 19,674 | 1,346 |
| 321 | 423 | 23,444 | 9,666 | 74,618 | 3,707 |
| 322 | 606 | 4,824 | 1,849 | 39,954 | 919 |
| 323 | 86 | 1,740 | 500 | 6,324 | 211 |
| 324 | 187 | 834 | 336 | 7,328 | 172 |
| 331 | 251 | 1,371 | 658 | 8,630 | 231 |
| 332 | 217 | 824 | 377 | 7,674 | 186 |
| 341 | 146 | 7,494 | 2,557 | 10,859 | 649 |
| 342 | 298 | 3,538 | 1,561 | 16,989 | 764 |
| 351 | 96 | 11,051 | 4,798 | 10,875 | 758 |
| 352 | 273 | 10,703 | 4,915 | 23,747 | 1,491 |
| 353 | 13 | 4,481 | 1,847 | 4,049 | 671 |
| 354 | 9 | 60 | 25 | 352 | 8 |
| 355 | 72 | 3,599 | 1,506 | 9,199 | 560 |
| 356 | 163 | 3,490 | 1,429 | 10,562 | 415 |
| 361 | 36 | 596 | 313 | 4,988 | 189 |
| 362 | 48 | 1,303 | 732 | 6,340 | 306 |
| 369 | 349 | 4,792 | 2,629 | 19,280 | 859 |
| 371 | 51 | 4,584 | 2,142 | 13,017 | 881 |
| 372 | 26 | 1,156 | 381 | 2,223 | 111 |
| 381 | 574 | 6,756 | 2,758 | 29,604 | 1,082 |
| 382 | 286 | 3,441 | 1,505 | 15,223 | 627 |
| 383 | 164 | 4,597 | 1,899 | 13,064 | 675 |
| 384 | 192 | 7,792 | 2,833 | 17,030 | 757 |
| 385 | 53 | 328 | 138 | 2,177 | 58 |
| 390 | 168 | 1,324 | 620 | 8,244 | 241 |

TABLE 59--Continued

| Industry | National Managerial Personnel 1972 | Foreign Managerial Personnel 1972 | Office Workers 1972 | Laborers 1972 | Average 1973 |
|---|---|---|---|---|---|
| Total | 121 | 176 | 49 | 26 | 36 |
| 311-2 | 112 | 164 | 41 | 20 | 30 |
| 313 | 191 | 186 | 65 | 33 | 55 |
| 321 | 137 | 165 | 53 | 31 | 39 |
| 322 | 62 | 70 | 33 | 14 | 19 |
| 323 | 134 | 184 | 41 | 22 | 29 |
| 324 | 55 | 178 | 40 | 19 | 32 |
| 331 | 76 | 107 | 34 | 18 | 23 |
| 332 | 79 | 130 | 26 | 17 | 20 |
| 341 | 151 | 232 | 68 | 33 | 31 |
| 342 | 122 | 181 | 47 | 27 | 38 |
| 351 | 142 | 185 | 71 | 38 | 62 |
| 352 | 132 | 220 | 54 | 24 | 53 |
| 353 | 178 | 621 | 89 | 132 | 152 |
| 354 | 106 | --- | 43 | 15 | 29 |
| 355 | 148 | 313 | 73 | 34 | 52 |
| 356 | 108 | 119 | 39 | 19 | 31 |
| 361 | 66 | 67 | 48 | 22 | 29 |
| 362 | 130 | 119 | 60 | 29 | 38 |
| 369 | 113 | 249 | 46 | 28 | 37 |
| 371 | 87 | 86 | 51 | 42 | 58 |
| 372 | 142 | 221 | 53 | 27 | 40 |
| 381 | 98 | 163 | 38 | 21 | 29 |
| 382 | 107 | 260 | 42 | 27 | 36 |
| 383 | 109 | 193 | 53 | 24 | 40 |
| 384 | 103 | 145 | 47 | 24 | 38 |
| 385 | 89 | 118 | 34 | 16 | 26 |
| 391 | 87 | 154 | 40 | 17 | 24 |

TABLE 59--Continued (1972 Figures)

| Industry | Remuneration/ Personnel (1,000s Pesos) | Per Capita Remunerat/ Per Capita Value Added | Fixed Assets/ Remuneration | Value Added/ Fixed Assets | Fixed Assets/ Personnel (1,000s Pesos) |
|---|---|---|---|---|---|
| Total | 33 | .33 | 2.1 | 1.4 | 70 |
| 311-2 | 27 | .29 | 2.9 | 1.2 | 79 |
| 313 | 50 | .17 | 2.4 | 2.4 | 121 |
| 321 | 37 | .39 | 1.6 | 1.6 | 59 |
| 322 | 17 | .46 | 0.9 | 2.3 | 16 |
| 323 | 27 | .44 | 0.9 | 2.4 | 25 |
| 324 | 21 | .58 | 0.7 | 2.3 | 15 |
| 331 | 20 | .46 | 2.0 | 1.1 | 40 |
| 332 | 19 | .61 | 0.9 | 1.9 | 17 |
| 341 | 45 | .35 | 2.9 | 0.9 | 135 |
| 342 | 35 | .49 | 1.3 | 1.5 | 47 |
| 351 | 52 | .32 | 6.0 | 0.5 | 321 |
| 352 | 43 | .30 | 1.0 | 3.1 | 45 |
| 353 | 129 | .17 | 5.9 | 0.9 | 768 |
| 354 | 22 | .25 | 2.8 | 1.3 | 64 |
| 355 | 44 | .38 | 1.1 | 2.2 | 51 |
| 356 | 25 | .35 | 2.4 | 1.2 | 61 |
| 361 | 26 | .63 | 1.4 | 1.1 | 37 |
| 362 | 35 | .38 | 1.2 | 2.2 | 41 |
| 369 | 32 | .39 | 2.7 | 0.9 | 88 |
| 371 | 47 | .54 | 2.7 | 0.7 | 129 |
| 372 | 35 | .45 | 1.9 | 1.2 | 66 |
| 381 | 26 | .45 | 1.4 | 1.5 | 37 |
| 382 | 34 | .46 | 1.2 | 1.7 | 42 |
| 383 | 36 | .44 | 1.3 | 1.7 | 47 |
| 384 | 30 | .33 | 1.3 | 2.2 | 40 |
| 385 | 23 | .39 | 1.3 | 1.9 | 30 |
| 390 | 22 | .43 | 2.1 | 1.6 | 32 |

TABLE 59—Continued

| Industry | Value Added/ Personnel (Thousands | Production/ Personnel of Pesos) | Value Added/ Production | Produc- tion/ Plant (Millions | Value Added/ Plant Pesos) |
|---|---|---|---|---|---|
| Total | 99 | 228 | .43 | 16 | 7 |
| 311-2 | 93 | 374 | .25 | 19 | 5 |
| 313 | 293 | 385 | .76 | 63 | 47 |
| 321 | 95 | 192 | .49 | 37 | 18 |
| 322 | 37 | 95 | .40 | 6 | 2 |
| 323 | 61 | 211 | .29 | 18 | 4 |
| 324 | 36 | 80 | .45 | 3 | 1 |
| 331 | 43 | 98 | .44 | 3 | 1 |
| 332 | 31 | 68 | .46 | 2 | 1 |
| 341 | 126 | 383 | .32 | 26 | 8 |
| 342 | 71 | 134 | .52 | 7 | 3 |
| 351 | 160 | 413 | .39 | 46 | 17 |
| 352 | 141 | 280 | .50 | 21 | 10 |
| 353 | 743 | 1635 | .45 | 392 | 178 |
| 354 | 86 | 543 | .16 | 19 | 3 |
| 355 | 114 | 242 | .47 | 27 | 13 |
| 356 | 71 | 166 | .43 | 11 | 4 |
| 361 | 41 | 71 | .58 | 8 | 5 |
| 362 | 91 | 148 | .61 | 18 | 11 |
| 369 | 81 | 154 | .53 | 8 | 4 |
| 371 | 87 | 185 | .47 | 52 | 24 |
| 372 | 77 | 223 | .35 | 20 | 6 |
| 381 | 57 | 128 | .45 | 6 | 2 |
| 382 | 73 | 150 | .49 | 8 | 4 |
| 383 | 81 | 197 | .41 | 13 | 5 |
| 384 | 89 | 281 | .32 | 20 | 6 |
| 385 | 58 | 121 | .48 | 4 | 2 |
| 390 | 51 | 102 | .50 | 5 | 2 |

TABLE 59—Continued

| Industry | 1974 Value Added/ Personnel (Thousands | 1974 Production/ Personnel of Pesos) | 1974 Value Added/ Production | 1974 Production/ Plant (Millions | 1974 Value Added/ Plant Pesos) |
|---|---|---|---|---|---|
| Total | 150 | 372 | .403 | 27.5 | 11.1 |
| 311-2 | 150 | 616 | .243 | 33.6 | 8.2 |
| 313 | 398 | 615 | .647 | 99.2 | 64.2 |
| 321 | 130 | 314 | .412 | 55.4 | 22.9 |
| 322 | 46 | 121 | .383 | 8.0 | 3.1 |
| 323 | 79 | 275 | .287 | 20.2 | 5.8 |
| 324 | 46 | 114 | .403 | 4.5 | 1.8 |
| 331 | 76 | 159 | .480 | 5.5 | 2.6 |
| 332 | 49 | 107 | .458 | 3.8 | 1.8 |
| 341 | 235 | 690 | .341 | 51.3 | 17.5 |
| 342 | 92 | 208 | .441 | 11.9 | 5.2 |
| 351 | 441 | 1016 | .434 | 115.1 | 50.0 |
| 352 | 207 | 451 | .459 | 39.2 | 18.0 |
| 353 | 456 | 1107 | .412 | 344.7 | 142.1 |
| 354 | 71 | 170 | .417 | 6.7 | 2.8 |
| 355 | 164 | 391 | .418 | 50.0 | 20.9 |
| 356 | 135 | 330 | .409 | 21.4 | 8.8 |
| 361 | 63 | 119 | .525 | 16.6 | 8.7 |
| 362 | 115 | 206 | .562 | 27.1 | 15.3 |
| 369 | 136 | 249 | .549 | 13.7 | 7.5 |
| 371 | 165 | 352 | .467 | 89.9 | 42.0 |
| 372 | 171 | 520 | .330 | 44.5 | 14.7 |
| 381 | 93 | 228 | .408 | 11.8 | 4.8 |
| 382 | 99 | 226 | .437 | 12.0 | 5.3 |
| 383 | 145 | 352 | .413 | 28.0 | 11.6 |
| 384 | 166 | 458 | .364 | 40.6 | 14.7 |
| 385 | 65 | 155 | .421 | 6.2 | 2.6 |
| 390 | 75 | 161 | .468 | 7.9 | 3.7 |

TABLE 59--Continued

| Industry | Manufactured Direct Exports, 1974 (Millions of Pesos) | Total Use of Raw Materials, 1970 (Millions of Pesos) | Use of Foreign Raw Materials, 1970 (Millions of Pesos) | Foreign Raw Materials/ Total Raw Materials, 1970 |
|---|---|---|---|---|
| Total | 9,510 | 30,465 | 7,660 | .251 |
| 311-2 | 2,574 | 9,486 | 1,078 | .113 |
| 313 | 57 | 1,371 | 348 | .253 |
| 321 | 2,310 | 4,155 | 688 | .165 |
| 322 | 478 | 1,121 | 8 | .007 |
| 323 | 261 | 404 | 31 | .076 |
| 324 | 27 | 176 | 2 | .010 |
| 331 | 95 | 291 | 19 | .064 |
| 332 | 44 | 152 | 0 | .002 |
| 341 | 470 | 1,254 | 291 | .231 |
| 342 | 37 | 555 | 260 | .470 |
| 351 | 653 | 971 | 530 | .545 |
| 352 | 242 | 1,725 | 907 | .525 |
| 353 | 0 | 1,066 | 22 | .020 |
| 354 | 0 | 11 | 0 | .002 |
| 355 | 89 | 631 | 305 | .483 |
| 356 | 192 | 384 | 122 | .317 |
| 361 | 71 | 61 | 13 | .207 |
| 362 | 60 | 93 | 19 | .205 |
| 369 | 370 | 647 | 131 | .203 |
| 371 | 136 | 705 | 356 | .504 |
| 372 | 14 | 209 | 143 | .686 |
| 381 | 430 | 1,238 | 414 | .334 |
| 382 | 328 | 702 | 311 | .443 |
| 383 | 138 | 817 | 360 | .440 |
| 384 | 109 | 1,625 | 1,170 | .720 |
| 385 | 41 | 51 | 20 | .404 |
| 390 | 117 | 257 | 87 | .340 |

TABLE 60
421 PLANTS WITH DIRECT FOREIGN INVESTMENT: 1974 (SET F)
(Figures in Millions of Pesos)

| Industry | # of Plants | Gross Production | Value Added | Employment | Total Remuneration |
|---|---|---|---|---|---|
| Total | 421 | 72,358 | 30,043 | 127,821 | 8,883 |
| 311-2 | 51 | 8,251 | 2,694 | 10,778 | 742 |
| 313 | 2 | 381 | 189 | 1,294 | 63 |
| 321 | 34 | 14,523 | 5,930 | 34,418 | 2,323 |
| 322 | 9 | 452 | 188 | 3,303 | 132 |
| 323 | 1 | 321 | 94 | 622 | 35 |
| 324 | 2 | 189 | 81 | 827 | 24 |
| 331 | 5 | 460 | 254 | 1,880 | 69 |
| 332 | 2 | 49 | 15 | 242 | 7 |
| 341 | 20 | 5,946 | 2,089 | 5,797 | 666 |
| 342 | 6 | 212 | 136 | 1,033 | 54 |
| 351 | 46 | 8,788 | 3,731 | 5,578 | 446 |
| 352 | 63 | 6,453 | 3,346 | 12,289 | 992 |
| 353 | 7 | 986 | 349 | 407 | 63 |
| 354 | 2 | 6 | 4 | 8 | 0 |
| 355 | 6 | 2,953 | 1,261 | 6,459 | 442 |
| 356 | 8 | 1,649 | 783 | 2,936 | 143 |
| 361 | 2 | 99 | 59 | 771 | 29 |
| 362 | 7 | 1,095 | 628 | 3,658 | 232 |
| 369 | 20 | 2,715 | 1,545 | 5,446 | 384 |
| 371 | 8 | 2,287 | 904 | 3,881 | 247 |
| 372 | 5 | 851 | 313 | 1,407 | 88 |
| 381 | 39 | 2,891 | 1,224 | 7,007 | 406 |
| 382 | 24 | 1,020 | 470 | 2,686 | 180 |
| 383 | 25 | 3,093 | 1,307 | 6,223 | 424 |
| 384 | 11 | 6,215 | 2,217 | 6,724 | 432 |
| 385 | 7 | 126 | 49 | 428 | 19 |
| 390 | 9 | 310 | 168 | 1,228 | 59 |

TABLE 60--Continued

| Industry | National Managerial Personnel 1972 | Foreign Managerial Personnel 1972 | Office Workers 1972 | Laborers 1972 | Average 1973 |
|---|---|---|---|---|---|
| Total | 164 | 242 | 64 | 35 | 55 |
| 311-2 | 186 | 215 | 50 | 31 | 54 |
| 313 | 161 | 194 | 50 | 14 | 39 |
| 321 | 160 | 218 | 64 | 37 | 53 |
| 322 | 149 | 165 | 50 | 23 | 33 |
| 323 | 260 | 193 | 69 | 32 | 50 |
| 324 | 206 | 162 | 58 | 29 | 41 |
| 331 | 231 | 243 | 48 | 29 | 31 |
| 332 | 201 | 381 | 42 | 12 | 28 |
| 341 | 197 | 271 | 84 | 45 | 77 |
| 342 | 197 | 200 | 41 | 35 | 46 |
| 351 | 164 | 183 | 68 | 40 | 71 |
| 352 | 161 | 244 | 68 | 31 | 68 |
| 353 | 203 | 621 | 92 | 53 | 142 |
| 354 | 123 | --- | 59 | 23 | 48 |
| 355 | 183 | 414 | 92 | 41 | 58 |
| 356 | 157 | 150 | 47 | 24 | 39 |
| 361 | 56 | 57 | 33 | 16 | 28 |
| 362 | 177 | 112 | 67 | 39 | 49 |
| 369 | 163 | 384 | 65 | 44 | 59 |
| 371 | 232 | 202 | 57 | 36 | 54 |
| 372 | 188 | 272 | 61 | 34 | 50 |
| 381 | 152 | 218 | 49 | 31 | 46 |
| 382 | 128 | 449 | 52 | 29 | 58 |
| 383 | 150 | 211 | 68 | 34 | 53 |
| 384 | 150 | 159 | 63 | 31 | 55 |
| 385 | 138 | 173 | 41 | 20 | 44 |
| 390 | 144 | 234 | 52 | 17 | 40 |

TABLE 60--Continued

| Industry | 1972 Remuneration/ Personnel (Thousands of Pesos) | 1972 Per Capita Remuneration/Per Capita Value Added | 1972 Fixed Assets/ Remuneration | 1972 Value Added/ Fixed Assets | 1972 Fixed Assets/ Personnel (Thousands of Pesos) |
|---|---|---|---|---|---|
| Total | 48 | .32 | 1.75 | 1.75 | 80 |
| 311-2 | 46 | .26 | 1.5 | 2.5 | 69 |
| 313 | 35 | .12 | 3.0 | 3.3 | 92 |
| 321 | 45 | .34 | 1.7 | 1.7 | 78 |
| 322 | 32 | .46 | 0.6 | 3.6 | 20 |
| 323 | 42 | .51 | 0.6 | 3.1 | 27 |
| 324 | 37 | .54 | 0.6 | 3.2 | 22 |
| 331 | 37 | .44 | 2.0 | 1.1 | 75 |
| 332 | 25 | .76 | 2.3 | 0.6 | 50 |
| 341 | 64 | .36 | 3.3 | 0.8 | 209 |
| 342 | 42 | .48 | 1.4 | 1.5 | 58 |
| 351 | 59 | .24 | 2.9 | 1.4 | 175 |
| 352 | 59 | .30 | 0.7 | 4.9 | 40 |
| 353 | 123 | .08 | 5.8 | 2.2 | 712 |
| 354 | 42 | .18 | 6.0 | 1.3 | 173 |
| 355 | 54 | .39 | 1.0 | 2.3 | 59 |
| 356 | 35 | .32 | 2.9 | 1.0 | 101 |
| 361 | 20 | .42 | 3.3 | 0.7 | 63 |
| 362 | 47 | .40 | 1.7 | 1.4 | 81 |
| 369 | 53 | .35 | 3.2 | 0.9 | 173 |
| 371 | 45 | .41 | 2.0 | 1.2 | 90 |
| 372 | 45 | .47 | 1.7 | 1.2 | 77 |
| 381 | 43 | .45 | 1.4 | 1.6 | 59 |
| 382 | 51 | .44 | 1.1 | 2.0 | 58 |
| 383 | 52 | .46 | 1.3 | 1.7 | 66 |
| 384 | 45 | .23 | 1.5 | 2.9 | 67 |
| 385 | 33 | .34 | 1.1 | 2.7 | 37 |
| 390 | 29 | .28 | 1.1 | 2.0 | 50 |

TABLE 60-- Continued

| Industry | 1972 Value Added/ Personnel (Thousands | 1972 Production/ Personnel of Pesos) | 1972 Value Added/ Production | 1972 Produc- tion/ Plant (Millions | 1972 Value Added/ Plant Pesos) |
|---|---|---|---|---|---|
| Total | 149 | 338 | .44 | 84 | 37 |
| 311-2 | 177 | 487 | .36 | 89 | 32 |
| 313 | 282 | 370 | .76 | 14 | 10 |
| 321 | 134 | 268 | .50 | 234 | 116 |
| 322 | 70 | 126 | .56 | 33 | 18 |
| 323 | 82 | 250 | .33 | 156 | 50 |
| 324 | 69 | 136 | .51 | 51 | 26 |
| 331 | 84 | 164 | .51 | 55 | 28 |
| 332 | 33 | 79 | .42 | 56 | 23 |
| 341 | 179 | 539 | .33 | 131 | 43 |
| 342 | 88 | 170 | .52 | 193 | 10 |
| 351 | 241 | 617 | .39 | 58 | 23 |
| 352 | 197 | 386 | .51 | 64 | 33 |
| 353 | 1,592 | 3,585 | .44 | 214 | 95 |
| 354 | 231 | 2,116 | .11 | 39 | 42 |
| 355 | 139 | 281 | .49 | 241 | 119 |
| 356 | 108 | 240 | .45 | 65 | 29 |
| 361 | 48 | 74 | .65 | 22 | 14 |
| 362 | 117 | 188 | .62 | 68 | 42 |
| 369 | 151 | 296 | .51 | 73 | 37 |
| 371 | 110 | 290 | .38 | 105 | 40 |
| 372 | 95 | 273 | .35 | 73 | 25 |
| 381 | 96 | 196 | .49 | 31 | 15 |
| 382 | 117 | 237 | .49 | 31 | 15 |
| 383 | 112 | 287 | .39 | 56 | 21 |
| 384 | 194 | 637 | .30 | 170 | 51 |
| 385 | 98 | 218 | .45 | 21 | 10 |
| 390 | 102 | 186 | .55 | 18 | 10 |

TABLE 60--Continued

| Industry | 1974 Value Added/ Personnel (Thousands | 1974 Production/ Personnel of Pesos) | 1974 Value Added/ Production | 1974 Production /Plant (Millions | 1974 Value Added/ Plant of Pesos) |
|---|---|---|---|---|---|
| Total | 235 | 566 | .415 | 171.9 | 714.0 |
| 311-2 | 250 | 766 | .327 | 161.8 | 52.9 |
| 313 | 146 | 294 | .496 | 190.5 | 94.5 |
| 321 | 172 | 422 | .408 | 427.1 | 174.4 |
| 322 | 57 | 139 | .4416 | 50.2 | 20.9 |
| 323 | 151 | 516 | .293 | 321.0 | 94.0 |
| 324 | 98 | 229 | .429 | 94.5 | 40.5 |
| 331 | 135 | 245 | .552 | 92.0 | 50.8 |
| 332 | 62 | 202 | .306 | 24.5 | 7.5 |
| 341 | 360 | 1,026 | .351 | 297.3 | 104.5 |
| 342 | 132 | 205 | .642 | 35.3 | 22.7 |
| 351 | 669 | 1,575 | .425 | 191.0 | 81.1 |
| 352 | 272 | 525 | .519 | 102.4 | 53.1 |
| 353 | 857 | 2,423 | .354 | 140.9 | 49.9 |
| 354 | 500 | 750 | .667 | 3.0 | 2.0 |
| 355 | 195 | 457 | .427 | 492.2 | 210.2 |
| 356 | 267 | 562 | .475 | 206.1 | 97.9 |
| 361 | 77 | 128 | .596 | 49.5 | 29.5 |
| 362 | 172 | 299 | .574 | 156.4 | 89.7 |
| 369 | 284 | 499 | .569 | 135.8 | 77.3 |
| 371 | 233 | 589 | .395 | 285.9 | 113.0 |
| 372 | 222 | 605 | .368 | 170.2 | 62.6 |
| 381 | 175 | 413 | .423 | 74.1 | 31.4 |
| 382 | 175 | 380 | .461 | 42.5 | 19.6 |
| 383 | 210 | 497 | .423 | 123.7 | 52.3 |
| 384 | 330 | 924 | .357 | 565.0 | 210.5 |
| 385 | 114 | 294 | .389 | 18.0 | 7.0 |
| 391 | 137 | 252 | .542 | 34.4 | 18.7 |

TABLE 60--Continued

| Industry | Manufactured Direct Exports 1974 | Total Use of Raw Materials 1970 | Use of Foreign Raw Materials 1970 | Foreign Raw Materials/ Total Raw Materials 1970 |
|---|---|---|---|---|
| | (MILLIONS OF COLOMBIAN PESOS) | | | |
| Total | 4,722 | 12,149 | 4,548 | .374 |
| 311-2 | 473 | 1,762 | 226 | .128 |
| 313 | 0 | 4 | 1 | .176 |
| 321 | 1,535 | 2,552 | 552 | .216 |
| 322 | 97 | 109 | 0 | .001 |
| 323 | 48 | 71 | 5 | .070 |
| 324 | 2 | 28 | 0 | .017 |
| 331 | 40 | 90 | 17 | .191 |
| 332 | 4 | 3 | 0 | .000 |
| 341 | 287 | 1,011 | 273 | .270 |
| 342 | 4 | 17 | 10 | .551 |
| 351 | 562 | 874 | 509 | .582 |
| 352 | 211 | 981 | 601 | .612 |
| 353 | 0 | 530 | 14 | .027 |
| 354 | 0 | 59 | 16 | .262 |
| 355 | 85 | 524 | 259 | .495 |
| 356 | 142 | 152 | 53 | .350 |
| 361 | 25 | 6 | 1 | .151 |
| 362 | 43 | 82 | 5 | .066 |
| 369 | 357 | 310 | 58 | .187 |
| 371 | 72 | 471 | 273 | .578 |
| 372 | 10 | 148 | 105 | .706 |
| 381 | 354 | 447 | 241 | .537 |
| 382 | 97 | 246 | 158 | .644 |
| 383 | 121 | 533 | 287 | .537 |
| 384 | 54 | 1,053 | 829 | .787 |
| 385 | 19 | 39 | 21 | .543 |
| 391 | 18 | 47 | 33 | .708 |

TABLE 61
DOMESTIC PLANTS 1974: SET D

| Industry | # of Plants | Gross Production, 1974 (MILLIONS OF PESOS) | Value Added, 1974 (MILLIONS OF PESOS) | Employment 1974 |
|---|---|---|---|---|
| Total | 5,645 | 94,499 | 37,237 | 320,353 |
| 311-2 | 1,062 | 29,126 | 6,387 | 49,885 |
| 313 | 120 | 11,719 | 7,641 | 18,380 |
| 321 | 389 | 8,921 | 3,736 | 40,200 |
| 322 | 597 | 4,372 | 1,661 | 36,651 |
| 323 | 85 | 1,419 | 406 | 5,702 |
| 324 | 185 | 645 | 255 | 6,501 |
| 331 | 246 | 911 | 404 | 6,750 |
| 332 | 215 | 775 | 362 | 7,432 |
| 341 | 126 | 1,548 | 468 | 5,062 |
| 342 | 292 | 3,326 | 1,425 | 15,956 |
| 351 | 50 | 2,263 | 1,067 | 5,297 |
| 352 | 210 | 4,250 | 1,569 | 11,458 |
| 353 | 6 | 3,495 | 1,498 | 3,642 |
| 354 | 7 | 54 | 21 | 344 |
| 355 | 66 | 646 | 245 | 2,740 |
| 356 | 155 | 1,841 | 646 | 7,626 |
| 361 | 34 | 497 | 254 | 4,217 |
| 362 | 41 | 208 | 104 | 2,682 |
| 369 | 329 | 2,077 | 1,084 | 13,834 |
| 371 | 43 | 2,297 | 1,238 | 9,136 |
| 372 | 21 | 305 | 68 | 816 |
| 381 | 535 | 3,865 | 1,534 | 22,597 |
| 382 | 262 | 2,421 | 1,035 | 12,537 |
| 383 | 139 | 1,504 | 592 | 6,841 |
| 384 | 181 | 1,577 | 616 | 10,306 |
| 385 | 46 | 202 | 89 | 1,689 |
| 391 | 159 | 1,014 | 452 | 7,016 |

TABLE 61—Continued

| Industry | 1974 Value Added/ Personnel (THOUSANDS | 1974 Production/ Personnel OF PESOS) | 1974 Value Added/ Production | 1974 Production/ Plant (MILLIONS OF | 1974 Value Added/ Plant PESOS) |
|---|---|---|---|---|---|
| Total | 116.2 | 295.0 | .394 | 16.7 | 6.6 |
| 311-2 | 128.0 | 583.9 | .219 | 27.4 | 6.0 |
| 313 | 415.7 | 637.6 | .652 | 97.7 | 63.7 |
| 321 | 92.9 | 221.9 | .419 | 22.9 | 9.6 |
| 322 | 45.3 | 119.3 | .380 | 7.3 | 2.8 |
| 323 | 71.2 | 248.9 | .286 | 16.7 | 4.8 |
| 324 | 39.2 | 99.2 | .395 | 3.5 | 1.4 |
| 331 | 59.9 | 135.0 | .443 | 3.7 | 1.6 |
| 332 | 48.7 | 104.3 | .467 | 3.6 | 1.7 |
| 341 | 92.5 | 305.8 | .302 | 12.3 | 3.7 |
| 342 | 89.3 | 208.4 | .428 | 11.4 | 4.9 |
| 351 | 201.4 | 427.2 | .471 | 45.3 | 21.3 |
| 352 | 136.9 | 370.9 | .369 | 20.2 | 7.5 |
| 353 | 411.3 | 959.6 | .429 | 582.5 | 249.7 |
| 354 | 61.0 | 157.0 | .389 | 7.7 | 3.0 |
| 355 | 89.4 | 235.8 | .379 | 9.8 | 3.7 |
| 356 | 84.7 | 241.4 | .351 | 11.9 | 4.2 |
| 361 | 60.2 | 117.9 | .511 | 14.6 | 7.5 |
| 362 | 38.8 | 77.6 | .500 | 5.1 | 2.5 |
| 369 | 78.4 | 150.1 | .522 | 6.3 | 3.3 |
| 371 | 135.5 | 251.4 | .539 | 53.4 | 28.8 |
| 372 | 83.3 | 373.8 | .223 | 14.5 | 3.2 |
| 381 | 67.9 | 171.0 | .397 | 7.2 | 2.9 |
| 382 | 82.6 | 193.1 | .428 | 9.2 | 4.0 |
| 383 | 86.5 | 219.9 | .394 | 10.8 | 4.3 |
| 384 | 59.8 | 153.0 | .391 | 8.7 | 3.4 |
| 385 | 52.7 | 119.6 | .441 | 4.4 | 1.9 |
| 391 | 64.4 | 144.5 | .446 | 6.4 | 2.8 |

TABLE 61--Continued

| Industry | Manufactured Direct Exports | Total Use of Raw Materials | Use of Foreign Raw Materials | Foreign Raw Materials/ Total Raw 1970 |
|---|---|---|---|---|
| | (MILLIONS OF COLOMBIAN PESOS, 1974) | | | |
| Total | 4,788 | 18,362 | 3,124 | .170 |
| 311-2 | 2,101 | 7,724 | 852 | .110 |
| 313 | 57 | 1,367 | 347 | .254 |
| 321 | 775 | 1,603 | 136 | .085 |
| 322 | 381 | 1,012 | 8 | .008 |
| 323 | 213 | 333 | 26 | .078 |
| 324 | 25 | 148 | 2 | .014 |
| 331 | 54 | 201 | 2 | .010 |
| 332 | 40 | 149 | 0 | .000 |
| 341 | 183 | 243 | 18 | .074 |
| 342 | 33 | 538 | 250 | .465 |
| 351 | 91 | 97 | 21 | .216 |
| 352 | 31 | 744 | 306 | .411 |
| 353 | 0 | 536 | 8 | .015 |
| 354 | 0 | 0 | a | a |
| 355 | 4 | 107 | 46 | .430 |
| 356 | 50 | 232 | 69 | .297 |
| 361 | 46 | 55 | 12 | .218 |
| 362 | 17 | 11 | a | a |
| 369 | 13 | 337 | 73 | .217 |
| 371 | 64 | 234 | 83 | .355 |
| 372 | 4 | 61 | 38 | .623 |
| 381 | 76 | 791 | 173 | .219 |
| 382 | 231 | 456 | 153 | .336 |
| 383 | 17 | 284 | 73 | .257 |
| 384 | 55 | 572 | 341 | .596 |
| 385 | 22 | 12 | 1 | .083 |
| 391 | 99 | 210 | 54 | .257 |

(a) Because of inconsistencies in the original data, these industrial groupings may not be comparable.

TABLE 62
421 DFI PLANTS AS A PERCENTAGE OF
TOTAL MANUFACTURING, 1974
(SET F / SET N X 100)

| Industry | Production | Value Added | Employment |
|---|---|---|---|
| Total | 43.37% | 44.65% | 28.52 |
| 311-2 | 22.08 | 29.67 | 17.77 |
| 313 | 3.15 | 2.41 | 6.58 |
| 321 | 61.95 | 61.35 | 46.13 |
| 322 | 9.37 | 10.17 | 8.27 |
| 323 | 18.45 | 18.80 | 9.84 |
| 324 | 22.66 | 24.11 | 11.29 |
| 331 | 33.55 | 38.60 | 21.78 |
| 332 | 5.95 | 3.98 | 3.15 |
| 341 | 79.34 | 81.70 | 53.38 |
| 342 | 5.99 | 8.71 | 6.08 |
| 351 | 79.52 | 77.76 | 51.29 |
| 352 | 60.29 | 68.08 | 51.75 |
| 353 | 22.00 | 18.90 | 10.05 |
| 354 | 10.00 | 16.00 | 2.27 |
| 355 | 82.05 | 83.73 | 70.21 |
| 356 | 47.25 | 54.79 | 27.80 |
| 361 | 16.61 | 18.85 | 15.45 |
| 362 | 84.04 | 85.79 | 57.70 |
| 369 | 56.66 | 58.77 | 28.25 |
| 371 | 49.89 | 42.20 | 29.81 |
| 372 | 73.62 | 82.15 | 63.29 |
| 381 | 42.79 | 44.38 | 23.67 |
| 382 | 29.64 | 31.23 | 17.64 |
| 383 | 67.28 | 68.83 | 47.63 |
| 384 | 79.76 | 78.26 | 39.48 |
| 385 | 38.41 | 35.51 | 20.22 |
| 391 | 23.41 | 27.10 | 14.90 |

## LIST OF WORKS CITED


Adams, Frederick.
1914. Conquest of the Tropics. Garden City, N.J.: Doubleday, Page and Co.

Adelman, Irma and Cynthia Taft Morris.
1974. "Who Benefits from Economic Development?" In Organization for Economic Cooperation and Development, ed., Planning, Income Distribution, Private Foreign Investment. Paris: OECD.

Aldana, Efrain; Louis Ignacio Aguilar; Catalina H. de Trujillo; and Ernesto Parra.
1977. Las Multinacionales en el Mundo y en Colombia. Bogota: Centro de Investigacion y Educacion Popular.

Alschuler, Lawrence.
1976. "Satellization and Stagnation in Latin America." International Studies Quarterly 20 (March): 39-82.

ANDI (Asociacion Nacional de Industriales).
1976. La Industria Colombiana, 1975. Bogota: Asociacion Nacional de Industrialies.

1977. La Economia Colombiana 1976. Medellin: Asociacion Nacional de Industriales.

Armendariz, Amadeo.
1977. "Inversion Extranjera y Saqueo Nacional." In Amadeo Armendariz and T. Varela, eds., Imperialismo y Dependencia Economica en Colombia. Bogota: Ediciones Suramerica.

Arrubla, Mario.
1977. Estudios sobre el Subdessarrollo Colombiano. 9th ed. Medellin: Libros de Bolsilla de la Carreta.

Banco de la Republica, Colombia.
1974a. Financiamiento de la Industria Manufacturera con Inversion Extranjera Directa. Bogota: Banco de la Republica.

1974b. Importaciones y Balanza Comercial de la Industria Manufacturera con Inversion Extranjera Directa. Bogota: Banco de la Republica.

1977. Registro de Inversiones Extranjeras.

Barnet, Richard J.
1973-4. "Comment." Foreign Policy 13 (Winter): 118-22.

Barrett, Gerald and Bernard Bass.
1976. Handbook of Industrial and Organizational Psychology. Chicago: Rand McNally.

Bass, Bernard and Philip Burger.
1979. Assessment of Managers: An International Comparison. New York: The Free Press.

---------- and Edward Ryterband.
1979. Organizational Psychology. 2nd ed. Boston: Allyn and Bacon.

Behrman, Jack.
1972. "International Divestment: Panacea or Pitfall?" In A. Kapoor and Phillip Grub, eds., The Multinational Enterprise in Transition. Princeton: The Darwin Press.

Bennett, Douglas and Kenneth Sharpe.
1976. "The Logic of Mexicanization." Paper presented to the Continuing Working Group on Latin America, Social Science Research Council. New York.

Berry, R. Albert.
1975. "Open Unemployment as a Social Problem in Urban Colombia: Myth and Reality." Economic Development and Cultural Change 23 (Janurary): 276-291.

no date a. "A Descriptive History of Colombian Industrial Development in the Twentieth Century." (mimeographed).

no date b. "Summary and Conclusions on the Experience of Industrialization in Colombia." (mimeographed).

---------------and Miguel Urrutia.
1976. Income Distribution in Colombia. New Haven: Yale University Press.

1977. "Import Substitution and Beyond: Colombia." World Development 5 (#1-2): 89-109.

Biersteker, Thomas.
1978. Distortion or Development? Contending Perspectives on the Multinational Corporation. Cambridge, Mass.: MIT Press.

Blutstein, Howard.
1977. Area Handbook for Colombia. 3rd ed. Washington, D.C.: U.S. Government Printing Office.

Bolsa de Bogota.
1977. *Manual del Mercado Bursatil 1977.* Bogota: Bolsa de Bogota.

Bornschier, Volker, Christopher Chase-Dunn, and Richard Rubinson.
1978. "Cross-National Evidence of the Effects of Foreign Investment and Aid on Economic Growth and Inequality." (mimeo)

Boyce, James and Francois Lombard.
1976. *Colombia's Treatment of Foreign Banks: A Precedent-Setting Case?* Washington, D.C.: American Enterprise Institute.

Brazilian Government Trade Bureau.
1975. *Guide to Investing in Brazil.* New York: Brazilian Government Trade Bureau.

Business International Corporation.
1970. *Nationalism in Latin America: The Challenge and Corporate Response.* New York: Business International Corporation.

1977. *Investing, Licensing and Trading Conditions Abroad: Colombia.* New York: Business International Corporation.

Camacho Guizado, Alvaro.
1977. *Capital Extranjero: Subdessarrollo Colombiano.* 2nd ed. Bogota: Punta de Lanza.

Cardoso, Fernando Henrique.
1970. "The Industrial Elite." In Seymour Martin Lipset and Aldo Solari, eds., *Elites in Latin America.* New York: Oxford University Press.

Champion, Dean.
1970. *Basic Statistics for Social Research.* no place: Chandler Publishing Company.

Chase-Dunn, Christopher.
1975. "The Effects of International Dependence on Development and Inequality: A Cross-National Study." *American Sociological Review* 40 (December): 720-738.

Chu, David.
1977. *The Great Depression and Industrialization in Colombia.* Santa Monica, Calif.: Rand Corporation.

Chudson, Walter.
1975. "Multinational Enterprises in Developing Countries: Some Issues in the Manufacturing Sector." In Patrick Boarman and Hans Schollhammer, eds., Multinational Corporations and Governments. New York: Praeger Publishers.

Clark, John.
1975. Economic Institutions and Human Welfare. New York: Alfred A. Knopf.

Cline, William
1972. Potential Effects of Income Redistribution on Economic Growth: Latin American Cases. New York: Praeger Publishers.

Cohen, Benjamin.
1973. "Comparative Behavior of Foreign and Domestic Export Firms in a Developing Economy." The Review of Economics and Statistics 40 (May): 190-7.

Commission of the Cartegena Agreement.
1973. "Common Regime of Treatment of Foreign Capital and of Trademarks, Patents, Licenses, and Royalties." In U.S. House of Representatives Committee on Foreign Affairs, ed., Inter-American Relations. Washington, D.C.: U.S. Government Printing Office.

Consejo Nacional de Politica Economica y Social, Colombia.
1972. Resolucion Numero 17 de 1972.

Constantino, Renato.
1978. Neocolonial Identity and Counter-Consciousness Essays in Cultural Decolonization. Edited by Istvan Meszaros. White Plains, N.Y.: M.E. Sharpe.

Cooper, Richard.
1977. "Speech: Investment Flow in the International Economic System." Washington, D.C.: U.S. Department of State (July 27).

Currie, Lauchlin.
1950. The Basics of a Development Program for Colombia. Baltimore: Johns Hopkins Press.

DANE (Departamento Administrativo Nacional de Estadistica, Colombia).
1971. "Inversion Extranjera en Colombia." Boletin Mensual de Estadistica 239 (June): 51-90.

1976a. Industria Manufacturera 1974. Bogota: DANE.

1976b. "Inversion Extranjera en la Industria Colombiana: I." Boletin Mensual de Estadistica. 302 (September): 111-223.

DeCarvalho, Livio.
1977. "Comparative Performance of Domestic and Foreign Firms in Latin America." Ph.D. Dissertation, Cornell University.

Diaz-Alejandro, Carlos.
1976. Foreign Trade Regimes and Economic Development: Colombia. New York: Columbia University Press.

Diebold, John.
1973. "Why Be Scared of Them?" Foreign Policy 12 (Fall): 79-95.

Dix, Robert.
1971. Colombia: The Political Dimensions of Change. New Haven: Yale University Press.

DNP (Departamento Nacional de Planeacion, Colombia).
1973. Formulario para Solicitud de Inversion Extranjera Directa. Bogota: DNP.

1977. Interviews with employees (November-December).

Edfelt, Ralph.
1975. "Direct Foreign Investment in a Developing Economy: Toward Evaluating the Human Resource Development Impact in Brazil." Ph.D. Dissertation, University of California, Los Angeles.

Erb, Guy and Valeriana Kallab.
1975. Beyond Dependency: The Developing World Speaks Out. Washington, D.C.: Overseas Development Council.

Evans, Peter.
1971. "National Autonomy and Economic Development: Critical Perspectives on Multinational Corporations in Poor Countries." In Robert Keohane and Joseph Nye, Jr., eds., Transnational Relations and World Politics. Cambridge, Mass.: Harvard University Press.

Fairchild, Loretta.
1977. "Performance and Technology of United States and National Firms in Mexico." Journal of Development Studies 14 (October): 14-34.

Fajnzylber, Fernando.
1975. "Las Empresas Transnacionales y el Sistema Industrial de Mexico." Trimestre Economica 42 (October-December): 903-931.

Falero, Frank.
1974. "Foreign Investment and the Balance of Payments." Inter-American Economic Affairs 28 (Autumn): 77-85.

Fedesarrollo.
1976. "Colombia." Coyuntura Andina 1 (October).

Forsythe, David and Robert Solomon.
1977. "Nationality of Ownership and Choice of Technique in Manufacturing in a Less Developed Country." Oxford Economic Papers 22: 265-278.

Freeman, Roger.
1968. Socialism and Private Enterprise in Equatorial Asia: The Case of Malaysia and Indonesia. Stanford: The Hoover Institution on War, Revolution, and Peace.

Freire, Paulo.
no date. Pedagogy of the Oppressed. Translated by Myra Bergman Ramos. New York: Herder and Herder.

Gaitan, Jorge Eliecer.
1972. 1928: La Massacre en las Bananeras. 2nd ed. Bogota: Los Comuneros.

Garcia Marquez, Gabriel.
1971. One Hundred Years of Solitude. Translated by Gregory Rabassa. New York: Avon Books.

Geraffi, Gary.
1978. "Drug Firms and Dependency in Mexico: The Case of the Steroid Hormone Industry." International Organization 32 (Winter): 237-86.

Gobalet, Jeanne and Larry Diamond.
1979. "Effects of Investment Dependence on Economic Growth: The Role of Internal Structural Characteristics and Periods in the World Economy." International Studies Quarterly 23 (September): 412-444.

Haire, M., E. Ghiselli and L. Porter.
1966. Managerial Thinking: An International Study. New York: Wiley.

Hayter, Teresa.
1971. Aid as Imperialism. Baltimore: Penguin Books.

Hirschman, Albert.
1971. A Bias for Hope: Essays on Development and Latin America. New Haven: Yale University Press.

Ingles, Jerry and Loretta Fairchild.
1977. "Evaluating the Impact of Foreign Investment: Methodology and Evidence from Mexico, Colombia, and Brazil." Latin American Research Review 12 (#3): 57-70.

Inter-American Economic Affairs.
1971. "How Will Multinational Firms React to the Andean Pact's Decision 24?" Inter-American Economic Affairs 25 (Autumn): 55-65.

International Labor Office.
1971. Towards Full Employment: A Programme for Colombia. Geneva: International Labor Office.

1976. Wages and Working Conditions in Multinational Enterprises. Geneva: International Labor Office.

Iyanda, Olukunle.
1975. "Impact of Foreign Direct Investment in Manufacturing on the Nigerian Economy." Ph.D. Dissertation, New York University.

Jacoby, Neil H.
1970. "The Multinational Corporation." Center Magazine 3 (May/June): 37-55.

Jolly, Richard.
1974. "International Dimensions." In Hollis Chenery, et. al., eds., Redistribution with Growth. London: Oxford University Press.

Joshi, Vijay.
1976. "Two-Gap Analysis." In Gerald Meier, ed., Leading Issues in Economic Development. 3rd ed. New York: Oxford University Press.

Kepner, Charles and Jay Soothill.
1935. The Banana Empire: A Case Study of Economic Imperialism. New York: The Vanguard Press.

Kierans, Eric.
1973. "The Cosmocorporation: An Unsympathetic View." In H.R. Halho, et. al. eds. Nationalism and the Multinational Enterprise. Dobbs Ferry, N.Y.: Oceanea Publications.

Koopman, Georg.
1975. "Foreign Enterprises in Colombia." Intereconomics 11: 349-352.

Lall, Sanjaya and Paul Streeten.
1977. Foreign Investment, Transnationals and Developing Countries. Boulder, Colorado: Westview Press.

Latin American Newsletters.
1977. Latin America Special Report: Colombia. (August).

Leys, Colin.
1975. Underdevelopment in Kenya: The Political Economy of Neo-Colonialism. Berkeley: University of California Press.

Lin, Steven.
1978. "Comparative Quality of Life." in N. M. Kamrany ed. The New Economics of Less Developed Countries. Boulder: Westview Press.

Little, Ian and J. Mirlees.
1974. Project Appraisal and Planning for Developing Countries. London: Heinemann Education Books.

Lipman, Aaron.
1969. The Colombian Entrepreneur in Bogota. Coral Gables: University of Miami Press.

Lombard, Francois.
1978. "Screening Foreign Direct Investment in LDCs: Empirical Findings of the Colombian Case (1967-1975)." Journal of International Business Studies 9 (Winter): 66-80.

1979. The Foreign Investment Screening Process in LDCs: The Case of Colombia, 1967-1975. Boulder: Westview Press.

Lopez Arias, Cesar.
1977. Empresas Multinacionales. Bogota: Tercer Mundo.

McGowan, Patrick and Dale Smith.
1978. "Economic Dependency in Black Africa: An Analysis of Competing Theories." International Organization 32: 179-235.

McGreevey, William.
1971. An Economic History of Colombia, 1845-1930. Cambridge, England: Cambridge University Press.

Mason, R. Hal.
1973. "Some Observations on the Choice of Technology by Multinational Firms in Developing Countries." Review of Economics and Statistics 55: 349-55.

Matter, Konrad.
1977. Inversiones Extranjeras en la Economia Colombiana. Medellin: Ediciones Nombre Nuevo.

Maullin, Richard.
1972. "The Colombia-IMF Disagreement of November-December 1966: An Interpretation of Its Place in Colombian Politics." In Yale Ferguson, ed., Contemporary Inter-American Relations. Englewood Cliffs, N.J.: Prentice-Hall.

May, Herbert.
no date. The Role of Foreign Investment in Latin America: Some Considerations and Definitions. New York: Fund for Multinational Management Education.

May, Stacy and Galo Plaza.
1958. The United Fruit Company in Latin America. Washington, D.C.: National Planning Association.

Montana Cuellar, Diego.
no date. Colombia: Pais Real o Pais Formal? Bogota: Editorial Latina.

Morawetz, David.
1981. Why the Emperor's New Clothes Are Not Made in Colombia. New York: Oxford University Press.

Moreno, Felix.
1976. "Application of Colombian Technology Legislation." In Fernando Robles ed. The Andean Common Market: Management Implications of Application of Technology Legislation. New York: Fund for Multinational Management Education.

Morgenstern, Richard and Ronald Muller.
1974. "Multinational Corporations and Balance of Payments Impacts in LDCs: An Econometric Analysis of Export Pricing Behavior." Kyklos 27 (#2): 304-321.

1976. "Multinational Versus Local Corporations in LDCs: An Econometric Analysis of Export Performance in Latin America." Southern Economic Journal 42 (January): 399-406.

Muller, Ronald E.
1973-4. "Poverty Is the Product." Foreign Policy 13 (Winter): 71-103.

Myrdal, Gunnar.
1970. The Challenge of World Poverty: A World Anti-Poverty Program in Outline. New York: Vintage Books.

Mytelka, Lynn.
1978. "Technological Dependence in the Andean Group." International Organization 32 (Winter): 101-139.

Negandhi, Anant.
1974. "Cross-Cultural Management Studies: Too Many Conclusions, Not Enough Conceptualization." Management International Review 14: 59-67.

OAS (Organization of American States).
1975. Situacion Economica, Principales Problemas y Perspectivas de Desarrollo de Colombia. Washington, D.C.: OAS.

Petras, James and Thomas Cook.
1973a. "Dependency and the Industrial Bourgeoisie: Attitudes of Argentine Executives toward Foreign Economic Investment and U.S. Policy." In James Petras, ed., Latin America: From Dependence to Revolution. New York: John Wiley and Sons.

1973b. "Politics in a Nondemocratic State: The Argentine Industrial Elite." In James Petras, ed., Latin America: From Dependence to Revolution. New York: John Wiley and Sons.

Pohlman, Randolph, James Ang and Syed Ali.
1976. "Policies of Multinational Firms: A Survey." Business Horizons 19 (December): 14-8.

Poitras, Guy.
1974. "Mexico's 'New' Foreign Policy." Inter-American Economic Affairs 28 (Winter): 59-77.

Presidente de Colombia.
1967. Decreto Ley 444 de 1967.

1973. Decreto Numero 1900 de 1973.

1977. Decreto Numero 170 de 1977.

Randall, Stephen.
1977. The Diplomacy of Modernization: Colombian-American Relations, 1920-1940. Toronto: University of Toronto Press.

Ray, James Lee and Thomas Webster.
1978. "Dependency and Economic Growth in Latin America." International Studies Quarterly 22 (September): 409-434.

Reuber, Grant.
1974. "Private Foreign Investment in Less Developed Countries." In Organization of Economic Cooperation and Development, ed. Planning, Income Distribution, Private Foreign Investment. Paris: OECD.

Rippy, James Fred.
1947. Latin America and the Industrial Age. New York: G.P. Putnam's Sons.

Rodriguez Acosta, Hugo.
1973. Elementos Criticos para una Nueva Interpretacion de la Historia Colombiana. 5th ed. Bogota: Editorial Tupac-Amaru Ltda.

Ronen, Simcha and Allen I. Kraut.
1977. "Similarities among Countries Based on Employee Work Values and Attitudes." Columbia Journal of World Business 12 (Summer): 89-96.

Rood, Leslie.
1976. "Nationalization and Indigenization in Africa." Journal of Modern African Studies 14 (September): 427-47.

Rubinson, Richard.
1976. "The World-Economy and the Distribution of Income Within States: A Cross-National Study." American Sociological Review 41 (August): 638-659.

Russett, Bruce and Elizabeth Hanson.
1975. Interest and Ideology: The Foreign Policy Beliefs of American Businessmen. San Francisco: W.H. Freeman and Company.

Salinas, Raquel and Leena Paldan.
1979. "Culture in the Process of Dependent Development: Theoretical Perspectives." In Kaarle Nordenstreng and Herbert Schiller, eds., National Sovereignty and International Communication: A Reader. Norwood, N.J.: Ablex Publishing.

Samuelson, Paul.
1970. Economics. 8th ed. New York: McGraw Hill Book Company.

Sauvant, Karl.
1979. "Sociocultural Emancipation." In Kaarle Nordenstreng and Herbert Schiller, eds., National Sovereignty and International Communication: A Reader. Norwood, N.J.: Ablex Publishing.

Schmidt, Steffan.
1971. "Consumer Nationalism and Development in Colombia: Preliminary Observations on Its Significance." University of Arizona, Institute of Government Research Series No. 5.

Scitovsky, Tibor.
1977. The Joyless Economy: An Inquiry into Human Satisfaction and Dissatisfaction. New York: Oxford University Press.

Sharpless, Richard.
1978. Gaitan of Colombia: A Political Biography. Pittsburgh: University of Pittsburgh Press.

Sheahan, John.
1968. "Imports, Investment, and Growth--Colombia." In Gustav Papanek, ed., Development Policy--Theory and Practice. Cambridge, Mass.: Harvard University Press.

Sherman, Gail.
1973. "Colombian Political Bases of the Andean Pact Statute on Foreign Capital: National Influences on International Regulation of Foreign Investment." Journal of Inter-American Studies and World Affairs 15 (February): 102-121.

Silva, Jaime.
1976. "Direct Foreign Investment in the Manufacturing Sector of Colombia." Ph.D. Dissertation, Northwestern University.

Silva Colmenares, Julio.
1977. Los Verdaderos Duenos del Pais: Oligarquia y Monopolios en Colombia. 2nd ed. Bogota: Fondo Editorial Suramerica.

Sirota, David and Michael Greenwood.
1971. "Understanding Your Overseas Work Force." Harvard Business Review 49 (January-February): 53-60.

Smetanka, John.
1977. "Political Socialization in the Multinational Corporation: The Impact of Multinational Business on the International Orientations of Host-Country Executives." (Paper presented at the annual meeting of the International Studies Assocation, March 17).

Sorpa, Miguel.
1976. Neoimperialismo y Subdesarrollo Colombiano. Bogota: Fundacion Centro de Investigacion y Educacion Popular.

Tambunlertchai, Somsak.
1976. "Foreign Direct Investment in Thailand's Manufacturing Industries." Ph.D. Dissertation, Duke University.

Thoumi, Francisco.
no date. "Plant Size, Factor Proportions and Efficiency in Colombian Industry." (mimeo).

Tironi, Ernesto.
1978. "Politicas frente al Capital Extranjero en la Integracion Andina." Trimestre Economico 45 (Noviembre-Diciembre): 965-996.

United Nations.
1955. Foreign Capital in Latin America. New York: United Nations.

USDC (United States Department of Commerce).
1976. "Marketing in the Philippines." Overseas Business Reports (March).

1977a. "Marketing in Indonesia." Overseas Business Reports (March).

1977b. "Marketing in Malaysia." Overseas Business Reports (January).

1977c. "Marketing in Mexico." Overseas Business Reports (March).

1977d. Survey of Current Business 57 (February).

USDS (United States Department of State).
1977a. "Colombia." Foreign Economic Trends. (May).

1977b. The Planetary Product in 1975. Washington, D.C.: Department of State.

US FBIS (United States, Foreign Broadcast Information Service).
1976. FBIS Latin America. (22 October).

USIA (United States Information Agency Office of Research).
1971. Opinions Regarding Foreign Investment in Colombia. (USIA Report R-34-71 of December 27).

1977. Colombian Elite Attitudes Toward Foreign Investment and Related Issues. (USIA Report R-4-77 of March 7).

Urrutia, Miguel.
1969. The Development of the Colombian Labor Movement. New Haven: Yale University Press.

Vaitsos, Constantine.
1973. "Foreign Investment Policies and Economic Development in Latin America." Journal of World Trade Law 7 (November-December): 619-665.

1974a. "Employment Effects of Foreign Direct Investments in Developing Countries." In Edgar Edwards, ed., Employment in Developing Nations. New York: Columbia University Press.

1974b. Intercountry Income Distribution and Transnational Enterprises. Oxford: Clarendon Press.

Vaupel, James and Joan Cuhran.
1969. The Making of Multinational Enterprise. Boston: Harvard School of Business Adminsitration.

Vernon, Raymond.
1973-4. "Does Society Also Profit?" Foreign Policy 13 (Winter): 103-118.

Weisner Duran, Eduardo.
no date. "Control Personal de la Economia Colombiana." Centro de Estudios sobre Desarrollo Economico Monografia No. 6. Bogota: Universidad de los Andes.

Weisskopf, Richard.
1976. "Income Distribution and Economic Growth in Puerto Rico, Argentina, and Mexico." In Alejandro Foxley, ed., Income Distribution in Latin America. Cambridge, England: Cambridge University Press.

Weisskopf, Walter.
1977. "The Moral Predicament of the Market Economy." In Gerald Dworkin, Gordon Bermant, and Peter Brown, eds., Markets and Morals. New York: John Wiley and Sons.

Wells, Louis.
1973. "Economic Man and Engineering Man: Choice of Technology in a Low Wage Country." Public Policy 21: 319-42.

Whyte, George.
1949. Industry in Latin America. 2nd ed. New York: Columbia University Press.

Wilkins, Mira.
1970. The Emergence of Multinational Enterprise. Cambridge, Mass.: Harvard University Press.

1974. The Maturing of Multinational Enterprise. Cambridge, Mass.: Harvard University Press.

Winkler, Max.
1928. Investments of United States Capital in Latin America. Boston: World Peace Foundation.

Wurfel, Seymour W.
1965. Foreign Enterprise in Colombia: Laws and Policies. Chapel Hill: University of North Carolina Press.

Zschock, Dieter.
1977. "Inequality in Colombia." Current History. 72 (February): 68-72 & 86.

MONOGRAPHS IN INTERNATIONAL STUDIES

ISBN Prefix 0-89680-

Africa Series

16. Weisfelder, Richard F. THE BASOTHO MONARCHY: A Spent Force or Dynamic Political Factor? 1972. 106pp.
049-0 (82-91676) $ 7.00*

19. Huntsberger, Paul E., compiler. HIGHLAND MOSAIC: A Critical Anthology of Ethiopian Literature in English. 1973. 122pp.
052-0 (82-91700) $ 7.00*

21. Silberfein, Marilyn. CONSTRAINTS ON THE EXPANSION OF COMMERCIAL AGRICULTURE: Iringa District, Tanzania. 1974. 51pp.
054-7 (82-91726) $ 4.50*

22. Pieterse, Cosmo. ECHO AND CHORUSES: "Ballad of the Cells" and Selected Shorter Poems. 1974. 66pp.
055-5 (82-91734) $ 5.00*

23. Thom, Derrick J. THE NIGER-NIGERIA BOUNDARY: A Study of Ethnic Frontiers and a Colonial Boundary. 1975. 50pp.
056-3 (82-91742) $ 4.75*

24. Baum, Edward, compiler. A COMPREHENSIVE PERIODICAL BIBLIOGRAPHY OF NIGERIA, 1960-1970. 1975. 250pp.
057-1 (82-91759) $13.00*

25. Kircherr, Eugene C. ABBYSSINIA TO ZIMBABWE: A Guide to the Political Units of Africa in the Period 1947-1978. 1979. 3rd ed. 80pp.
100-4 (82-91908) $ 8.00*

27. Fadiman, Jeffrey A. MOUNTAIN WARRIORS: The Pre-Colonial Meru of Mt. Kenya. 1976. 82pp.
060-1 (82-91783) $ 4.75*

32. Wright, Donald R. THE EARLY HISTORY OF THE NIUMI: Settlement and Foundation of a Mandinka State on the Gambia River. 1977. 122pp.
064-4 (82-91833) $ 8.00*

36. Fadiman, Jeffrey A. THE MOMENT OF CONQUEST: Meru, Kenya, 1907. 1979. 70pp.
081-4 (82-91874) $ 5.50*

37. Wright, Donald R. ORAL TRADITIONS FROM THE GAMBIA: Volume I, Mandinka Griots. 1979. 176pp.
083-0 (82-91882) $12.00*

38. Wright, Donald R. ORAL TRADITIONS FROM THE GAMBIA: Volume II, Family Elders. 1980. 200pp.
084-9 (82-91890) $15.00*

39. Reining, Priscilla. CHALLENGING DESERTIFICATION IN WEST AFRICA: Insights from Landsat into Carrying Capacity, Cultivation and Settlement Site Identification in Upper Volta and Niger. 1979. 180pp., illus.
102-0 (82-91916) $12.00*

41. Lindfors, Bernth. MAZUNGUMZO: Interviews with East African Writers, Publishers, Editors, and Scholars. 1981. 179pp.
108-X (82-91932) $13.00*

42. Spear, Thomas J. TRADITIONS OF ORIGIN AND THEIR INTERPRETATION: The Mijikenda of Kenya. 1982. xii, 163pp.
109-8 (82-91940) $13.50*

43. Harik, Elsa M. and Donald G. Schilling. THE POLITICS OF EDUCATION IN COLONIAL ALGERIA AND KENYA. 1984. 102pp.
117-9 (82-91957) $11.50*

44. Smith, Daniel R. THE INFLUENCE OF THE FABIAN COLONIAL BUREAU ON THE INDEPENDENCE MOVEMENT IN TANGANYIKA. 1985. x, 98pp.
125-X (82-91965) $ 9.00*

45. Keto, C. Tsehloane. AMERICAN-SOUTH AFRICAN RELATIONS 1784-1980: Review and Select Bibliography. 1985. 159pp.
128-4 (82-91973) $11.00*

46. Burness, Don, and Mary-Lou Burness, ed. WANASEMA: Conversations with African Writers. 1985. 95pp.
129-2 (82-91981) $ 9.00*

47. Switzer, Les. MEDIA AND DEPENDENCY IN SOUTH AFRICA: A Case Study of the Press and the Ciskei "Homeland". 1985. 80pp.
130-6 (82-91999) $ 9.00*

48. Heggoy, Alf Andrew. THE FRENCH CONQUEST OF ALGIERS, 1830: An Algerian Oral Tradition. 1986. 101pp.
131-4 (82-92005) $ 9.00

Latin America Series

1. Frei, Eduardo M. THE MANDATE OF HISTORY AND CHILE'S FUTURE. Tr. by Miguel d'Escoto. Intro. by Thomas Walker. 1977. 79pp.
066-0 (82-92526) $ 8.00*

2. Irish, Donald P., ed. MULTINATIONAL CORPORATIONS IN LATIN AMERICA: Private Rights--Public Responsibilities. 1978. 135pp.
067-9 (82-92534) $ 9.00*

4. Martz, Mary Jeanne Reid. THE CENTRAL AMERICAN SOCCER WAR: Historical Patterns and Internal Dynamics of OAS Settlement Procedures. 1979. 118pp.
077-6 (82-92559) $ 8.00*

5. Wiarda, Howard J. CRITICAL ELECTIONS AND CRITICAL COUPS: State, Society, and the Military in the Processes of Latin American Development. 1979. 83pp.
082-2 (82-92567) $ 7.00*

6. Dietz, Henry A., and Richard Moore. POLITICAL PARTICIPATION IN A NON-ELECTORAL SETTING: The Urban Poor in Lima, Peru. 1979. viii, 102pp.
085-7 (82-92575) $ 9.00*

7. Hopgood, James F. SETTLERS OF BAJAVISTA: Social and Economic Adaptation in a Mexican Squatter Settlement. 1979. xii, 145pp.
101-2 (82-92583) $11.00*

8. Clayton, Lawrence A. CAULKERS AND CARPENTERS IN A NEW WORLD: The Shipyards of Colonial Guayaquil. 1980. 189pp., illus.
103-9 (82-92591) $15.00*

9. Tata, Robert J. STRUCTURAL CHANGES IN PUERTO RICO'S ECONOMY: 1947-1976. 1981. xiv, 104pp.
107-1 (82-92609) $11.75*

10. McCreery, David. DEVELOPMENT AND THE STATE IN REFORMA GUATEMALA, 1871-1885. 1983. viii, 120pp.
113-6 (82-92617) $ 8.50*

11. O'Shaughnessy, Laura N., and Louis H. Serra. CHURCH AND REVOLUTION IN NICARAGUA. 1986. 118pp.
126-8 (82-92625) $11.00*

Southeast Asia Series

31. Nash, Manning. PEASANT CITIZENS: Politics, Religion, and Modernization in Kelantan, Malaysia. 1974. 181pp.
018-0 (82-90322) $12.00*

44. Collier, William L., et al. INCOME, EMPLOYMENT AND FOOD SYSTEMS IN JAVANESE COASTAL VILLAGES. 1977. 160pp.
031-8 (82-90454) $10.00*

47. Wessing, Robert. COSMOLOGY AND SOCIAL BEHAVIOR IN A WEST JAVANESE SETTLEMENT. 1978. 200pp.
072-5 (82-90488) $12.00*

48. Willer, Thomas F., ed. SOUTHEAST ASIAN REFERENCES IN THE BRITISH PARLIAMENTARY PAPERS, 1801-1972/73: An Index. 1977. 110pp.
033-4 (82-90496) $ 8.50*

50. Echauz, Robustiano. SKETCHES OF THE ISLAND OF NEGROS. 1978. 174pp.
070-9 (82-90512) $10.00*

51. Krannich, Ronald L. MAYORS AND MANAGERS IN THAILAND: The Struggle for Political Life in Administrative Settings. 1978. 139pp.
073-3 (82-90520) $ 9.00*

52. Davis, Glora, ed. WHAT IS MODERN INDONESIAN CULTURE? 1978. 300pp.
075-X (82-90538) $18.00*

54. Ayal, Eliezar B., ed. THE STUDY OF THAILAND: Analyses of Knowledge, Approaches, and Prospects in Anthropology, Art History, Economics, History and Political Science. 1979. 257pp.
079-2 (82-90553) $13.50*

56. Duiker, William J. VIETNAM SINCE THE FALL OF SAIGON. Second edition, revised and enlarged. 1985. 281pp.
133-0 (82-90744) $12.00*

57. Siregar, Susan Rodgers. ADAT, ISLAM, AND CHRISTIANITY IN A BATAK HOMELAND. 1981. 108pp.
110-1 (82-90587) $10.00*

58. Van Esterik, Penny. COGNITION AND DESIGN PRODUCTION IN BAN CHIANG POTTERY. 1981. 90pp.
078-4 (82-90595) $12.00*

59. Foster, Brian L. COMMERCE AND ETHNIC DIFFERENCES: The Case of the Mons in Thailand. 1982. x, 93pp.
112-8 (82-90603) $10.00*

60. Frederick, William H., and John H. McGlynn. REFLECTIONS ON REBELLION: Stories from the Indonesian Upheavals of 1948 and 1965. 1983. vi, 168pp.
111-X (82-90611) $ 9.00*

61. Cady, John F. CONTACTS WITH BURMA, 1935-1949: A Personal Account. 1983. x, 117pp.
114-4 (82-90629) $ 9.00*

62. Kipp, Rita Smith, and Richard D. Kipp, eds. BEYOND SAMOSIR: Recent Studies of the Batak Peoples of Sumatra. 1983. viii, 155pp.
115-2 (82-90637) $ 9.00*

63. Carstens, Sharon, ed. CULTURAL IDENTITY IN NORTHERN PENINSULAR MALAYSIA. 1985. 91pp.
116-0 (82-90645) $ 9.00*

64. Dardjowidjojo, Soenjono. VOCABULARY BUILDING IN INDONESIAN: An Advanced Reader. 1984. xviii, 256pp.
118-7 (82-90652) $18.00*

65. Errington, J. Joseph. LANGUAGE AND SOCIAL CHANGE IN JAVA: Linguistic Reflexes of Modernization in a Traditional Royal Polity. 1985. xiv, 198pp.
120-9 (82-90660) $12.00*

66. Binh, Tran Tu. THE RED EARTH: A Vietnamese Memoir of Life on a Colonial Rubber Plantation. Tr. by John Spragens. Ed. by David Marr. 1985. xii, 98pp.
119-5 (82-90678) $ 9.00*

67. Pane, Armijn. SHACKLES. Tr. by John McGlynn. Intro. by William H. Frederick. 1985. xvi, 108pp.
122-5 (82-90686) $ 9.00*

68. Syukri, Ibrahim. HISTORY OF THE MALAY KINGDOM OF PATANI. Tr. by Conner Bailey and John N. Miksic. 1985. xx, 98pp.
123-3 (82-90694) $10.50*

69. Keeler, Ward. JAVANESE: A Cultural Approach. 1984. xxxvi, 523pp.
121-7 (82-90702) $18.00*

70. Wilson, Constance M., and Lucien M. Hanks. BURMA-THAILAND FRONTIER OVER SIXTEEN DECADES: Three Descriptive Documents. 1985. x, 128pp.
124-1 (82-90710) $10.50*

71. Thomas, Lynn L., and Franz von Benda-Beckmann, eds. CHANGE AND CONTINUITY IN MINANGKABAU: Local, Regional, and Historical Perspectives on West Sumatra. 1985. 363pp.
127-6 (82-90728) $14.00*

72. Reid, Anthony, and Oki Akira, eds. THE JAPANESE EXPERIENCE IN INDONESIA: Selected Memoirs of 1942-1945. 1985. 411pp., 20 illus.
132-2 (82-90736) $18.00*

73. Smirenskaia, Ahanna D. PEASANTS IN ASIA: Social Consciousness and Social Struggle. Tr. by Michael J. Buckley. 1986. 248pp.
134-9 (82-90751) $12.50

80. Nguyen Anh Tuan. SOUTH VIETNAM TRIAL AND EXPERIENCE: A Challenge for Development. 1987. 482pp.
141-1 (82-90827) $15.00

## ORDERING INFORMATION

Orders for titles in the Monographs in International Studies series should be placed through the Ohio University Press/ Scott Quadrangle/ Athens, Ohio 45701-2979. Individuals must remit prepayment via check, VISA, MasterCard, CHOICE, or American Express. Individuals ordering from outside of the U.S., please remit in U.S. funds by either International Money Order or check drawn on a U.S. bank. Residents of Ohio please add sales tax. Postage and handling is $2.00 for the first book and $.50 for each additional book. Prices and availability are subject to change without notice.